PENGUIN BOOKS
Death of the Rainbow Warrior

Michael King was born in Wellington in 1945. He has a B.A. from Victoria University (1967), an M.A. from Waikato University (1968) and a D.Phil. from Waikato University (1978). He has won a number of awards for his journalism and writing, including the Cowan Prize for Journalism (1976), a Feltex Award for television writing (1975), the National Book Award for Non-fiction (1978) and the Wattie Book of the Year Award (1984). He spent most of 1976 in France as the Katherine Mansfield Memorial Fellow.

Michael King lives in Auckland and works as a freelance writer, teacher and broadcaster. His books have explored new areas in New Zealand writing and publishing. They include: *Te Puea* (1977), *New Zealanders at War* (1981), *The Collector: A Biography of Andreas Reischek* (1981), *Maori: A Photographic and Social History* (1983), *Whina: A Biography of Whina Cooper* (1983), *Being Pakeha* (1985), and a major contribution to *The Oxford History of New Zealand*. He scripted and narrated the prize-winning television documentary series *Tangata Whenua* (1974).

Death of
the Rainbow Warrior

MICHAEL KING

PENGUIN BOOKS

Penguin Books (N.Z.) Ltd, 182–190 Wairau Road,
Auckland 10, New Zealand
Penguin Books Ltd, Harmondsworth,
Middlesex, England
Penguin Books, 40 West 23rd Street,
New York, N.Y.10010, U.S.A.
Penguin Books Australia Ltd, Ringwood,
Victoria, Australia
Penguin Books Canada Limited, 2801 John Street,
Markham, Ontario, Canada L3R 1B4

First published 1986
Copyright © Michael King 1986
All rights reserved

Designed by Richard King
Typeset in English Times by Typocrafters Ltd, Auckland
Printed and bound in Great Britain by
Cox & Wyman Ltd, Reading

AUTHOR'S NOTE

There were several reasons for writing this book, and for writing it the way I have. Like most people, I was shocked at the blowing up of the *Rainbow Warrior*, the first act of international terrorism in New Zealand waters. I wanted to know how and why it happened.

Second, I wanted to put the explosion in perspective and show that it was not an isolated and momentarily diverting act of destruction. The context for the sabotage of the *Rainbow Warrior* can be found in 40 years' use of the Pacific Ocean as a nuclear testing and dumping ground; and in the belief of one nuclear power that it had the right to use any means to safeguard its own testing programme.

The focus of the book is on the Greenpeace people who inadvertently provoked the bombing, and on the agents who carried it out. I have gone to considerable lengths to depict, from evidence, what kind of people came to a country friendly to their own to blow up the flagship of a pacifist organisation: what they ate and drank, what they believed, how they behaved under stress. I doubt if any other non-fiction book has been able to present such a detailed picture of agents recently at work for a major Western intelligence agency.

The book is also marked off from the ones that preceded it by close attention to accuracy and detail. This was achieved by spending long hours with Greenpeace members, police investigators and those who associated with the French agents. It names for the first time the agent who actually placed the bombs on the *Rainbow Warrior* and explains how this was done. It comes as close as any book can to being the full story of what happened in New Zealand in the course of Operation Rainbow Warrior.

Writing it brought me into contact with other activities that I can't speak of in detail here, but which reminded me constantly that the book involved higher stakes than any literary project with which I had been previously involved. Apparent attempts at seduction, industrial sabotage, French surveillance of my own activities and competition for film rights made the period after the bombing almost as eventful for the author as it was for the people about whom I was writing.

I am indebted to dozens of individuals and organisations for assistance in the preparation of this book, especially members of Greenpeace and the New Zealand Police Department. Those who can be named are identified in a separate section. I thank them warmly, but stress that the book's conclusions are my own.

Michael King

CONTENTS

Tree let your arms fall:
raise them not sharply in supplication . . .
This is no gallant monsoon's flash,
no dashing trade wind's blast.
The fading green of your magic
emanations shall not make pure again
these polluted skies . . . for this
is no ordinary sun.

    Hone Tuwhare

Let there be no war.
For the man who wants war there is never enough.
Let my son be, instead, a man of wisdom and learning,
a keeper of the good traditions of his house.

    Tahitian traditional song

ONE

Voyage of the Warrior

1 March, 1954

The wind blew across the lagoon in the pre-dawn darkness. Small waves agitated the coral sand and palm fronds rattled, as if some animal stranded in their branches was trying to escape. It seemed to make all things tremble and sent oscillations through the heavy air inside the open-windowed huts. But it did not reduce the heat, which was already oppressive.

Unable to sleep for the drumming in his ears, Billiet Edmond got up to clean his house and boil coffee. Aged 22, he was sole-charge teacher on Rongelap, largest island in the Rongelap Atoll. On this as on most mornings, he was happy to wake on his father's homeland. It was large as atoll islands go – seven kilometres long, one wide – and it was endowed plentifully with water, gardens, coconut palms and pandanus trees.

The lagoon too – which seemed opalised when the sun came out – was well stocked with fish, crab and shellfish, sometimes turtles. From land or sea, Rongelap matched the outsiders' vision of Pacific paradise: white sands, drooping palms, hibiscus plants, clear safe waters encircled by a coral reef. The people, 82 residents in 1954, were brown rather than dark, heavy-set but not tall, more Polynesian-looking than most Micronesians, oblique in their communication with one another and shyly friendly towards strangers. Most were Edmond's relatives, though he had been born 160 kilometres away on Kwajalein, in the centre of the Marshalls group.

The house he shared with his pregnant wife and infant son was the largest on the island. Framed with timber abandoned by the Japanese and American occupations, the walls and roofs

– like those elsewhere in the village, strung along the edge of the lagoon – were thatched pandanus leaves. He whistled as he swept the floor, and he looked forward to sharing coffee with the village magistrate and swimming in the lagoon before classes.

At six o'clock, just as light had begun to filter through the door and windows, he was blinded by a flash that penetrated the walls. It was seconds before he regained his sight. When he did, he rushed outside to find other villagers, already awake and standing among the canoes drawn up at the edge of the water, looking across the lagoon where the lightning had come from. What he saw then made him sick with fear. He recorded it that day in his diary:

> . . . a huge and fiery sun-like object rose up in the western part of the lagoon. It was a sun, for it was round, but it was much bigger than our sun. It was a sun, for it was illuminating and giving off heat like the sun, yet its intense heat was far greater and much brighter . . .

As Edmond watched from the beach he was joined by his wife, who held their one-year-old son, and by magistrate John Anjain. Anjain was about to ask a question when new horrors erupted before them. The upper portion of the fireball exploded and threw burning particles higher into the sky. Then the bright light went out altogether and the formation consolidated into an orange mushroom cloud, then another which shot into the air above the first, then another, and then another, as if a mighty staircase were being thrust into the heavens.

Meanwhile the atmosphere between the clouds and the onlookers turned the colour of blood and they were hit by an immense wave of heat, which scorched their skins like severe sunburn. At Edmond's shouted command, the villagers nearest to him retreated to the fragile shelter of their huts. Before they reached them, however, they were overtaken by the sound of an explosion so loud that it split many eardrums, and immediately afterwards by what seemed like a tornado roaring across the island:

. . . twisting coconut trees, uprooting bushes, smashing windows, doors and overturning one house . . . John, the magistrate, my wife still clasping our son, and myself were forcefully pushed against the wall. Thatched roofs of most houses were blown out.

The wind passed as rapidly as it had arrived. And now the air was completely still. But for the burns on their skins and damage to their houses, conditions could have been normal again. But they were not. The Rongelapese did not yet know it but they had just witnessed and survived the explosion of the world's first deliverable hydrogen bomb over Bikini Atoll. This 15-metagon weapon had a destructive power equivalent to more than 1,000 uranium bombs of the kind that had destroyed Hiroshima in 1945. Its use signalled for the first time the capacity of man to destroy life on earth and even the planet itself. Eighty-two Rongelap Islanders had been involuntary spectators at the birth of this power, at a distance of 150 kilometres.

Later, informed of what had occurred, they were to suspect that they had been more than spectators – guinea-pigs, perhaps, in an experiment on the effects of radiation. They knew already about the American nuclear testing programme in the Marshall Islands and were aware that their neighbours on Bikini and Enewetak had been forcibly removed from their homes so that those islands could be pulverised by American weapons. All this was somehow sanctioned by the United Nations Trusteeship Charter* that required the American Government to 'promote the development of the inhabitants of the Trust

---

*'Of eleven United Nations Trusteeships created after World War II, Micronesia was the sole "strategic trust", and is the only one that remains in the 1980s. All the other trust territories have become independent . . . Only Micronesia – now in four separate political units: the Republic of the Marshall Islands, Federated States of Micronesia, Republic of Palau, and Commonwealth of the Northern Marianas – will not become independent. Nor is independence on the horizon, as the US is in the final stages of cementing long-term military authority in the islands.'
Giff Johnson, *Collision Course at Kwajalein*, p6.

Territory toward self-government or independence', and to 'protect the inhabitants against the loss of their lands and resources'.

Under the mantle of this 'protection', the inhabitants of Rongelap had themselves been evacuated in 1946 when a Hiroshima-sized atomic blast was ignited over Bikini. But in March 1954, when the test was 1,000 times more powerful, there was no evacuation. There was not even notice that something dangerous was about to occur.

Lulled by the absence of warnings, the adult Rongelapese set about repairing their homes. Billiet Edmond, meanwhile, summoned his 21 pupils to the thatched classroom in the centre of the village and began morning classes. He tried to anaesthetise the shock of what they had experienced that morning by an immediate imposition of normal routine. Also as usual, he dismissed the students at 11.30 to return home for lunch.

> . . . [We] went out and were greeted by powder-like particles as they began to fall . . . it did not alarm the islanders whom I met on my way back home. Even the children who were accompanying me on the way were playing with it. They ran through it, and they turned to catch it as if to see who could collect the most . . .

The ash shower continued to fall gently, like powdered snow. By mid-afternoon it was five centimetres deep over the entire island. As it drifted to the ground, it touched bare heads, arms and feet. It settled in tanks and wells and turned drinking water blackish-yellow. By 6 p.m., everyone exposed to the ash had developed an agonising itch over their earlier burns. 'Grown-ups were too old to have cried,' Edmond reported, 'but the kids were violently crying, scratching, and more scratching; kicking, twisting and more, but nothing could we do. My one-year-old was worse than everyone else . . .'

Magistrate Anjain remembered:

'About 10 p.m. many of the islanders became sick. They were vomiting, felt nausea or had diarrhoea. On the second day, people were really sick and couldn't move around. Just a few strong men tried staggering from home to home to check on everybody and get food . . . all they could do was lie down and wait.' At 5 p.m. that day an American seaplane landed on the lagoon and two servicemen in uniform came ashore. Watched by the lethargic villagers, they used Geiger counters to check ground and water radiation levels. They said nothing and left within 20 minutes of their arrival.

The following day, the third since the explosion, an American destroyer entered the south passage into the Rongelap lagoon and anchored offshore. A landing craft raced to the beach and the officer in charge asked John Anjain to summon the villagers. Through an interpreter, he told them that the atoll was contaminated by radiation and that many of them were already showing signs of high-level radiation exposure. Another day on the atoll and they could die. To prevent this, they were to be moved at once, first to the Kwajalein navy base, later to Ejit Island, in Majuro Lagoon. They were allowed to take nothing other than the clothes they were wearing. All other personal possessions – homes, graves and sacred sites, everything that connected them to the land of their forefathers – had to be abandoned.

Billiet Edmond noted later:

> Like a military invasion, the evacuation was conducted in a most dramatic and forceful fashion . . . everyone was oblivious to what was really happening. Everyone was in a complete state of shock. How could it be otherwise when they were still afresh with what they had experienced during the past two days? I, for one, had seen that flash, I saw that fireball, I saw the fiery mushroom, that storm, and I had seen and been showered by that fallout . . . I was, like other islanders were, waiting for what would happen next . . .

What happened next was a long unfolding of consequences of that 1 March test, which the Americans code-named Bravo. According to the United States Department of Energy, the explosion had snowed Rongelap with 175 'rads' of radiation – the worst-ever contamination of human beings other than that which had occurred at Hiroshima and Nagasaki.

Contaminated too were 157 inhabitants of Utirik Atoll down wind of the explosion, 28 American Army and Air Force technicians monitoring Bravo from Rongerik Atoll, and the 23-man crew of the Japanese tuna fishing vessel *Lucky Dragon*, one of whom subsequently died.*

More sinister than the simple fact of radiation exposure was a later admission by one of the senior American technicians responsible for monitoring the weather at the time of the test. Gene Curbow told the *New York Times* in 1982 that there had been no sudden change of wind before the test, as American authorities had claimed, and that it was difficult to regard the consequences as an accident. 'The wind had been blowing straight at us for four days,' said Curbow, who had been stationed on Rongerik with other Army and Air Force personnel. 'It was blowing straight at us during the test, and straight at us after it. The wind never shifted.' Asked why he had taken so long to come forward with this information, Curbow cited 'a mixture of patriotism and ignorance.'

An official report on the Bravo test, compiled in 1954 and made public under American freedom of information legislation in 1982, confirmed Curbow's allegations that the decision to ignite the bomb was made in full knowledge that winds were blowing directly towards inhabited atolls. It provided evidence that the Marshallese may indeed have been used as guinea-pigs for testing the effects of strong doses of radiation on people. Their island had become a microcosm for the aftermath of nuclear war.

Those effects were more frightful than anything the Rongelapese had encountered before. In the four years following Bravo, miscarriages and deformed births among Rongelap women doubled. Most distressing were the 'jellyfish

---

*It was the contamination of the Japanese fisherman that was reported most widely in the world's press. The public outcry about the condition of the fishermen forced an official but guarded American announcement about the effects of Bravo ('. . . individuals were exposed to some radioactivity. There were no burns. All were reported well . . .'), and it led in England to the formation of the group that later came to be known as the Campaign for Nuclear Disarmament.

babies', born without faces and bones, who lived for about half a day. These were a phenomenon previously unknown to the islanders.

The Americans made no attempt to decontaminate Rongelap. In 1957 they told the islanders it was safe to return home. The Brookhaven National Laboratories reported, however (to the authorities, not to the Rongelapese), that levels of radioactivity on Rongelap were 'higher than those found in other inhabited locations in the world. The habitation of these people on the island will afford most valuable ecological radiation data on human beings.'

The nature of that data began to become apparent after the population of the island had been living off lagoon food, bread-fruit and coconuts for six more years. By 1963, the first thyroid tumour had appeared. Each successive year the number of islanders with similar growths increased. By 1985, 77 per cent of all Rongelapese under ten at the time of the Bravo test had had tumours requiring surgery. A smaller number developed other forms of cancer. The first to die (of leukaemia) was Lekoj Anjain, son of former magistrate John Anjain. In an admission that this death was directly attributable to fallout from Bravo, Anjain received $100,000 compensation from the American Government. Both his surviving sons subsequently required surgery for thyroid cancers. Another man died in 1974 from gastric carcinoma, a further cancer attributable to radiation exposure.

Even these horrors did not represent the full extent of the new health problems faced by the Rongelapese after 1957. Growth retardation became common among young children, as did the incidence of physical and mental deformity. Older people aged prematurely. The medical director of the Brookhaven National Laboratories revealed in *Science Magazine* that more than half of the Rongelap Islanders were suffering from a rare form of 'double breakage' chromosome damage, believed to be caused by radiation and source of the islanders' high proportion of physical and mental disorders.

'. . . the Marshall Islanders are the first victims of World War Three,' wrote Australian film maker Dennis O'Rourke, who made a documentary on Rongelap. 'They are the first culture in the history of our race which has been effectively destroyed by radiation. And they are a small culture – the end of the line . . . decisions were made to . . . allow these gentle and trusting people to be exposed to radioactivity. In the name of national security the United States has irreversibly destroyed the fragile world of the Marshall Islanders, for countless generations . . .'

Alarming data continued to accumulate on Rongelap. In 1978, an aerial survey of the northern Marshalls revealed that parts of Rongelap were as radioactive as – or even more so than – Bikini, which had been declared off limits for up to 100 years. Following this report, Rongelap residents were warned not to take food from the northern islands in their atoll – and this 22 years after they had been assured by the Americans that the whole atoll was a safe place on which to live.

By 1983, the elders of Rongelap had reached a reluctant consensus. However strong their cultural and emotional ties to the island (and atoll dwellers, because they have so little land, are attached to it more intimately); however dismal the prospect of exile; they would have to abandon Rongelap if their culture and their people – especially their children – were to survive.

That same year Senator Jeton Anjain, brother of the former magistrate, won from the Marshallese Parliament a unanimous resolution of support for the evacuation and resettlement of his people. In 1985 he and his supporters secured a promise from the American Congress of two grants: $300,000 to pay for an independent radiological survey of the island; and $3.2 million for resettlement of its poplation of 300 to Mejato Island to the south, if the survey proved the move was justified.

There was a catch, however. The grants were dependent on all Marshallese accepting a compact of free association with the United States, which would allow the Americans to continue to use their missile base at Kwajalein Atoll for a further 30 years and retain military and strategic control of the region; and it would deprive the Marshallese of any right to sue the United States over the physical and environmental effects of earlier nuclear testing.

The compact was approved by the Marshallese in general, but rejected by the people of Rongelap and Kwajalein. Consequently the Rongelap Islanders had to look beyond the United States for deliverance. The Greenpeace environmental organisation was scheduled to send its protest vessel *Rainbow Warrior* to the Marshall Islands in May 1985. The Rongelapese decided to ask Greenpeace for assistance with their evacuation.

The *Rainbow Warrior* had formed a chain of attachment to Rongelap long before it dropped anchor in the island's lagoon in May 1985. The vessel, a 30-year-old converted research trawler, had been bought by Greenpeace in 1977 with a £40,000 grant from the Dutch branch of the World Wildlife Fund. She was named after a Greenpeace version of an apocryphal North American Indian legend: 'When the Earth is sick and the animals disappear, the Warriors of the Rainbow will join together to protect the wild creatures and to heal the Earth.'*

Crewed by men and women of deliberately varied nationality, the *Rainbow Warrior* became the flagship of the organisation's small fleet of four protest vessels. It was propelled at once into the kinds of environmental campaigns that Greenpeace had

---

*In fact there is no such Indian legend. The story is an interpolation of Indian ideas worked into a millennial vision by a European and an Eskimo writer, Vinson Brown and William Willoya. They close their book *Warriors Of The Rainbow* (1962) with these words: 'Among the Indians of old, children and youth respected the elders and were taught love and unity, strength of character, love of the Great Chief in the Sky and good deeds from babyhood. Today young people, who should be the hope of mankind, have wandered far from the strength of soul in their pursuit of pleasure and "success". The Warriors of the Rainbow will bring back this lost spirit before it is too late and the youth shall once more do great deeds of selflessness and heroism. The glory and the purity of their lives shall light the world.'

been evolving and refining over the previous six years, since
the organisation had grown out of the Canadian Don't Make
a Wave Committee. The *Warrior* sailed to Iceland, Spain and
Peru to confront commercial whaling operations, to Canada
to draw attention to the slaughter of harp seal pups on the
icepacks, to the North Atlantic to impede the dumping of
nuclear waste, to the United States to protest against chemical
dumping and offshore oil and gas development, and to Siberia
to document illegal Russian whaling operations at Lorino.

All these campaigns attracted extensive publicity, which was
their immediate objective. Some provoked conflict with commercial and national authorities. This required Greenpeace in
turn to devise non-violent 'guerilla' tactics, which contributed
to public perception of the organisation as a highly macho
group flirting with adventure and danger in the cause of conservation. Toxic-waste drums were dropped into the sea peril-
ously close to Greenpeace Zodiacs weaving in and out of their
path. *Rainbow Warrior* crew members interposed themselves
between whales and whaler's harpoons, and between seals and
sealers' knives.

In June 1980 the ship was seized by the Spanish Navy and
held under arrest in the military harbour of El Ferrol. To prevent its escape, Spanish marines removed sections of the vessel's
propulsion system. Five months later Greenpeace members
smuggled replacement parts aboard and the *Rainbow Warrior*
made a dramatic and successful night-time run for freedom.
Off Siberia in July 1983, seven crew members were arrested
by the Soviets but the *Rainbow Warrior* itself outmanoeuvred
a Russian destroyer and other pursuit vessels and returned
safely to Alaska. Diplomatic manoeuvres secured the release
of the captives five days later.

Successive *Rainbow Warrior* crews fought these campaigns
to highlight and repair damage to the earth's ecosystem with
an even-handedness that ignored national boundaries and ideological loyalties. The letter they handed to the Spanish whaler
Ibsa Tres in 1980 was characteristic of their motivation and
their tactics. They drew attention to the fact that those on board

the *Rainbow Warrior* represented nine nationalities and millions of people throughout the world, and they appealed to the whalers on behalf of those people to stop killing whales before there were none left to save. They were tools of neither East nor West, of neither capitalism nor communism. And the considerable funding to support their activities came from hundreds of thousands of members and donors in Europe and North America.*

Their most spectacular successes came in the form of publicity (journalists, delighted by the heightened combination of news elements and racy pictures Greenpeace generated, dubbed the organisation's activists 'commandos of conservation'). But specific objectives were also achieved, at least in the short term: the European Parliament voted against the dumping of radioactive waste in the sea, the bottom dropped out of the fur seal market, Peru closed its whaling industry after the *Rainbow Warrior* campaigned there in 1982, and international support for a whaling moratorium grew as a direct consequence of the attention Greenpeace had drawn to the issue.

These campaigns were small and spontaneous operations in comparison with that planned for 1985, however. In 1985, the annual general meeting of Greenpeace International agreed to make 1985 Greenpeace's Year of the Pacific, thus turning attention back to the region of its earliest targets (American nuclear testing in the Aleutians in 1971 and French nuclear testing on Moruroa Atoll in 1972/73). The highlight of the year would be the dispatch of a group of protest vessels from New Zealand to Moruroa; and the *Rainbow Warrior* would lead the fleet and enable it to remain at sea longer than previous flotillas or individual yachts. The *Warrior*'s size, storage capacity and desalinisation plant would support the smaller boats; and its sophisticated communication facilities would enable crew members to inform the world instantaneously about French

---

*By 1985 Greenpeace had 1.3 million members in 15 countries, more than 30 offices, a paid staff of 150, and a projected budget of $NZ25 million.

responses to the Greenpeace presence.

In all, the *Warrior* would make a 30,000-kilometre voyage from the United States to the Marshall Islands, to highlight the effects of American military installations at Kwajalein Atoll, cornerstone of President Reagan's Strategic Defence Initiative (or 'Star Wars') programme; to Kiribati and Vanuatu to encourage those newly independent nations to continue their anti-nuclear stands; to New Zealand, to express solidarity with that country's decision to close its ports to nuclear-propelled and weapons-carrying ships, and to stock up for the Peace Flotilla voyage; to Rarotonga, for a meeting of the South Pacific forum countries; and to Moruroa, aiming to rendezvous there with other protest vessels in the first week in August, thus marking the 40th anniversary of the atomic bombing of Hiroshima and Nagasaki. Such at least was the initial plan, drawn up by campaign director Steve Sawyer in consultation with other Greenpeace organisations, especially Greenpeace New Zealand.

Sawyer was a bearded and serious-minded American who blushed easily when he was embarrassed or under pressure. In age (28), background (a college degree in philosophy and love of the outdoors) and motivation, he was typical of the recruits Greenpeace had made in England and North America in the previous decade. But he was distinguished by extraordinary stamina, level-headedness, a gift for administration that had previously been employed to sort out the tangled affairs of Greenpeace USA, and a contagious sense of commitment to ecological causes. Sawyer prepared details for the 1985 campaign at the headquarters of Greenpeace International in Lewes, Sussex. There he worked intently in the centre of a noisy confusion of computers, teleprinters, VDUs and telephones. He was helped by an administrative and secretarial staff of about ten, all of whom were paid £45 per week plus rent, transport and clothing allowances. Sawyer himself was paid a small salary, to allow him to work off college debts and support his mother back in New Hampshire. Like Greenpeace offices in other parts of the world, that in Lewes seemed to outsiders to be almost wilfully disorganised. In fact, the workers and their equipment – as modern as that found in any international business – produced results and produced them quickly.

By mid-October 1984, however, Sawyer was beginning to alter the focus of the *Rainbow Warrior*'s planned voyage. In Seattle he met with Giff Johnson, an American journalist married to a Marshall Islander. They discussed the cultural difficulties presented by a Greenpeace direct action campaign in or around Kwajalein Atoll. Marshall Islanders would be unlikely to understand or appreciate such a gesture, which might make life difficult for those who worked on Kwajalein. What was needed was a programme involving the islanders, and of immediate benefit to them. At the end of a three-day consultation, the two Americans talked about Rongelap's difficulties and the possibility of what Sawyer then conceived as 'some kind of symbolic evacuation of the atoll.'

Before the end of October, Johnson was back on the phone to Sawyer from Hawaii. He had with him Senator Jeton Anjain, the 55-year-old former cabinet minister in the Marshall Islands Government and effective leader of the Rongelap people. 'To hell with this symbolic business,' Anjain told Sawyer, who took the call at the Greenpeace office in Washington. 'I've talked with my people about this. We want to move. You've got a big boat. Can't you help us?'

'Well, Jesus,' Sawyer said, thrown momentarily by the implications. 'That's a pretty heavy thing to get involved in. But in principle it sounds okay. We'll see what we can really do.'

From that moment the determination of the Rongelap people to escape their contaminated atoll and find a safe home assumed as much importance for Sawyer as the scheduled Moruroa project. He shifted his base to Honolulu, and flew to the Marshalls in January 1985. There, in consultation with Rongelapese and other sympathetic Marshallese, he began to work out details of a more ambitious plan than that originally envisaged by Greenpeace: the removal of the Rongelap people

:

to Mejato, a small uninhabited island 160 kilometres away in
the Kwajalein Atoll.

Two factors drove the Greenpeace campaign director to make
a success of this potentially difficult operation. One was the
awareness that – for once – Greenpeace would be doing something for real people rather than simply for a principle or for
the benefit of marine life. Secondly, a Rongelap evacuation
would nonetheless attract media attention and hold enormous
symbolic value: the Rongelapese were the innocent victims of
nuclear testing. Like other Pacific peoples, including those in
French Polynesia, they had neither wanted such weapons in
their neighbourhood, nor had any control over them once a
superpower brought them there. The consequences had been
catastrophic for their health and their culture. The plight of
the Rongelapese reflected everything Greenpeace alleged and
felt about the callous use of the Pacific by Britain, the United
States and France. Evacuation might not only give those people
a future, it could also be an opportunity for the victims to tell
their story to a global audience. Or so Sawyer believed.

Arrangements made in the Marshalls (though he was unable
to visit Rongelap itself), Sawyer returned to Hawaii to continue planning the wider Pacific Peace Voyage and to await
the arrival of the *Warrior*.

The *Rainbow Warrior*, meanwhile, rusting and neglected
between campaigns, was undergoing a spectacular $130,000
refit at Green Cove Springs, Jacksonville, Florida. The new
crew – two Americans, two Dutchmen, two Swiss, and one
German, Dane, an Englishman, an Irishwoman and a New
Zealander – was carefully selected by Greenpeace International's marine division director Maureen Falloon for its
combination of boat skills, experience, international represent-
ativeness and compatibility. Members assembled at Jacksonville from October 1984 to begin stripping, cleaning and paint-
ing the vessel. They overhauled the engines (one main for
propulsion and three auxiliaries for electricity and navigation
gear), laid in new radar and radio equipment, rebuilt the bridge,

and converted the *Warrior* into a sailing vessel, to economise on fuel.

Two of the ship's crew, including its skipper of four years, Peter Willcox, had sailed on her previously. Most had worked on other Greenpeace vessels on projects as varied as anti-whaling campaigns and the prevention of the dumping of radio-active waste. Three had sailed on the *Fri*, which, while not a Greenpeace boat, was probably the world's best-known protest vessel;* and three had been on earlier Moruroa protests.

The immediate job that promised the most attractive gain – the ability to cruise under sail power and save as much as 35 per cent on fuel – was also the most difficult. Two masts, a 33-metre main and a 26-metre mizzen, had to be fitted and secured below decks. Ballast had to be calculated and added; rigging, booms, winches and other paraphernalia accommodated among existing features and equipment; sails had to be prepared. And then the crew – all the crew – had to master the new system. For while sailing was far more pleasant and reduced the overall workload, the business of raising and lowering sails and booms was cumbersome and required the assistance of virtually all hands.

By the time the *Warrior* sailed out of Mayport, Jacksonville's harbour, for sea trials in February 1985, the crew had more than a shipshape vessel. They had come to know one another intimately as a result of the co-operative labours of the previous four months; and they felt extraordinarily attached to their vessel, as if they had built it from scratch. Two weeks at sea ironed out most of the creases in the sail system, and the ship's company were delighted with the boat's performance. Its rounded lines responded well to windpower, and there was little difficulty in moving up to eleven knots under sail.

---

*The *Fri* – a 30-metre ketch built in Denmark in 1912 – had been undertaking nautical protests for twelve years. It had sailed to the Moruroa testing zone in 1973, and subsequently to Pacific islands affected by earlier nuclear testing; to the Soviet Union and China to deliver anti-nuclear messages from the Pacific; to impoverished Caribbean countries in need of food and equipment; and to block the dumping of nuclear waste on the high seas.

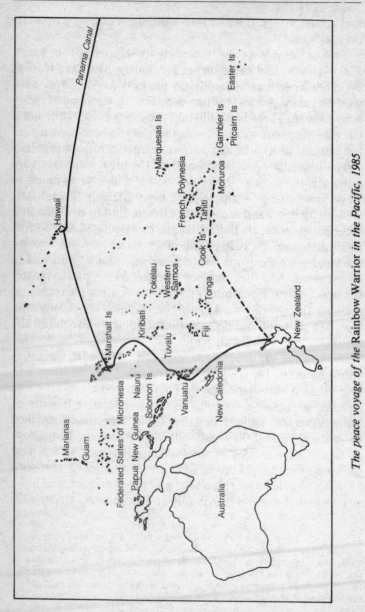

Panama Canal

Hawaii

Marquesas Is

French Polynesia

Gambier Is

Easter Is

Pitcairn Is

Moruroa

Tahiti

Cook Is

Marshall Is

Tokelau

Western Samoa

Tonga

Kiribati

Tuvalu

Fiji

New Zealand

Marianas

Guam

Federated States of Micronesia

Nauru

Solomon Is

Papua New Guinea

Vanuatu

New Caledonia

Australia

The peace voyage of the Rainbow Warrior in the Pacific, 1985

The *Rainbow Warrior* felt comfortable, steady and safe; its crew at one with one another and with their vessel.

On 15 March 1985 they took their leave of Jacksonville happily (they had not encountered much support from the local community) and just under one month later, on 19 April, the *Rainbow Warrior* sailed into Honolulu making ten knots, after a stop at the Bahamas for minor repairs, and passage through the Panama Canal.

En route for Hawaii, the crew established rhythms and dynamics of its own. It worked six four-hour watches a day, each consisting of three or four people. The basic grouping for running the ship was skipper Willcox, one engineer, one mate and one deckhand. But at any time more or fewer than this number might be engaged, according to weather and circumstances. All available hands turned out to help with the heavy hauling and lowering of sails; under windpower, duties were largely reduced to trimming sails and steering.

In age, they ranged over two decades. Willcox, a quiet, authoritative 32-year-old, was the dominant member, though in an understated manner. Greenpeace boats are never sharply hierarchical. Crew know that there has to be a system and a line of authority to make a vessel function safely, and generally they observe such a system willingly; but also relaxedly. This was the case on the *Rainbow Warrior*'s 1985 voyage. Willcox consulted his crew on all major decisions, such as the need to put into Nassau for repairs. They for their part felt at all times secure about his direction; there was general agreement that he was the most able Greenpeace skipper with whom they had sailed.

First mate was Martini Gotje, a tall, spare, 36-year-old Dutchman, ex-Merchant Service. He was the most overtly forceful personality on board, and the most experienced seaman. But he too wore his authority (and his strength) lightly. In the course of the voyage he teamed with Hanne Sorensen, a handsome 25-year-old Danish second engineer with piercing eyes, and they shared a cabin. Also sharing accommodation were Henk Haazen aged 31, Dutch and third engineer, and Bunny McDiarmid from New Zealand, a 28-year-old sociology graduate who signed on as a deckhand. They had joined the crew as a couple and had sailed previously in the Caribbean with Gotje on the *Fri*.

Davey Edward, a gnomish 32-year-old Yorkshireman and also an ex-merchantman, was chief engineer and the one individual close to rivalling Gotje and Willcox in experience and confidence. Except when exasperated, he too was not inclined to pull rank. He liked things shipshape, especially in his engineroom, but he was not needlessly fussy. He was also a forceful optimist.

Lloyd Anderson, a laconic New Yorker, was radio engineer and – at 41 – oldest of the company. Nathalie Mestre, at 20, was the youngest: Swiss, vegetarian and ship's cook. She shared a cabin with Grace O'Sullivan, 23, an Irish deckhand. Andy Biedermann, 29, was ship's doctor and also Swiss. And the eleventh crew member was Bene Hoffmann, the 33-year-old German second mate. Fernando Pereira, who would double as photographer and deckhand and make up the third four-person watch, was to join the vessel at Hawaii.

There were minor strains on the voyage out, but nothing serious. Some bad weather in the Bahamas, which damaged radio antenna insulators; some difficulties with the sail system which caused chaffing; a small degree of tension between meat eaters and vegetarians.

The daily routine for crew members was a variation on sleeping, taking watch turns, helping with general maintenance, participating in boat, fire and man-overboard drills, reading, resting, and talking. They were not all rabid conversationalists. But they did think and talk a great deal – either over the evening dinner, the one time of the day when most of them were together; or while they were sitting on the deck in the sun between watches or doing relaxed jobs, such as modifying the sails and sail rig.

The most common topics of conversation were group examination of motives (what they were doing there, and why); and attempts to equip themselves with as much information and theory as possible on Greenpeace issues, especially on the issues raised by the 1985 Pacific Peace Voyage.

Lloyd Anderson, for example, would emerge from the darkness of the radio room on the upper deck, bearded, blinking like a badger, to slowly articulate the value of Greenpeace (of which he, incidentally, was not a member). 'The big thing about Greenpeace, what it's got going beyond other environmental groups, is that it enables you to *act* on your beliefs. They have big meetings, Man, and they stand around and talk, and they push around bits of paper, and then nothing happens. Greenpeace pushes paper too, but something happens at the end of it. It allows me to feel personally effective as well as personally involved.

'I don't expect to change anything overnight,' insisted Anderson, who had been to Moruroa once before. 'But I can feel that I am helping to move things along in the direction in which they should be moving.' On this, he spoke for all the crew.

Gotje had read widely on the nuclear issue, especially on the militarisation of the Pacific, and he quickly became heated and visionary in discussion, even when there was no obvious adversary. 'A few people in Paris, and in Moscow and Washington and London, make decisions that are disastrous for the rest of the world. Who the hell are they? What makes them so special? Why should we accept it? Especially, why should we accept any of those countries making a nuclear garbage heap out of the Pacific, a place to go and dump all the things they don't want on their own land? They don't even ask people. They just do it.'

Time and again conversation returned to Moruroa: how the French authorities might respond to the Greenpeace presence; what initiatives the crew might take to register that presence, to record their disapproval, and to deal with whatever the French Navy threw at them. In the past there had been rammings of protest vessels, boardings, beatings and arrests. At

least this time there would be independent observers along –
journalists, and perhaps even cabinet ministers from sympathetic countries such as Vanuatu or New Zealand; and the
means for Lloyd Anderson to remain in continuous radio contact with the outside world, including the media wire services,
and to instantly transmit photographs and documents.

The question of tactics at Moruroa was to be an open one
until the vessel got there. The first step was to sail the *Warrior* and its accompanying flotilla up to the 12-mile territorial
limit and to stay there. From that point there was a range of
options. Individual yachts might spread themselves around the
atoll to make it as difficult as possible for the French Navy
to keep track of them. Past experience had shown that French
surveillance would be intensive, because the authorities were
frightened of unauthorised landings and attempts to collect
coral samples. There was also the possibility (though an unlikely
one) of all the boats converging on Moruroa and risking simultaneous arrest.

Some *Rainbow Warrior* crew members had hoped that they
might be able to launch outrigger canoes crewed by Polynesians
– preferably Tahitian Polynesians – to sail towards the atoll.*
But this was dependent on the *Warrior* being able to pick up
Polynesian protestors, either in the Cook Islands or, surrep-
titiously, in French Polynesia, west of Tahiti. In April 1985,
such a course was purely theoretical; no arrangements had been
made with indigenous protestors. And back in Lewes, Greenpeace International chairman David McTaggart was to veto
the idea.

Other ideas bandied about included launching the *Rainbow
Warrior*'s own Zodiacs for a dash to the atoll, or for a harassing
game of hide and seek with larger, less manoeuvrable French
Navy vessels; or the release of balloons carrying anti-nuclear

---

*It was this possibility, apparently communicated to the DGSE in May 1985 by
its agent who infiltrated the Greenpeace office in Auckland, that most angered
the French military and intelligence services and triggered the disaster that followed.
The option of involving indigenous people in the protest was one that had always
appealed strongly to Greenpeace New Zealand.

messages to fly over the atoll. The crew also talked about what they might do beyond the Moruroa vigil. It was intended to keep the *Warrior* in the Pacific for several years and to visit other islands and countries to dramatise her peace message. After Moruroa, the crew hoped, the vessel would be well known; people would turn out to see her and to hear what information and experience the crew had gathered.

All such possibilities (and some impossibilities) were canvassed in crew discussion. Some were dismissed as risky or unnecessarily counter-productive; others retained for future consideration with Greenpeace members in Auckland, and with campaign director Sawyer in particular. But it was never the role of the *Warrior* crew to plan tactics. Their job was to get the boat to Moruroa and keep it there as long as possible: as long as it *was* there, it had the oppportunity to hold world attention on the nuclear tests that were expected to take place from August 1985.

In situ, they would watch and report what was happening, particularly the movements of French vessels. Decisions about actual operations would be made by Sawyer (who would be on board) in radio consultation with the Greenpeace organisation. The crew might have to carry out the tactics eventually agreed upon; they might have to modify them in the face of circumstances that could change from minute to minute. But the major decisions would not be made by them alone.

From Jacksonville to Hawaii, such considerations remained near the surface of the crew's preoccupations because they were at the heart of the purpose of the voyage, and because they might involve risk and personal danger. But just being at sea was important too. That circumstance brought profound satisfaction to all of them. And so at dawn and dusk, Willcox and Anderson would take position readings with sextants, enjoying the employment of old maritime skills, even though the vessel had satellite navigation. As an antidote to work or stale conversation, Davey Edward would sling a fishing line over the side or scan the horizon for his beloved dolphins and whales. And Hanne Sorensen would take her favourite position at the bow and look into the depths and turbulence of the Pacific as the *Warrior* ploughed towards Hawaii.

The two-week voyage from Hawaii to the Marshall Islands had a different quality from the first leg. Fernando Pereira, the 34-year-old Portuguese-born photographer, had to be integrated into a crew that had already formed links and loyalties. David Robie from New Zealand, the first of the independent journalists who was to report on their activities, was also on board. So were three Rongelap islanders – Kotak Loeak, a traditional chief; Julian Riklon, treasurer of a Marshallese landowners' association; and Jolbo Samuel, from Riklon's office on Ebeye Island in the Kwajalein Atoll. These passengers would perform the crew's introduction to Pacific culture; in particular to the culture of the people with whom they were going to interact most intimately on the next stage of the voyage.

In Hawaii, Sawyer and Robie (who, while paying his way, would file stories for *Pacific Islands Monthly*, the *New Zealand Times* and Radio New Zealand) had been struck immediately by the crew's cohesion and rapport, and by their absolute and uncritical confidence in Peter Willcox. Both had sailed in other boats and knew that – however responsible and co-operative people were capable of being as individuals – weeks of being cooped up in a small space at sea inevitably created tensions. But, apart from differing feelings about food, there was no sign of such feeling on board the *Rainbow Warrior*. People were genuinely attached to and considerate of one another, and they welcomed the newcomers with an almost palpable sense of comradeship. If Robie was surprised at this, Sawyer was delighted. It augured well for the rest of the campaign.

Pereira's presence caused some unease after the boat left Hawaii, however. The photographer was – in temperament and choice of lifestyle – somewhat out of phase with the rest of the crew. Although he had left Portugal 15 years earlier, to avoid military service under the Salazar regime, he had retained what others on board identified as a 'Latin temperament'. He was moustached and walked with a swagger. As Henk Haazen noted with some distaste, he liked tight trousers and fast sports cars. He was wide-eyed, light-hearted and easygoing at times when the mood of the others was more businesslike. He was slow to respond to his duties as a deckhand, moving at his own pace and nobody else's. He liked the company of women, and he sought out and flirted shamelessly and happily with those on board. He was in a party mood at mealtimes when, at sea, most of his shipmates were ready for sleep.

Four of the crew – Gotje, Sorensen, O'Sullivan and Mestre – had sailed with him before and knew him and liked him. Some of the others feared at first that Pereira would not fit in. He seemed too frivolous for the purpose and work of the voyage. This impression was to change, particularly when the photographer began to talk about the children of his broken marriage – Marelle aged eight and Paul aged five – who lived with their mother in Amsterdam and to whom he was devoted. And, as he got to know other crew members individually, he showed sensitivity and a capacity for lifting the spirits of others when they were tired or temporarily deflated, which he seemed never to be. He was also to display, on Rongelap, superb professional qualities, honed when he worked for a Dutch news agency, a communist daily paper in Amsterdam, and then on European Greenpeace campaigns. But from Hawaii to the Marshalls, there were doubts about his suitability and dedication.*

There were other minor difficulties. While the Rongelapese

---

*Later allegations by right-wing French and Dutch publications that Pereira was an undercover communist – and possibly even a KGB agent – were laughed at by Greenpeace people who had known him and worked with him. Certainly his sympathies were 'left' rather than 'right', a consequence of his adolescence in fascist Portugal. In spite of his working for *De Waarheid*, no evidence was ever produced that he was a communist. On the contrary, his temperament made him hostile towards totalitarianism of any kind, fascist or communist; and he enjoyed luxuries that revolutionaries could only regard as decadent. In addition, he lacked utterly the quality of discretion that an agent would require. The accusation was disinformation disseminated by right-wing French sources, originating within the DGSE, to discredit Pereira and justify the bombing of the *Rainbow Warrior* in Auckland.

on board were able to brief the crew about conditions on the island and the effects of radiation contamination, they did so shyly, hesitantly. They were not accustomed to confrontation – however friendly – with so many forceful, garrulous Europeans. They found the largely vegetarian diet difficult to digest and even more difficult to look forward to (being accustomed to seafood, tinned fish and tinned meat). And they were disconcerted at the number of women on board (five) doing what Marshall Islanders regarded as men's work – apart from Nathalie Mestre cooking – and often doing it topless in the sun and heat. Rongelap, like many other Pacific cultures, had long since jettisoned its pre-European *mores* in favour of missionary-induced modesty.

The newcomers strengthened the muscles of the carnivorous contingent. So in addition to pressing for variety in the general diet – beans and lentils, rice, lasagne, fresh fruit for as long as possible, fish when Davey Edward was later able to catch it – a small group of dissenters formed a Breakfast Club. Whenever they could, they tried to sneak in a 'meaty breakfast' before the vegetarians were awake to be upset by the sight and the smell. In fact, the vegetarians tended not to mind – either because their culinary expectations were lower than those of the carnivores, or because their equability was a testament to the value of their diet.

The *Rainbow Warrior* reached Majuro, capital of the Marshall Islands, on 12 May. The first thing the crew learnt on docking and landing was that France had just exploded two further nuclear devices at Moruroa. Angrily, they sent a telex to President Mitterrand:

> We wish to express our outrage over these tests, not only for what they represent in terms of the nuclear weapons race, but also because of France's callous disregard for the wish of Pacific peoples everywhere to make their ocean a nuclear-free zone. We are now engaged in an evacuation of the people of Rongelap Atoll . . . [who] were heavily contaminated by American nuclear tests in the 1940s and 1950s – and their islands remain dangerously

radioactive to this day. Must France continually repeat the mistakes of the United States and Britain in the Pacific? Must France continue to pompously ignore the tide of public opinion regionally and around the world which says, 'enough'?

During the four-day stopover the crew held an open day on board and used local radio to invite the Marshallese to visit the *Warrior*. They came in their hundreds and included the Republic's foreign minister, Tony deBrum. Crew members showed locals over the boat, played videotapes in the old fish hold, converted into a theatre, and gave away T-shirts proclaiming 'Save Our Seas'. The local newspaper gave front page publicity to the boat's mission and to the forthcoming evacuation of the Rongelapese.

At Majuro the *Warrior* also put ashore two of the Rongelap islanders who had travelled from Hawaii and took on five others, including Senator Anjain. It acquired more journalists: Paul Brown writing for the *Guardian* and the *Washington Post*; two French writers, Phillipe Chatenay of *Le Point* and Walter Guerin, making a documentary for Par France television; Kousei Shimada, a freelance Japanese photojournalist; and John Perulis, a film maker working for Greenpeace Productions. Like Robie, they would pay for food, help with the running of the vessel, and file their stories through radio operator Lloyd Anderson. The ship's total complement was now 25, and almost everybody was in shared cabins.

David Robie found Majuro a picture-postcard Pacific port, perching on a narrow atoll. It seemed a peaceful and contented community. There was no sign of the slum conditions that characterised Ebeye, nor of the military hardware that bristled on Roi-Namur and Kwajalein Island to the north. But a notice outside the post office caught his attention just before the boat left. 'Listen to Your Bodies' it was headed. Then it listed the symptoms of cancer.

The *Rainbow Warrior* motored into Rongelap lagoon a little

after ten o'clock on the morning of Friday 17 May. The main island looked little different from the way Billiet Edmond had described and enjoyed it some 30 years before. The crew were stunned by the almost unreal beauty of turquoise water, teeming fish life, white sand, and coconut palms etched against a bright blue sky. The village was strung along the edge of the lagoon among palms and outrigger canoes pulled up on the shore.

There had been some changes, however. A white concrete church now dominated the village. The houses were built predominantly of plywood and corrugated iron, a result of the resettlement of the community by the Americans in 1957. There was a rough airstrip cut through the coconut palms, with a small sign saying 'Welcome to Rongelap'. And the inhabitants were traumatised by 30 years of sickness and deformity and trying to fight an enemy that was all the more fearsome for being unseen. Rongelap not only looked safe for human habitation; it looked inviting, irresistible. But within it crawled an invisible, malevolent force.

All the *Warrior* crew saw, however, was the beauty. The boat anchored well offshore at first, because of uncertainty about the location of coral heads. As they looked towards the village, a group of 11 women and girls in bright red and floral dresses pulled out into the lagoon in one of their inboard motorboats, known as *bum bums*. As they approached and then circled the *Warrior*, they waved and sang welcoming songs in Marshallese:

> 'I love my home island, where I was born
> I will never leave it.
> This is my home, my only home
> And it is better that I die on it.'

The stern of the small craft trailed a home-made banner reading 'We love the future of our kids'. All the *Warrior* crew were on deck and watching; all were affected. Three of the European women began to cry. The Rongelapese then boarded the visiting boat and – in the manner of atoll dwellers who have been separated from friends and relatives – greeted Jeton

Anjain, Julian Riklon and the other islanders with warm hugs and kisses.

Ashore, a further welcome awaited the strangers who had sailed half way round the world for this encounter. On the beach was an archway of coconut trunks and pandanus leaves, and a sign across the top which proclaimed: 'Welcome to Rongelap. Ba Eman Kabjere. We Love the Future of our Kids.' The crew, transferring to the shore in their inflatables, walked under the sign and were garlanded with leis and *wus* (floral crowns). The air was heavy with hibiscus scent.

As in most Pacific cultures, the women were responsible for the rituals of welcome. The men remained at a distance, 'checking us out', some of the crew felt. The visitors were handed fresh coconut milk to drink and bananas to eat as the hosts continued to sing songs of welcome.

The food and drink presented the ecologists with their first dilemma. They knew the island and its foods were contaminated; that was why they had come there, that was why the Rongelapese were leaving. Should they risk their own health by eating? To refuse, in these circumstances, would be an insult to their hosts. After murmured consultations, they ate and drank.

Philippe Chatenay and Walter Guerin were late coming ashore and missed the ceremony. They asked the Rongelap women to do it again. 'It's for a special film for French television.' The women were not moved by this plea and politely declined to perform.

Steve Sawyer was now on the edge of an anxiety attack. Like the others, he was awed by the beauty of the island and by the fact that the inhabitants felt so strongly about the dangers that they were ready to abandon it. He was moved by the trust and warmth of the Rongelapese welcome, which transcended language differences. But he was alarmed at the number of houses that had already been dismantled. The village looked like a ghost town, an archaeological ruin. Lashed bundles of timber, plywood and corrugated iron lay on the beach ready for removal. It hit him forcefully. The *Rainbow Warrior* was to move 304 people, their homes and their possessions. How the hell could they do it?

In previous discussions, including those that took place on the boat between Majuro and Rongelap, Jeton Anjain had been vague about how much 'cargo' was to be shifted. 'Just take the people,' the senator kept saying. 'That's all we ask.' 'No,' Sawyer had said, 'we can take *some* cargo. How much do you want us to move?' But the Marshallese had not wanted to impose, to appear to ask for too much, and had kept talking about passengers.

Now it was apparent that cargo was indeed to be shifted, some 100 tonnes of it, over about ten days. Could they do it? 'Oh my God,' Sawyer kept saying to himself. 'This is for real.' Expectations had been raised that would have to be met.

A meeting had been called for 2 p.m. to formally present the visitors to the islanders, and to allow the Rongelapese to discuss details of the shift with Anjain and other community leaders. For some older people too, it appeared, it was time to make a final decision about whether they would leave the only home their ancestors had ever known.

At two o'clock sharp the crew began to assemble outside the church, on benches under a shadehouse and under a giant breadfruit tree. No islanders appeared. Was it a bad sign? Had they changed their minds? They had not. They were observing Pacific time. The villagers began to arrive in twos and threes and virtually the whole community was assembled by three o'clock. David Robie recorded the course of the meeting:

Senator Anjain began. He introduced the *Warrior* crew and spelled out the atoll's legacy of deaths and illnesses from the Bravo fallout. 'American scientists have been lying to us for 30 years about radiation on our islands,' he said. 'The poison from the Bravo monster is still felt today. Our people suffered then, and we are suffering now from radiation diseases such as thyroid tumours, cancer, leukaemia, birth defects, stillbirths and miscarriages. As we all decided last year, the time has come for us to leave for Mejato. For the sake of our children and grandchildren.'

Not a stir among the men. But an elderly woman asked: 'How are we going to eat – there are few coconuts and no breadfruit growing on Mejato? How are we going to get money?' 'It will be hard, but we'll find a way,' said Anjain.

Now it was Julian Riklon's turn. 'We know it's going to be tough, trying to make a new life, to become alienated from our land and our spiritual roots. But we also have no choice. The future of our children is most important – by staying here they have no hope. They are bound to die from cancer.'

A fisherman asked what was going to happen to his outrigger canoe. He was assured it would be taken to Mejato. Then somebody cracked a joke and suddenly it was all over. A logistics meeting between Anjain, Riklon, mayor Randy Thomas and other island leaders was set for the next afternoon with Sawyer, skipper Willcox and first mate Gotje to fine tune Operation Exodus.

'The people looked to me to find a way to save them, but they didn't really believe a ship would come all the way from Britain,' said Anjain later. 'It wasn't until they saw the *Rainbow Warrior* in their lagoon that they really believed me. They thought I might be bluffing.'

The crew spent most of Saturday and Sunday wandering around the island, trying to get to know the people they had come to help. To the European eye, the Rongelapese seemed to combine Malayan and Polynesian features, at least facially. But they tended to be short and solid. The women wore long floral dresses, the men mainly denims and T-shirts or sports shirts. In deference to local custom, the *Rainbow Warrior* women wore dresses ashore.

Adults were friendly but reticent with strangers, and at first avoided eye contact. Bunny McDiarmid spent an afternoon with the women weaving pandanus mats. 'They *were* shy, they'd giggle a lot. But every now and then one would grab your hand and hold it and squeeze it as an expression of friendship.' Communication with children was easier. They seemed more open, more curious and playful; to the crew, devoid of all but adult company for two months, they were engaging.

Language was also a barrier. While some adults spoke English, most Rongelapese knew only three or four words. So all the crew, like McDiarmid, tried to get by with gestures, smiles and laughs. But they felt like intruders. Atoll islands are small and walking into an island community is like entering somebody's living room.

The journalists meanwhile sought out victims of the Bravo blast with the help of interpreters. They also found that all the evacuees were desolate to be leaving their homes, but saw no alternative.

Kiosang Kios was 15 in 1954. After the Bravo explosion her hair fell out, her feet ached and burned, and she suffered vomiting and diarrhoea. Three years later she bore her first child. It was a boneless 'jellyfish baby' and survived only half a day. After further stillbirths and miscarriages she had a daughter in 1959, who has a thyroid disease and malformed legs and feet.

The journalists watched, listened and scribbled. Later they would give their stories to Lloyd Anderson to radio to an outside world only mildly interested.

At one o'clock on Monday morning loading began. With it, any barriers between the islanders and the outsiders started to dissolve. The *Warrior* had moved closer to the shore, standing off about 800 metres, and the *bum bums* motored out stacked high with building materials, generators, furniture, suitcases and sleeping mats. The whole day and the next was spent passing cargo up from the motorboats and stowing or fastening it down on the larger vessel. As they worked, the two groups talked, jested, smiled at shared mishaps, frowned together while mishandling or dropping difficult bundles. During breaks from work, they ate and drank together. A bond began to form.

At dusk on Tuesday the first 75 passengers came aboard, mainly the elderly (many of them aged prematurely), pregnant mothers, and children, handed up from the *bum bums* to the

Warrior and handled with care. Four of the children were seriously deformed; a dozen of the adults had operation scars on their necks, the result of thyroid cancers. With them they brought suitcases held together with string, carry-all bags, pots and pans, kettles, and rolled plaited sleeping mats. The crew rigged a tarpaulin over the deck to shelter most of the evacuees. Other Rongelapese took over cabins vacated by the Europeans or laid sleeping mats in spare spaces such as the workshop hold. Thus loaded, the *Rainbow Warrior* turned south-east and motored towards Mejato, 160 kilometres away.

Mejato lies near the eastern tip of Kwajalein Atoll – a 240-kilometre circle of coral and 93 islands. It is close to the American bases at Roi-Namur and Kwajalein Island, and within 40 kilometres of the area where American test missiles launched from as far away as Vandenberg Air Force Base in California splash down. The island is about half the size of Rongelap and was uninhabited. The soil is bad by comparison; it had no cultivations when the evacuees arrived; but the water supply was adequate and the shallow reef offshore thick with fish.

There was one massive shelter, erected in March at Jeton Anjain's direction. It was a concrete slab, about 9 metres by 12 metres, covered with corrugated iron. The roof had gutters and fed water barrels. Eventually the structure would be walled and used as the school. Initially it served as the community house for the children and older people.

The first *bum bum* which had set out from Rongelap ahead of the *Rainbow Warrior* had not arrived. So the crew began unloading with their own inflatables. First they carried passengers to the beach, where they were welcomed with songs and food by relatives from Ebeye, an island at the opposite corner of the atoll. Then they began the laborious task of moving bundles of cargo ashore. A heavy swell made the job even more difficult, and one of the islanders was injured after the *bum bum* arrived when he fell between the *Warrior* and the smaller vessel.

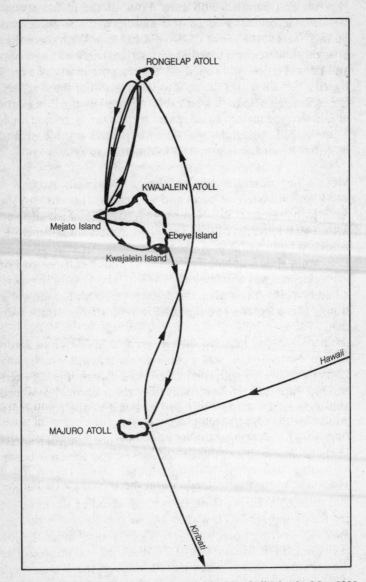

RONGELAP ATOLL

KWAJALEIN ATOLL

Mejato Island

Ebeye Island

Kwajalein Island

Hawaii

MAJURO ATOLL

Kiribati

The Rainbow Warrior*'s movements in the Marshall Islands, May 1985*

On shore, the Rongelapese were putting tarpaulins around
the community house for additional shelter and building tem-
porary cookhouses from traditional materials. Even as the
cargo was being unloaded, the site began to look like a village:
food was prepared, children ran about and explored, old people
rested in the shade, trying to come to terms with what for many
of them was their third forced evacuation, and probably their
last.

There were no animals, however. Pigs, dogs and fowls had
been left on Rongelap in case they carried radiation-induced
disease. Thus, for their greater safety, the refugees had denied
themselves a major source of food.

It was soon apparent to Willcox and Sawyer that the pace of
removal was too slow. The first load had taken five days to
assemble and deliver, and there were to be at least three more
removals. And yet, to make its other connections, the *Rainbow
Warrior* had allowed ten days for the entire evacuation. And
so the crew began to work harder and move faster. For subsequent trips they used their Zodiacs to load *and* unload the
Warrior; with practice they became more adept at packing
cargo. The second voyage moved 114 people, the third about
40.

As the vessel left Rongelap for the fourth and final time with
70 passengers, Martini Gotje looked back at the bolted and
shuttered church – the only building left standing – and at the
whitewashed graves surrounding it. It was still a beautiful place,
he realised, as near to paradise as he had seen. But those were
the only people who could stay there: the dead.

Relations between the islanders and the *Warrior* crew had become open and strong. The visitors were now unwilling to leave
the Marshalls, some of them believing that the work of reset-
tling the evacuees was more important than the Moruroa demonstration: because it involved real people; and because Greenpeace
had helped set in motion something that was far from finished
and possibly even dangerous (there was a likelihood of a severe

food shortage on Mejato). Haazen, McDiarmid, Biedermann and others felt a sense of responsibility that could not be ignored when the last evacuees were abandoned.

Davey Edward sat down and wrote one of his rare letters, to Maureen Falloon, and said that he did not think anyone in Greenpeace International realised the magnitude of what the *Warrior* crew had done. It established the possibility of humanitarian missions in conjunction with environmental campaigns. 'We found out what had happened to these people, the consequences of nuclear games on their lives. And we lived with them, worked with them, ate and drank with them, handled the kiddies and the old folk. And finally we cried with them. We finished up with a relationship with people who are usually very aloof with outsiders.'

As the *Rainbow Warrior* approached Mejato for the last time, four young men asked Nathalie Mestre for a pen. 'We, the people of Rongelap, love our homeland,' they wrote in English. 'But how can we live in a place which is dangerous and poisonous . . . why didn't those American people test Bravo in a state capital? Why? *Rainbow Warrior*, thank you for being so nice to us.'

In spite of feverish activities on the part of the journalists (who, in addition to filing stories, also helped with loading and unloading and cleaning the vessel), outside interest in the evacuation was minimal. Some stories appeared in papers in Germany, Belgium and the Netherlands, and in the *Guardian* in England; a few others, less prominently, in Japan, Australia and New Zealand. French television screened Chartenay's and Guerin's film weeks later. Pereira's photographs were taken and distributed by Associated Press's wire service, though not widely used. In the United States, source of the events that had caused the evacuation and of the political forces that should have taken care of the Rongelap people, the story was ignored.

By Thursday 30 May, the evacuation was complete. It was also

Fernando Pereira's 35th birthday. The crew decided to have a day of rest off Mejato to celebrate both events. Reservations about Pereira's presence on the boat had evaporated in the sweat of his efforts to help in the shift, his compilation of an intensively moving portfolio of photographs documenting the event, and his refusal to be angered or depressed by setbacks.

Full of affection for his contribution, and more appreciative now of his *joie de vivre*, his shipmates printed a T-shirt for him. The front read 'Rainbow Warrior Removals Inc. We move anything anywhere.' The back was decorated with the crew's signatures. That night there was a party on the boat with all the things Pereira valued most: music, drink, food, and women to dance with. And he danced with abandon, drenching his new shirt with perspiration.

The party emphasised something else. The crew had not only bonded with the Rongelap people, they were now even closer to one another. 'We are not simply a good crew,' Henk Haazen told himself. 'We are a good *operating* crew.' They felt more affection for one another, and more respect. They were pleased and grateful. It was a good feeling, a family feeling.

The following day the *Warrior* left for Ebeye with Sawyer an invalid. Visiting one of the wrecks on the reef, he had fallen ten metres into a rusty hold, dislocated his shoulder and lacerated his abdomen. He was the first casualty of the Pacific Peace Voyage.

The *Rainbow Warrior* still had unfinished business in the Marshalls. Anchored off Ebeye at the eastern corner of the Kwajalein Atoll (where it was to offload all the journalists apart from David Robie), the crew decided to do something about the American missile tracking station on adjacent Kwajalein Island. In characteristic Greenpeace fashion, they opted for an impromptu protest – one that would not risk arrest, impounding of the boat or embarrassment to the Marshallese.

Down in the engine-room they unfurled ten metres of canvas and painted on it in large letters, in English and Marshallese: 'We Can't Relocate the World – Stop Star Wars'. Then, early on the morning of 6 June, Bene Hoffmann, Andy Biedermann, Bunny McDiarmid and Grace O'Sullivan carried the banner across Kwajalein Harbour in a Zodiac, with Henk Haazen at the tiller. Another inflatable followed with Fernando Pereira to record the gesture.

Motoring into Kwajalein was a strange experience. The installation – radar dishes, domes, telescopes and antennae – looks like a set from a science fiction movie. It is the American 'bullseye' for intercontinental ballistic missile tracking and a key component in Strategic Defence Initiative research. Strategists have identified it as a high-priority target in the event of a nuclear war. Ironically, it even houses a highly sophisticated video camera used for part of the filming of the Hollywood blockbuster *Star Wars*.

The first Zodiac landed on the beach unmolested. Biedermann, O'Sullivan and McDiarmid scrambled out and carried the banner to a protective fence in front of one of the radar domes. They climbed the fence and strung the banner from it, about ten metres from the ground. While they clung there struggling to attach it, two elderly American women on their early morning walk passed underneath and called up politely, 'Good morning.' The protestors, breathless with anxiety, responded with equal politeness.

They climbed down, saw the sign was not straight, and climbed up again to rectify it, terrified all the while that military guards would get to them before they were finished. The security police did not come until they were back on the harbour, however, and Pereira had photographed the banner in place. Minutes later it was torn down. The protestors were allowed to return unmolested to Ebeye.

Back at the *Warrior*, the crew made up a photocopy pamphlet with a photograph of the banner and an explanation of the action in Marshallese. The people at Ebeye were amused and approving, even those who depended on the Kwajalein installation for work. Meanwhile officials at the base told Associated Press in Honolulu that the protest had taken place on the island's golf-course. 'Some golf ball,' Haazen commented, thinking of the 50-metre-high radar dome that had been the backdrop for the banner.

At Majuro the *Rainbow Warrior* put ashore Steve Sawyer (who would fly to Honolulu and thence to New Zealand) and took on Hans Guyt, 32-year-old director of Greenpeace Netherlands and close friend of Fernando Pereira. From there it turned south on 13 June for the next leg of the voyage, to New Zealand.

En route it called in at Kiribati, where – in spite of government approval of the visit – some crew members were detained by police and accused by the leader of the opposition of being communist; and Vanuatu. The welcome at Vanuatu on 27 June was spectacular and heart-warming: a flotilla of boats at Port Vila, 3,000 people at the waterfront, and a visit from Prime Minister Walter Lini, Greenpeace's strongest governmental supporter in the Pacific. Before the boat departed Lini sent aboard Charles Rara, a member of the Prime Minister's Department, to stay with the vessel for the Moruroa protest. Rara had been issued with a diplomatic passport for protection in the event of French interference with the voyage.

By the night of Saturday 6 July, the *Warrior* was off the New Zealand coast and everybody on board in a state of high excitement. For Bunny McDiarmid, returning home after seven years, there was the knowledge that many things had changed since her departure: the country's government and its policy on nuclear ship visits, which had attracted so much attention in Europe and North America, and the renaissance of Maori culture. David Robie too was coming home. And Edward, Gotje and Hoffmann had all visited New Zealand previously; they spoke well of the land and its people. For the others, it seemed as if they were reaching some kind of Mecca: one of the few countries in the Western world with a nuclear policy that matched that of Greenpeace.

A clear dawn and the sight of the east coast near the Hen and Chicken Islands intensified the exuberance. After nearly four months at sea and their recent experience of parched atolls, the crew were confronted by a massive coastline, seemingly lush and devoid of people – not merely a Mecca but an oasis. And they were looking forward to reunions with Greenpeace members and supporters whom they had met previously, in New Zealand, overseas and on earlier campaigns.

Everything on board was more shipshape than at any other time on the voyage: the deck freshly painted, varnish on the railings, brass polished on the bridge. This was in part an expression of the pride that the crew took in the boat, *their* boat; and partly a preparation for the short break they all planned before sailing for Moruroa, expected to be the most demanding section of the voyage. In New Zealand, each crew member would work on the boat for one week and holiday for another. Fernando Pereira, for example, was going to Mt Ruapehu in the centre of the North Island for a few days' skiing with Andy Biedermann. Others would be fishing at Taupo, crossing Cook Strait to visit the South Island, staying with friends on Waiheke Island. Bunny McDiarmid and Henk Haazen would stay with her parents in Herne Bay, Auckland. By 21 July, they would all rejoin the boat to sail for Rarotonga and Moruroa, in time to reach the atoll by Hiroshima Day, 6 August. After weeks of alertness and strain, the *Warrior* crew were on the edge of unwinding. As they approached Auckland, Haazen felt that he was not just entering a friendly harbour; it was *the* friendly harbour – the home of the Pacific Peace Flotilla in a nuclear-free country. For the first time in weeks they began to relax. They felt safe.

Auckland turned on a welcome as memorable as that in Vanuatu, though without a Prime Ministerial presence. It was a clear, bright winter's day. The *Warrior* cruised up the Rangitoto Channel into Waitemata Harbour, sails filled with air like the wings of a great bird, painted rainbow arching over the bow. The residents of the city, watching from homes, beaches and boat clubs, were impressed: the vessel had charisma. On the water, she was met by a festive flotilla of

20 yachts, launches and speedboats, members of the city's
Peace Squadron (originally formed to protest against the entry
of nuclear ships into the port). Among them was *Vega*, veteran
of the earliest Greenpeace protests to Moruroa in 1972 and
1973, when she had been owned and skippered by Canadian
David McTaggart, now chairman of Greenpeace International.
Vega too was heading for Moruroa in 1985.

The *Warrior* scarcely had time to acknowledge the welcome,
however. Just as the kauri scow *Te Aroha* and front-running
members of the Peace Squadron reached her, the port's pilot
boarded the vessel and said he was obliged to get her moored
as soon as possible. So the flotilla assembled in time to see
the *Rainbow Warrior* draw rapidly away in the direction of
Marsden Wharf on the city side of the harbour. Other Greenpeace supporters, gathered at Devonport on the north side for
a 'peace festival', could only wave as the *Rainbow Warrior*
passed by at speed.

On board *Te Aroha*, former nurse Elaine Shaw was as excited
as the *Rainbow Warrior* crew. The Greenpeace New Zealand
co-ordinator on nuclear issues had scarcely allowed herself to
believe the vessel was in the Pacific until she saw it enter Waitemata Harbour that morning. Its arrival was the culmination
of years of planning within the New Zealand organisation and
agitation within Greenpeace International. For Greenpeace New
Zealand, the nuclear issue was a Pacific one above all else and
its members had formed close links with the Nuclear-Free and
Independent Pacific Movement established in Hawaii in 1980.

This link was something of an embarrassment to Greenpeace
International, which is determinedly non-political so as to work
with all governments and political parties. In the Pacific, however, efforts on the part of indigenous peoples to resist
militarisation of the region by colonial powers had become inex-
tricably linked to efforts to secure independence from those
powers, especially in Tahiti and New Caledonia (and previously
in Vanuatu, which broke free from Britain and France in 1980).

Greenpeace New Zealand accepted the inevitability of this

link, although, curiously, it has few Maori members and activists. Working out of cheerfully chaotic headquarters in downtown Auckland, it is directed and staffed by women to a far greater extent than its counterparts. Formed originally in 1974 to support yachts going to Moruroa, its membership had grown to 2,500 by 1985, with an additional mailing list of more than 1,800. Perhaps because of the degree of female participation, it had not been involved in the kinds of high-profile direct action campaigns that had characterised Greenpeace elsewhere. Most of its efforts had been invested in public education, and in lobbying government and the Public Service on the nuclear issue, whaling, sealing, pollution from a chemical plant in New Plymouth, the problems of dolphins in captivity and the future of Antarctica.

Shaw and her colleagues, especially national co-ordinator Carol Stewart, had given a great deal of time and attention to campaigns objecting to nuclear testing in French Polynesia, however. They had helped organise the despatch of earlier protest vessels from New Zealand to Moruroa, and they had pleaded year after year with Greenpeace International to send the *Rainbow Warrior* into the region, to allow more sustained and more publicised protest. When authorisation for the 1985 Peace Voyage was finally won in 1984, the New Zealand organisation was ecstatic. From that time on it concentrated on assembling and arranging support for a fleet of vessels – *Vega*, *Alliance*, *Django* and *Kliss II* – to leave Auckland between Bastille Day (14 July) and Hiroshima Day, and rendezvous with the *Warrior* off Moruroa. On Sunday 7 July 1985, these efforts seemed to Shaw and Stewart, following on board *Vega*, on the verge of fruition. It was a moment of deep satisfaction.

Auckland turned on a series of welcomes for the *Rainbow Warrior* crew. There was a Greenpeace party on board the vessel the night of its arrival. The following evening, five government Members of Parliament came aboard to meet crew members, look over the vessel, and express support for the Moruroa campaign.

The next night, 9 July, there was a Maori reception on the boat. Local Maori leaders, including the leader of the Mana Motuhake Party, Matiu Rata, welcomed the crew on behalf of the country's tangata whenua (indigenous people). Rata praised Greenpeace members for their efforts to protect the earth and the sea, and said such ideals were close to those of the native peoples of the Pacific. The occasion was a further reminder to the crew of the Pacific nature of the peace voyage, and of the environmental complications which Western man and technology had introduced into the lives of Pacific peoples. Rata himself had been a Greenpeace ally for more than a decade, having sailed to Moruroa in 1973 on the protest yacht *Magic Isle*. The ceremony closed with a hymn for the protection of the *Warrior* and its crew on the high seas.

The evening of Wednesday 10 July was one of comings and goings. Half the crew was away from the ship, holidaying in other parts of the country. Willcox, Gotje and Anderson were staying on board for a meeting with skippers of the Moruroa Peace Flotilla. Biedermann and Sorensen too were there for a meal, prepared by relief cook Margaret Mills, a 55-year-old peace activist from Waiheke Island.

Steve Sawyer was ashore for dinner. He had been invited to the Mexican Café in downtown Auckland to celebrate his 29th birthday with New Zealand Greenpeace members, and with a handful of American and Canadian Greenpeace officials in town for a three-day regional conference of the organisation due to begin the following day.

Davey Edward and Fernando Pereira were not required for the skippers' meeting. They agreed that they were bored and decided to go ashore too, to look for some action in Auckland's sparse night-spots.

Edward and Pereira had not liked each other at first. The chief engineer had been one of the group offended by the laborious manner in which the photographer responded to calls to work. He had picked him as the kind of person who would happily drink what other people provided but be slow to put his hand in his pocket to buy his own round. Their respective manners and personal styles were also utterly at odds: Edward was matter-of-fact, undemonstrative and strictly non-sartorial in his choice of clothes; Pereira was a raver, a gesticulator and a careful dresser. As a person of authority on the *Warrior*, the Yorkshireman had found occasion to speak sharply to his 'Latin' colleague; Pereira for his part tried to steer clear of the man he regarded as a dour Anglo-Saxon.

In Vanuatu, each discovered he had misread the other. They had gone to a French-run nightclub one evening, hoping to be able to drink and dance for a couple of hours. They were wearing clean but scarcely formal clothes. After an hour, Pereira came over to Edward, crying.

'This guy's just told me to leave,' he said. 'Just because I'm wearing a T-shirt. Why should he want to throw me out? What have I done? I have not offended anyone? Why should he want to do this to me?'

Edward was surprised. He had picked Pereira as somebody who would not care about what other people thought or felt. Now he consoled the photographer and tried to calm him down. They spent the rest of the evening drinking and talking together (Pereira was not made to leave), and as they reminisced they found they had much in common – particularly a strong sense of family and a love of people and of the sea. They were, from that time on, close friends.

On 10 July they headed up town around eight o'clock, making for the Ponsonby Club Hotel (known locally as the Gluepot), in an old inner-city suburb characterised by restaurants and (among the locals) a strong community feeling. There was no music at the pub that night, however, and they found it a gloomy place. After having a beer they decided to move on.

It was a chilly evening with intermittent drizzle. They walked briskly along Ponsonby Road, wrapped in their heaviest coats, swinging their arms and slapping their hands together in an effort to keep out the cold. They spotted nothing else that appealed to them until they got to the Star Hotel on the other side of the suburb. There they had a few more drinks and shared stories about the friendliness of New Zealanders and the hopelessness of the country's night-life. Then they decided to return to the ship. There was a party scheduled for Steve Sawyer's birthday. Things might be more lively there. On the way they bought a bag of chips to warm them, some beer for the party, and a bottle of rum as a present for Sawyer. By that time, though, things were as quiet on the boat as they were in the city, which seemed to have shut down for the winter.

Sawyer had arrived back on board just after 7.30. He was greeted with a chocolate cake, decorated with a jellybean rainbow, which Margaret Mills had baked for his birthday. Before heading down to the theatre for the skippers' meeting, Sawyer shared the cake around with ice cream, and with wine left over from the reception the previous night. There was also a present for him from the crew: a brass bolt out of one of the *Rainbow Warrior*'s old engines that had been removed some years before (he had had such a bolt previously, but it had been stolen).

Among the 20 or so people milling about the messroom was a Frenchman, whom Peace Flotilla co-ordinator Rien Achterberg had spotted looking in the portholes from the wharf half an hour earlier. Achterberg, staying on board and long accustomed to playing a public relations role for Greenpeace, invited the stranger onto the ship and took him into the mess.

'What's your name?'

'François Verlet.'*

'Are you staying in New Zealand?'

'No. I am in transit from Singapore to Tahiti. I am here four more hours only.'

'What's your interest in Greenpeace?'

Verlet thought, then said he was a pacifist and that he had friends in Tahiti who worked on boats and could be helpful

---

*He did not, as other reports have claimed, give his name as François 'Verlon'.

to Greenpeace. They could perhaps assist in getting canoes from some of the French Polynesian islands to Moruroa.

All this struck Achterberg as odd, including Verlet's appearance. He was in his early twenties, well dressed (designer jeans), short hair brushed upwards. He looked too 'straight' to be a greeny. He could not name any peace organisations in France with which he had associations. And the idea of sending Polynesians onto Moruroa itself in canoes had been considered by Greenpeace only briefly, and then vetoed by international chairman David McTaggart. It had never been discussed publicly.

Verlet, by this time also in conversation with Chris Robinson, skipper of *Vega*, asked what else would be happening on board that night. He was told that the Peace Fleet skippers were conferring for a couple of hours in the hold, and that afterwards the birthday party would continue in the mess. He nodded, thanked Achterberg and Robinson and made to leave, in deference to the imminent meeting. As he was escorted from the messroom, he called back to Steve Sawyer: 'Happy birthday. And good luck on the campaign.'

The meeting, in the old fish hold forward of the engine-room, was literally in the bowels of the ship. It was an awkward place to get into (down a hatch which opened only from the outside, and then down a ladder), and from which to leave.

Attending were the skippers of *Vega*, *Alliance*, *Kliss II*, *Django* and *Varangian*; Willcox, Gotje, Anderson and Guyt from the *Warrior*; and Achterberg and a couple of others from the Auckland Greenpeace office.

They went over charts together, discussed routes and possible rendezvous points off Moruroa, and equipment. In cases of shortages, they talked about where additional gear might be acquired or borrowed. And they drew up a tentative schedule for leaving Auckland, to make allowances for variations in the speed of the vessels (which ranged from a flat-bottomed scow, the *Alliance*, to a sleek catamaran such as *Kliss II*). Those who had not been to Moruroa previously called upon the expertise of those who had.

Shortly before eleven they broke up. Sawyer was to go out to Piha – where the regional meeting was to begin the following morning – with the visiting Americans. They all had another drink in the messroom before dispersing around 11.20. Only those left of the crew were still on board; plus Achterberg and Russell Munro, skipper of *Django*, which was moored to the port side of the *Warrior*.

For Hanne Sorensen, the evening had been a restless one. She ate on board and did the dishes afterwards. Then, because the rest of the crew were either ashore or at the skippers' meeting, she went to the Seamen's Mission further along the waterfront. There she rang her parents in Denmark to tell them how she was and given them a résumé of the *Rainbow Warrior*'s programme for the coming months – the Moruroa leg of the voyage.

Back on the boat she still felt restless. She was in the messroom when the meeting broke up shortly after eleven. Nothing further seemed in prospect so she decided to go to bed. On her way to the cabin she shared with Gotje she changed her mind abruptly. She felt she had to get off the boat.

Afterwards, she had no explanation for her behaviour. She did not feel an acute sense of danger, simply that she ought not to be there. This had never happened previously; she had only been ashore once, in fact, since the boat arrived in Auckland.

And so she came back up to the deck, crossed the gangway on to the wharf and went for a walk, a long walk, along the Auckland waterfront.

By 11.50 Peter Willcox, Lloyd Anderson and Margaret Mills were in bed, asleep. Left in the messroom having a final drink were Edward and Pereira, disgruntled that their party had evaporated, Martini Gotje, Andy Biedermann, Hans Guyt, Rien Achterberg and Russell Munro.

And then the explosion.

Outside, it was heard as a dull boom that shook nearby

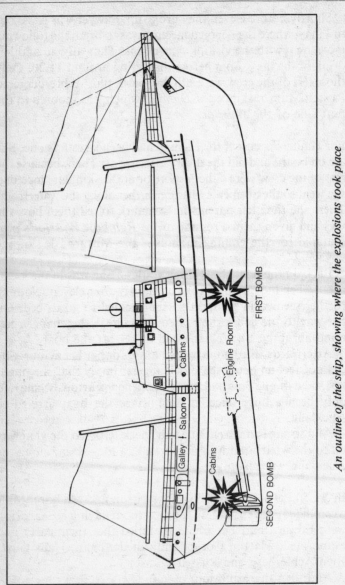

An outline of the ship, showing where the explosions took place

buildings and rattled window panes. The *Warrior* lifted slightly
in the water and then settled, the sea boiling and steaming on
its starboard side. Within seconds she was listing as thousands
of gallons of water rushed into the engine-room.

Inside, it came as a thump and a shiver. The lights went out
and those in the messroom were thrown off the chairs and
tables on which they perched.

Edward, accustomed to emergencies at sea, swore but kept
his head. His immediate thought was that something had blown
up in the engine-room, his engine-room. He yelled, 'Don't
panic,' and ran to the engine-room door. By the time he
wrenched it open the emergency lighting had come on. He got
three steps down the ladder before he saw the water, tonnes
of it. He could not believe it, but did not stop to speculate.

Back in the passageway he met a half-naked Willcox, who,
waking when the explosion occurred, thought the *Warrior* had
been involved in a collision at sea. 'The engine-room's full of
water. And it's still coming in.' That was all Willcox needed
to know. 'Abandon ship,' he shouted as he emerged from the
passage. 'Everybody get the hell off.'

Lloyd Anderson had woken in the radio room, dressed,
found his glasses in the dark and got out on to the bridge –
all within two minutes. Andy Biedermann made straight for
Margaret Mills's cabin and escorted her out forcibly when she
tried to find her glasses. Gotje had grabbed a torch and rushed
to his cabin to find Sorensen. And Pereira went below with
him, heading for his cameras.

The second explosion, at the stern, came minutes after the
first. Terisa Tutte, now on deck on the *Django*, saw a blue
flash underwater. Gotje and Pereira were still below. The others
were on the *Warrior*'s deck or had crossed the now precariously
tilting gangway on to the wharf. In less than another minute
Gotje was up too, saying he couldn't find Sorensen: 'Where's
Hanne? Where's Hanne?'

Willcox and Edward leaped on to the wheelhouse roof and
ripped the cover off the smokestack, in case anyone was trying

to get out that way. But they could see nothing. They too abandoned ship as the *Warrior* came to rest, four-fifths submerged, its wheelhouse roof touching the wharf, its mast at a 45-degree angle. Fernando Pereira, apparently stunned by the second explosion, drowned in the cabin next to his own, straps of a camera bag twined around his legs.

The first bomb had blown a hole two metres by three into the engine-room – big enough to drive a truck through; water had poured through this at the rate of six tonnes per second. The second, set near the propellor, had destroyed the ship's propulsion system. Carefully, the *Rainbow Warrior* had been sunk *and* disabled.

Many of the empty cabins were found later to be holed and mangled with shrapnel from the first explosion. Had the bombs gone off an hour later, when everybody on board had retired for the night, there could have been four deaths from the first explosion, five from the second. Had they detonated an hour earlier, the 14 people at the skippers' meeting would have been trapped in the fish hold. The entire leadership of the Greenpeace Peace Flotilla would have been eliminated.

Throughout the early hours of the morning, members of the *Warrior* crew sat on the steps of the Wharf Police Station, in sight of Marsden Wharf. All of them stared across at their ship, floodlit, slumped and sunken. All were stunned. All came to terms with grief in their own way. The dominant feelings were shock at the loss of Pereira; and numbness for the loss of the ship that they felt had become part of them and they part of it.

'I felt I just had to touch it,' Sorensen said afterwards. 'I hadn't been there when it happened, so I had to touch it: to see if it was really dead. And to say goodbye.' But she was not allowed back. Auckland Police had taken charge of what they already suspected was a homicide enquiry; and what was soon to become an investigation into international terrorism – New Zealand's first.

TWO

Operation Rainbow Warrior

April/May 1985

Four days after the *Rainbow Warrior* sailed into Honolulu, the first agent associated with the sabotage of the 1985 Pacific Peace Voyage arrived in New Zealand from France, via Fiji. She was Christine Huguette Cabon. She held the rank of lieutenant in the French Army and was 33 years old. Her instructions from the Direction Générale des Services Extérieurs (French Secret Service) were to infiltrate Greenpeace, to gather intelligence about the movements of the boats *Vega* and *Rainbow Warrior*, and to advise on ways of counteracting Greenpeace strategies for the Moruroa voyage.

Cabon was no svelte feminine charmer, out to woo information from unsuspecting male and female confidants. On the contrary. She was, in fact, lesbian. It is difficult to disassociate her selection by the DGSE for this particular mission from the fact that the active membership of Greenpeace in New Zealand in 1985 was overwhelmingly female. Inevitably, some of its supporters were lesbian. Whoever assigned Cabon to this aspect of the French Rainbow Warrior operation already had access to intelligence about the nature of the peace movement in Auckland. And Cabon was ready to employ more than her brains and her wits to gather further information about Greenpeace activities.

She was a tough and professional woman. Three years earlier she had been invalided out of a French Army commando unit after a parachute accident. From that time she had worked for the DGSE on infiltration assignments, including one in 1984 which took her into the Palestine Liberation Organisation,

gathering intelligence for France and for Mossad, the Israeli
Secret Service. She is reported to have helped select targets for
the Israeli bombing of PLO installations in Beirut. Afterwards,
to protect her from the attention of Arab assassins, she under-
went plastic surgery to change her appearance.

In New Zealand, Cabon was to travel under the name
Frédérique Bonlieu. She called herself a scientific consultant
and said initially that she was gathering information for travel
articles and for friends who would visit New Zealand as
tourists. After a Greenpeace official had sown the idea, she
also claimed to be writing articles on ecological issues for the
French press. She had already conned a French conservationist
and yachtsman known to New Zealand ecologists, a friend of
Jacques Cousteau, into giving her a testimonial. Jean-Marie
Vidal had written to Greenpeace New Zealand in March 1985
that Bonlieu 'is a scientist, an excellent sailor, and shares our
beliefs'. He added that she was 'coming to your country to
study geography . . . Help her and share your views and
activities with her.' Bonlieu herself sent a telegram announcing her imminent visit to Joan Cavaney, a Greenpeace supporter in South Auckland.

When she arrived in Auckland on 23 April she contacted
Cavaney, who gave her the Greenpeace office telephone number
and told her to ask for Elaine Shaw. Bonlieu then spent her
first night in New Zealand in a city youth hostel. The following
day, 24 April, she rang Shaw from the Chief Post Office.
Because Bonlieu's difficulty with English made directions a
problem, Shaw told her to wait there and she would come and
meet her. When she did she found an intense, thickset woman
in sweatshirt, scarf and jeans. 'You're looking very patriotic,'
Shaw said, noting the red, white and blue colours. Bonlieu did
not respond. She was to have difficulty penetrating the New
Zealand sense of humour, particularly when jokes seemed
directed against her country.

Shaw took the visitor back to the Greenpeace office in Nagel
House, a comfortably shabby suite of rooms on the fifth floor
overlooking Auckland city on one side and Albert Park on the

other. She sat her down on one of the well-used sofas, under posters of yachts, whales and peace symbols. There, while Shaw finished up work for the day, Bonlieu talked with Greenpeace workers who came and went. She was nervous, intense and (in the recollection of everyone who met her) exaggeratedly French in attitude and mannerism. Surprisingly, she seemed to have few overt sympathies for Greenpeace's anti-nuclear crusades.

At 7.00 p.m. she was still there, so Shaw took her to a café nearby for a meal. There, the earnest conversation continued. Bonlieu kept stressing that the French had as much right to be in the Pacific as Anglo-Saxon colonisers. And they had the right to defend themselves with their *force de frappe*. Shaw tried to explain how Pacific peoples felt about the French military presence and in particular about nuclear testing, and said it was difficult to register those feelings in France. That might have given Bonlieu the idea for further cover.

'Well,' she said, 'I could write some articles for you. I have good contacts. I could give my opinion in France of your point of view. I could research that here.'

Yes. Shaw agreed. That might be helpful. And – yes – she could use the Greenpeace office for her research.

After they had eaten, Bonlieu announced that she had no money. Shaw had to pay for both meals. This was to be a common experience for those who associated with the French-woman during her early weeks in New Zealand. She also told Shaw she was only allowed to sleep three nights in the youth hostel and would have to find somewhere else to stay. Could she recommend cheap accommodation?

The following morning Bonlieu was back in the Greenpeace office and Shaw introduced her to Carol Stewart. Stewart, a serious-minded 39-year-old former insurance claims clerk, was one of Greenpeace's first paid officials in New Zealand. By 1985 she was national co-ordinator for the local organisation and New Zealand trustee on the Greenpeace International council.

'Carol,' said Shaw carefully, 'Frédérique is looking for somewhere to stay. Do you know anywhere cheap?'

Stewart misunderstood. She leased a largish house in Grey Lynn and part of the rent was subsidised by Greenpeace when other officials or members were staying there. She thought Shaw was asking her to take in the Frenchwoman, and she resented it. Overhearing previous conversations, she had already decided that she had little in common with Bonlieu, and on some issues – such as independence of French colonial territories – their views were irreconcilable. None the less, believing that she was being called upon to be hospitable, she invited Bonlieu to stay with her. Shaw delivered the French-woman to her the following evening.

Frédérique Bonlieu was not a good guest. She helped herself to everything that was in the house – preparing her own breakfasts and eating dinner with the rest of the family – but did not offer to pay anything towards food or board. She did no housework. She tried to persuade a German woman also staying there to speak French all the time, when no one else in the house could understand the language. They all found her cold; in the words of Stewart's daughter, 'snooty'.

She was also left alone there for long periods when everyone else had departed for work or school. On several mornings she told Stewart she would stay behind because she was expecting phone calls from France. And she had ample opportunity to read the odd Greenpeace telex that Stewart may have brought home from time to time.

In the midst of benevolent disorder at the office, Bonlieu rolled up her sleeves and pitched in with whatever donkey-work had to be done: sorting address stickers, folding newsletters, sealing envelopes (Greenpeace New Zealand then had a mailing list of about 1,800 people). Shaw believed she kept coming in because she was accepted there and had nowhere else to go.

Her fellow workers, such as Judy Seaboyer and Jane Cooper, did not feel as negative about her as Shaw and Stewart had at the outset. When she got to know people by name she relaxed a little and began to talk as she worked – not so much conversation, Seaboyer felt, but a need to fill the silences with words. Although she was decidedly Eurocentric and pro-nuclear, this did not annoy everybody. They had already encountered such attitudes in visiting Europeans. And she *was* prepared to work for Greenpeace, however incongruous its views seemed alongside her own.

Ostensibly, she also got to work on her 'essays' for the French press, making use of whatever literature was lying around the office. No one was concerned about this. Greenpeace is an open organisation. There are no secrets. On occasions she was even left briefly alone, to mind the office and answer telephones while others went to meetings in different parts of the building.

She spoke with Rien Achterberg, organiser of the Peace Flotilla, about when the *Rainbow Warrior* would arrive and where it would berth. She read frequent telexes from the *Warrior* itself as it sailed from Hawaii to the Marshalls and began the Rongelap evacuation. She asked Achterberg too about the other flotilla boats, who would be sailing on them, their expected departure times from Auckland and arrival dates at Moruroa.

Bonlieu listened to speculation in the office about whether Tahitians would take part in the Moruroa protest; and she seemed to have confused this with discussion of a planned boycott (by participants, not Greenpeace) of the Pacific Arts Festival due to be held in Tahiti at the end of June.* All this information was passed back to the DGSE in Paris via written reports or phone calls, some of them from the Greenpeace office itself (they were always incoming and person-to-person to Bonlieu). She also made two calls to a contact in Los Angeles. Her own explanation for these communications was

---

*The Tricot report states that the DGSE was sent intelligence that some form of protest could possibly take place on 24 June during the Pacific Arts Festival; in fact the festival began on 29 June, and Greenpeace never planned to use it as part of the Moruroa protest.

that they were to and from friends who would soon be visiting New Zealand and wanted information about the country.

In addition to collecting maps for these 'friends', Bonlieu also began to write down the names, phone numbers and rates of hotels and vehicle hire firms, and to check the costs and conditions for hiring boats and underwater equipment. One afternoon she asked Carol Stewart to make some telephone calls for her to dive shops, on the ground that her own English was not adequate.

Stewart rang one shop and found what it cost to hire and refill diving tanks, and whether it was possible to rent small boats for individuals to take on diving expeditions (it was not). Once she had this information, Bonlieu said that was fine; she did not want comparative prices. But she seemed disappointed that boats were available for large charter trips only.

Another Greenpeace volunteer who worked alongside Bonlieu on several occasions was Monique Davis, an expatriate Dutchwoman who spoke fluent French. At their first meeting, Bonlieu overpowered her with one of her standard monologues; she was doing research on the French in the Pacific and putting together an essay for the French press. She spoked slowly, intensely, like a politician, Davis thought.

A few days later they got together to work on the draft of an open letter to President Mitterrand from French nationals in New Zealand. Bonlieu diluted the draft considerably, saying that France should not feel under siege. It would be better to use the slogan of the Revolution (liberty, fraternity, equality) as a basis for the document; to say that, although the French had a right to live in the Pacific, they should be careful not to violate the rights of Pacific peoples. The final draft was so bland that only two people signed and it was not sent.

Later still, Davis and Bonlieu went to Auckland University to translate a controversial video on Tahiti, *Behind the Flower Curtain*. Bonlieu seemed uneasy about the content, which dealt with France's cultural impact on French Polynesia. She did talk a little more with Davis, however. When the Dutchwoman said she had studied at the University of Pau, Bonlieu said that she knew Pau too but had lived mainly in Paris, where her university qualification had been in geography. She was not working at the moment, she added, other than on freelance projects for the peace movement. Davis wondered, but did not ask, how she was financing her trip.

Early in May Frédérique Bonlieu found herself in a situation she had wanted to avoid. She was interviewed by a journalist.

Jenny Little, a young reporter with the local community paper, *Inner City News*, came into the Greenpeace office for information on a visiting Kanak activist scheduled to speak at the university. Bonlieu was sitting on the couch in the reception area and Elaine Shaw introduced the two women. 'This is Frédérique who has just come from France. Why don't you have a word with her?'

It seemed a good idea to Little. She could balance the Kanak story she planned to write with opinions from an 'ordinary' French person; and she could get a French view of Greenpeace's anti-French testing activities. So she smiled and sat down next to Bonlieu. Frédérique, however, bristled with discomfort and hostility. She was obviously annoyed to be placed in such a situation. She began by asking the questions herself, grilling Little on what kind of paper she worked for and where it was distributed. She seemed less anxious when she discovered the limits of its circulation (25,000 and only within Auckland city), and gradually she opened out, choosing her words with care.

'Here you are very far from your enemies. In Europe we are very close to them. We need nuclear weapons to be safe and independent. Trying to find peace with weapons is a very big paradox, but without this defence, we risk becoming like Finland, which is so influenced by Russia. Since we have had nuclear weapons we haven't been threatened nationally.'

As the visitor talked, Little thought she looked more German than French: so solid, serious and austere. There was nothing chic about her, no trimmings or frills in the way she dressed. And she talked like an academic.

On New Caledonia, Bonlieu said the attitude of France's critics, including New Zealand, was hypocritical. Because *they* had a colonial tradition too. She emphasised that Kanaks and Tahitians showed far more signs of thriving on their own islands than Hawaiians did on theirs. 'Then the United States tries to tell us about civilisation. That is hypocrisy.'

She was warming to her subject when Little produced her camera. Could she take a photograph to go with the article? No. Bonlieu's whole manner changed. No pictures.

After staying with Carol Stewart for nearly a fortnight, Bonlieu moved into a house in the suburb of Kingsland with Jane Cooper, a technical institute tutor and Greenpeace volunteer, and Karen Mangnall, a journalist working for the *New Zealand Herald* and active in the peace movement (she had been a full-time co-ordinator for the Campaign for Nuclear Disarmament). Their flat was to be her home base for the rest of her stay in New Zealand. She became intimately involved with them and some of their circle of close friends, and they too became unwitting sources of further information for the DGSE about the activities of the peace movement in New Zealand, and about travel and accommodation arrangements within the country.

In addition to collecting dozens of maps of the North Island, particularly of harbours and estuaries, Bonlieu hired cars on at least three occasions for trips out of Auckland. It is known that she visited the coast immediately north and south of the city; she went to the Coromandel Peninsula with Cooper and Mangnall; she made a four-day journey down the east coast, the Bay of Plenty and Taupo. And she stayed a weekend on Waiheke Island with Rien Achterberg from the Greenpeace office. It has been assumed but not proven that she visited North Auckland.*

The trip to Coromandel took place on the weekend of 11

---

*Alleged sightings of her in that district occurred on dates when she was known to be elsewhere.

and 12 May. It was an important journey in the light of what was to happen on 10 July.

Bonlieu, Cooper and Mangnall left Auckland on Saturday, sharing the driving in one of the Frenchwoman's hired cars. They travelled to Thames, then up the west side of the peninsula to Coromandel township. From there they crossed the range to Kuaotunu, a beach resort on the eastern side, and stayed the night at a holiday home belonging to an acquaintance of Mangnall's.

The following morning Bonlieu got up before her New Zealand friends to ring France from a public telephone at the local motor camp. Her explanation was that she had been making inquiries for acquaintances who planned to come to New Zealand on their honeymoon. During the remainder of the day, as they travelled to Otama Beach, Whitianga and Hot Water Beach, Bonlieu took photographs of the coast. For Cooper and Mangnall it had been simply a holiday weekend; for Frédérique Bonlieu it was another reconnaissance trip.

One of the people who saw Bonlieu in the course of her long swing south was potter Helen Mason, who lives in the old harbourmaster's house at Tokomaru Bay on the North Island's east coast. Bonlieu had been given the address by one of her Auckland friends. She arrived at the bay in her white Toyota rental car mid-morning on 10 May. Mason, a kindly and placid middle-aged woman who always welcomes visitors, asked the Frenchwoman into her home and offered her coffee.

For the next hour, the potter was harangued. 'It is difficult being French,' Bonlieu told her. 'Everybody hates you.' She went on to say that she was an archaeologist working for Greenpeace; but that her father had been an admiral in the French Navy who had had to stand onshore at Toulon and watch his battleship scuttled during the Second World War.* Then, she

---

*None of these asertions was quite true (her father, for example, had been a lieutenant commander). Bonlieu was again putting up a smoke-screen, telling different stories to different people – a process that became risky only if they had the chance to compare accounts, which did not happen until much later.

said, the French had helped the British Army get as far as Dunkirk only to be told that they would have to return to their homes because there was no possibility of evacuating them too. She exuded bitterness and hostility.

Mason was confused. Bonlieu did not speak like Greenpeace members she had met previously, and she wondered why she – Bonlieu's hostess – should be the target for so much invective. It sounded as if Bonlieu was trying to convince herself that the French had just cause to feel that the rest of the world – especially Anglo-Saxons – was against them. Had the need been triggered by the kindness and acceptance she had encountered in the previous weeks? Had this treatment undermined her previous convictions to the point where they were now precarious?

Bonlieu eventually bought some wine cups from the potter, refused lunch, and left a trail of further false information. She put a non-existent French address in Mason's visitors' book and said she was going to stay that night in Wanganui, which she did not.

Helen Mason was not the only person to wonder if Bonlieu's beliefs were being altered by her association with New Zealanders. Greenpeace workers noted that, in the latter half of her month-long stay, she was less adamant in the expression of French points of view and more willing to listen to others. She looked occasionally confused, as if – Judy Seaboyer felt – she was beginning to appreciate that her French position was invidious to others; possibly even to herself. She became more demonstrably generous and took to slipping out of the office to buy pastries for afternoon teas.* Was this reparation for guilt engendered by the constant friendship she

---

*One Greenpeace member who came to know Bonlieu well attributed her progressive mellowing to the satisfaction she was deriving from gay company in New Zealand. In France she had found acceptance as a lesbian difficult to achieve; in New Zealand – according to this theory – she was more able to come to terms with that side of herself, in much the same way as a male homosexual might in San Francisco or New York.

encountered? Or simply a more rigorous application of her cover? Later, knowing her true identity, her New Zealand associates were unable to decide.

On 24 May, the day she was to leave New Zealand, Frédérique again spoke with Monique Davis in the Greenpeace office. This time the Frenchwoman opened up and told her that, like Davis, she had been to the University of Pau (she did not add that she had also grown up in that town in the Pyrenees, 30-odd kilometres from Lourdes, and that her mother lived there still). They discussed professors who had taught them both and found that they had liked and disliked the same ones. And Bonlieu knew a family who had been Davis's landlords. Davis wondered why Bonlieu had not told her all this earlier. It would have given them a degree of rapport. She realised afterwards that it was so that she would not have time to check these connections before Bonlieu left the country. Frédérique Bonlieu *did* know all the people she cited; but they knew *her* as Christine Cabon.

That afternoon, Bonlieu invited Greenpeace workers to a wine bar near the office for a farewell drink. She had had her hair cut very short by one of the volunteers, and this accentuated her features, especially her nose, and made her seem more Gallic.

The ecologists were all a little disconcerted when she bought them Beaujolais. As a matter of principle they did not drink French wine. Bonlieu, however, was good-humouredly dismissive of their reservations. It was her last day in New Zealand. She wanted to give them something, she said, and she wanted them to drink a *good* wine for a change. Most of her guests complied to please her; it seemed important to her. And for once Frédérique paid.

The last impression the Greenpeace people had of her was a good one. Her protective shield seemed to fall away and she was bouncy, good-humoured and acting as if she felt among friends. Had she genuinely come to like these New Zealanders?

They certainly felt she had. Was it the effects of the wine? Or was it simply the fact that she had completed her job, retained her cover, pleased her controller, and been recalled with compliments?

Whatever the reason, Bonlieu flew out of Auckland that night to attend a conference on coral reefs in Tahiti (which she turned out to know little about: it seems to have been yet another cover, this time to meet the Swedish Tahitian-based anthropologist and anti-nuclear activist Bengt Danielsson). From Papeete she returned to Paris, and by early July she was back on one of her old stamping grounds, the Middle East, working on an archaeological excavation at Pardes Hanna in Israel. Throughout this period she sent back a stream of letters, postcards and telephone calls to the Greenpeace office and to her recently acquired friends. These stopped abruptly shortly before the *Rainbow Warrior* was bombed on 10 July. After that there was one further letter to Elaine Shaw, expressing shock. 'Could you say to everybody in Auckland that I am with you, with all my heart.' And then silence. Neither Greenpeace nor her friends heard from Frédérique Bonlieu again. They heard *of* her within a month, however, when police investigations established that she was Christine Huguette Cabon, a trained infiltrator working for the DGSE. Greenpeace members felt betrayed; Bonlieu's 'friends' felt frightened and violated.

Three weeks after Christine Cabon left New Zealand – and days before eight more French spies were to arrive in the country – a rare ceremony was conducted on New Zealand's northernmost coast. This was a region in which Cabon had shown particular interest in the course of map collecting in Auckland and it was to be the scene of frenetic activity on the part of other DGSE agents in the coming month.

The ceremony commemorated the second landfall by French ships in New Zealand waters, in 1772. The vessels were the *Mascarin* and the *Marquis de Castries*, under the command of Captain Marc-Joseph Marion du Fresne. In April 1772,

Marion du Fresne's men had come ashore at Spirits Bay and
Tom Bowling Bay – literally at the 'top' of New Zealand –
in search of fresh water. Journals described what they saw:

> [M. Le Houx] came back at four o'clock in the afternoon and
> reported that he had found two coves where the bottom was not
> bad and it was easy to water. He said that in one of them he had
> seen abandoned huts which he had gone into and had seen
> windows decorated with latticework, several carved planks, a fairly
> large seine made of screw pine which had, instead of sinkers, little
> round pebbles in a casing of netting with very much smaller mesh
> than that of the seine, a marble slab for grinding paint – the one
> he found was red – a roundish stick and a lot of other trinkets
> which gave us a high regard for the industry of these people.

Marion du Fresne's crew were prevented from further
immediate investigation by a storm, which caused the vessels
to drag anchors and lose five of them. A comparable squall
had driven the first French navigator in the region, Jean
François Marie de Surville, to within kilometres of the English
explorer Cook off exactly the same coast three years before.
Only poor visibility prevented an historic encounter.

Returning to Spirits Bay in an effort to retrieve the anchors
on 26 April 1772, the Frenchmen this time sighted inhabitants
in a small cove. Marion du Fresne sent Jean Roux, ensign on
the *Mascarin*, close to shore to investigate the pa:

> When he returned we learnt that it was a very pretty little village
> surrounded by ditches and palisades. When the inhabitants saw
> him near the shore they came to meet him and gave him fish from
> a canoe which was on its way back from fishing. The officer gave
> them in his turn a handkerchief and a knife, which they tried out
> on the spot on one of their paddles. They were so pleased with
> it that they gave them a second lot of fish. They had invited him
> to go ashore and had seemed despondent to see that nobody went.
> These proceedings had given us a good opinion of the character
> of these people and we imagined we would be very well received
> among them.

On 15 June 1985, the French ambassador to New Zealand, M.

Jacques Bourgoin, unveiled a plaque at the foot of Mangapiko Hill (which Marion du Fresne had named Montagne de Pouce) among the descendants of those very people for whom the explorer had had such a high regard 213 years before.

On a warm and sunny winter's day, M. Bourgoin told his mixed Maori-Pakeha audience on the beach between Spirits and Tom Bowling Bays that one of Marion du Fresne's first assignments for the French Navy had been the rescue of Bonnie Prince Charlie from the Scottish coast after the failure of the Jacobite Rising in 1746.

'I have mentioned this episode,' said the ambassador, 'to point out that while still young [du Fresne] had cause to come into contact with our British friends at a time when our relations with them were not always as easy as they have become today.' Monsieur l'Ambassadeur's broad smile indicated that he included his audience in the category of 'British friends'.

After leaving North Cape, Marion du Fresne had made for the Bay of Islands, where he stayed more than two months. There, apparently as a consequence of breaking tapu, he was slain by local Maori in June 1772. In retribution, his second-in-command du Clesmeur shelled and burned the village he believed to be responsible and took more than 250 Maori lives. This was the contact which, 213 years later, M. Bourgoin identified as marking 'the beginning of relations between France and New Zealand.'

Symptoms of contemporary relations between France and New Zealand were evident on the day of the ceremony. Before the official party arrived, a member of Greenpeace had been over its route and stuck 'Nuclear-free and independent Pacific' stickers on fence posts and stiles. He placed another on the rock next to the plaque commemorating Marion du Fresne, after M. Bourgoin had unveiled it – a gesture the ambassador reportedly regarded as ill-mannered.

Later, the whole party repaired to the marae at Te Hapua on Parengarenga Harbour to be welcomed by local Maoris – members of Te Aupouri tribe – and to be fed.

A week to the day after the French ambassador had left Parengarenga, a French yacht from New Caledonia scraped over the harbour's dangerous bar, past the skeleton of another French vessel, *Drac II*, which had foundered there three years before. The *Ouvéa* was crewed by three further DGSE agents and one doctor, a navy reservist experienced in treating the victims of diving accidents. The agents were led by Chief Petty Officer Roland Verge, aged 31, who came from Lourdes, scene of miraculous cures attributed to the Blessed Virgin (and close to Pau, home of Christine Cabon). He had worked for the DGSE for eleven years and been based at the Centre d'Instruction des Naqueurs de Combat (CINC), the French Navy training centre for combat frogmen at Aspretto in Corsica. On this operation, he was to be known as Raymond Velche, professional yacht skipper, holidaying with friends in the South Pacific.

The others were Petty Officer Gerald Andries, 29, from Hyères on the French Riviera, also based at the CINC at Aspretto and a DGSE agent for six years, travelling as Eric Audrenc, photographer; and Petty Officer Jean-Michel Barcelo, 31, born in Algeria, a DGSE agent for four years and formerly at Aspretto. His passport identified him as Jean-Michel Berthelo, commercial agent.

The status of the fourth person is more difficult to define. He claimed later to be a passenger rather than crew member, and to have chartered the *Ouvéa* without prior knowledge of the identity or background of his shipmates. He was 38-year-old Xavier Christian Jean Maniguet, a freelance doctor and *bon vivant* who lived in bizarre bachelor quarters on an artificial lake near Dieppe which, with typical chauvinism, he called his 'pussycat trap'. His background in tropical, diving and aeronautic medicine (and his own experience as a scuba diver and pilot) had landed him lucrative jobs in exotic locations in Asia and the Middle East. Just prior to the *Ouvéa* expedition, for example, he had worked for a French oil company drilling near Abu Dhabi, treating underwater oil-rig operators affected by the bends or other diving mishaps.

There were odd links in Maniguet's life that brought him far closer to the DGSE's sphere of activities than he would admit, however. There was his status as a Navy reservist; the potential value of his experience in diving medicine on a mission that would involve frogmen using dangerous rebreather equipment; the fact that the man who had employed him at Zabco Oil in Abu Dhabi was the father of François Verlet, the agent who insinuated himself on board the *Rainbow Warrior* the night it was bombed. There were further associations – equally sinister or (cumulatively) unbelievably coincidental – that were to emerge over the following months.

Like the crew, Maniguet would claim to be simply on holiday. He had hired the yacht through a family travel agency in Paris that closed down temporarily after the *Rainbow Warrior* bombing to avoid scrutiny. He is said to have paid more than 110,000 francs for a 50-day charter. Velche, Audrenc and Berthelo, also on holiday, were allegedly available by chance to sail the yacht; however only Velche was an experienced sailor.

As it turned out, it was a most peculiar excursion. They had told Noumea Yacht Charters, owners of the *Ouvéa*, that they planned to visit Australia, New Zealand and Fiji, even though the middle of winter was the worst possible time for sailing in the southern Pacific. They had said it was a diving holiday, yet had to be persuaded to take the yacht's dinghy, an essential part of diving equipment. They had told staff at the Castaway Hotel in Norfolk Island (where they stayed two nights) that they were heading for Auckland and Tauranga. Later, in Whangarei, they would tell marine suppliers that they planned to fish in the harbour. They did none of these things apart from visit New Zealand. They even denied to New Zealanders that they had called at Norfolk on the way from Noumea. Maniguet was part of these deceptions (or confusions). They had not sorted out a consistent cover story among themselves; or they were deliberately laying a trail of confusion.* Either way, they neither told the truth about themselves nor about their reasons for being in New Zealand.

Parengarenga Harbour (Maori for 'place of many undulations')
has a deceptive entrance. There is a hill to the north, a dazzling
white silica sandspit to the south, and an 800-metre gap between
them. The notorious bar that has wrecked at least four boats
in recent years lies across that gap and is an underwater extension of the spit. Even the most experienced yachtsmen in New
Zealand hesitate to cross it without local guidance. That the
11.6-metre *Ouvéa* negotiated it safely on 22 June is little short
of a miracle.

In addition to being a dangerous port of entry, Parengarenga
is also an illegal one for foreign boats: there are no Customs
or quarantine facilities. Raymond Velche's excuse was that the
yacht had been battered by a severe storm the day before (winds
had risen to 30 knots) and that seas were still heavy when they
sighted the New Zealand coast. If he had a chart, as he subsequently claimed in France after giving the impression in New
Zealand that he did not, then it was an archaic one on which
the bar was not indicated.

Inside the heads, the yacht would have been carried by the
tide into one of two channels. The first is a blind one that would
have led them to grounding and wreckage. Purely by chance,
the *Ouvéa* found its way into the second – the channel proper.
From there, Velche reported later, he made use of the incoming
waves and his 40-horsepower engine to bounce the boat in when
he had enough water underneath him. Every few seconds the
yacht dropped onto the sand with a stomach-lurching thud from
the keel, only to be picked up and carried forward again.

The crew would have been anxious and exhausted by the
time they reached the inner channel – indeed, they were to make
jokes about this experience for the remainder of their stay in
New Zealand. Once there, however, they were able to motor
up to Te Hapua, anchoring off the village shortly before 4 p.m.

---

*That false trail had begun with Gerald Andries buying a French-made Zodiac
and a second-hand outboard motor from a marine supplier in London on 29 May
— both of which the DGSE could have acquired far more easily in France.

If the entrance is deceptive, so is Parengarenga itself. The harbour is nearly 20 kilometres wide, with dozens of inlets running like mangrove-covered fingers into folds in the hills. Apart from Te Hapua, it seems deserted. One headland is farmed, the other surrounding hills are covered in scrub, flax and lupin. Visitors have the illusion of being alone and unobserved. In fact the very isolation of the district makes strangers stand out like silhouettes. Although the village was largely deserted that afternoon in favour of a rugby game, it was only minutes before the Te Hapua residents who were home had noted the presence of the yacht, and the fact that it was considerably smarter and better equipped than most vessels that come into the harbour. This impression immediately aroused curiosity and comment. Who were these people (clearly not ordinary yachties)? Were they smugglers or drug runners (Te Hapua had seen more than its share of both)? Why had they come to the most isolated community in the country?

The first person to speak to the Frenchmen was 12-year-old Charlie Sucich, a Maori with freckles, who – with his sister Hope – had spotted the yacht heading up the channel towards Te Hapua's only wharf. Three men came ashore in an orange inflatable dinghy, making for the spot where he sat on the rocks in front of his parents' combined store and post office. One of them, blond and in his late thirties, said hello and asked if there was a shop nearby. Charlie Sucich was as shy of strangers as most children in a small village. He pointed to the store front and said he would fetch his mother.

Like many clans in the far north of New Zealand, the Sucichs are Maori-Yugoslav, a product of the turn-of-the-century days when single Dalmatian men invaded the region in large numbers to dig the swamps for kauri gum. Almost all Te Hapua families have some Dalmatian antecedents. But it is Maori language, culture and *mores* that dominate the community.

When Charlie rushed into the house behind the shop that Saturday afternoon, Jewel Sucich was watching television. It was a rare and precious occurrence, for two reasons. Transmission signals only reach Te Hapua for a couple of hours in the afternoons, and then only on clear days. That day's transmission was a rugby test, Australia versus Canada, important because Australia was to play the All Blacks the following Saturday. The earlier game would be a form guide to the opposition. Te Hapua is rugby mad. The only community facilities are the marae, the Ratana church, the school and the rugby ground. An international was not to be missed; it was of far more consequence than a royal wedding or a one-day cricket match. Jewel had a conscience, however. Customers had to be served. If they were yachties they probably wanted stores. So she padded out to the shop in her fluffy slippers to see what the Frenchmen needed.

Strangely, considering they had just completed a week-long sail from Noumea (with only a brief stopover at Norfolk Island) they did not want food. They wanted to know where they were. 'Parengarenga Harbour,' she told the shortish blond man who seemed to be the spokesman. The crew member next to him was much taller, about 1.8 metres, with a military bearing. But he said nothing. The third man, dark and short, stood in the background by the door.

'Do you have maps of the harbour?' Maniguet asked, in accented but easily intelligible English.

'No,' said Jewel. 'Just groceries and postcards.'

'Is there a hotel where we could get a shower?'

'No. But you could try the school for that, along the road and up the hill.'

'What about petrol?'

There was something odd about the men, Jewel Sucich thought. They were dirty and looked tired, apparently as a result of several days' hard sailing. But they were tidily groomed in well-fitting jeans and sweatshirts. They seemed formal and excessively polite. They were more 'posh' than most Parengarenga visitors – or residents. Strangest of all, they seemed uncertain about where they were. And yet the yacht outside looked as though it would be equipped with the most modern and expensive navigational gear.

Feeling uneasy, she rang the local ranger as soon as they had left for the schoolhouse.

Hec Crene, a burly 64-year-old with craggy features and an engaging manner, was the government's man-on-the-spot in the Far North. Officially, he was known as the ranger of Te Paki Farm Park. Unofficially he could be called upon to act as honorary policeman, ambulance driver or breakdown serviceman. The afternoon Jewel Sucich tried to contact him he was hauling a tourist minibus out of the soft sand on adjacent Ninety Mile Beach, to free the vehicle before it was inundated by the incoming tide. It was 6.30 by the time he was home and able to take Jewel's call. 'Can you come down?' she asked. (Te Paki Station is on a hill about 20 minutes' drive from Te Hapua).

'What's up?' said Crene.

'There's a yacht in down here with some foreigners on board. I'm not sure who they are or what's going on.'

Crene thought and decided against it. 'There's not much point in coming down now. It's dark. I'll do it in the morning.'

Then he rang Lew Sabin, a customs officer in Whangarei, to let him know about the vessel. Sabin was not worried. He suggested Crene ask the crew to ring him in the morning to report where they were from and where they were headed. Crene agreed and rang off.

Thus three French agents and their companion were left unmolested by officialdom for their first 18 hours in New Zealand. They were not seen to come ashore again. But nobody from Te Hapua was able to observe the boat that night.

Meanwhile at Houhora, 40 kilometres south, Police Constable Archie Clark was also left undisturbed. He had been acting as unofficial customs officer in the district for some years, and had inspected vessels previously in Parengarenga and Houhora Harbours and recorded particulars about the crews, including an earlier French one (whom he had invited to stay with him). On Saturday 22 June, however, nobody thought to call Arch Clark out. He spent a quiet evening at home watching television. Programmes included *So This is Paradise*, a look at 'copra, black pearls and nuclear testing' in French Polynesia; and *F. Comme Fairbanks*, a film about a Frenchman who tries to escape reality in fantasies based on movies.

The same day the *Ouvéa* reached Parengarenga, two more DGSE agents disembarked in New Zealand. Major Alain Mafart, aged 34, and Captain Dominique Prieur, 36, stepped off an Air New Zealand flight at Auckland Airport at 10 a.m. They were travelling as a holidaying Swiss couple, Alain and Sophie Turenge. They had reached New Zealand from Paris, via Los Angeles and Honolulu.

Both had worked as agents over the previous decade, Prieur infiltrating anti-nuclear groups in Europe and terrorist movements in Africa; Mafart also in Africa and in Lebanon. Interestingly, Prieur had a close asociation with Christine Cabon. Both women had joined the French Army together in December 1975, both had been promoted captain on the same day seven years later. Like the other male agents already in New Zealand, Mafart was a graduate of Aspretto and had risen to be second in command of the underwater combat school. He was drawn to strenuous outdoor recreation (on one occasion he had undertaken a single-handed expedition to the Greenland ice cap using a dog-sled), he had parachuted competitively, and he considered himself an ecologist, with a special interest in whales.

At Auckland Airport they looked like a typical bourgeois European couple. He was clean-cut, of medium height, dressed in sports clothes, and relaxed and affable in manner. His English was fluent and tinged with an American accent. Sophie appeared rather frumpish and wore slacks, cardigan and glasses. She had her hair cut in the close-cropped style more favoured among French women than elsewhere. Unlike her 'husband', her English was limited and she seemed nervous – her dark eyes darted from point to point and she frowned constantly. They did not appear as connected to or concerned about each other as another couple might.

Their documents identified them as a trading manager and a sociology lecturer who had been married for almost ten years and who (in spite of their Swiss nationality) lived in Paris. On rapid glance, both passports seemed in order. They had been issued on the same day eight years before by the Swiss consul-general in Lyon. Closer scrutiny (not applied until later) would reveal that the scroll patterns on both documents were forged. Further checks would show the Turenges's identities to be false. Had the passports been in order – or sufficiently well forged for other checks to verify them – the Turenges would have stayed in New Zealand a mere three weeks. As it turned out they were to remain in the country long after their colleagues had left, a consequence of shoddy documentation.

None of this was apparent on 22 June, however. At the air-port bank, Sophie methodically changed $US1,000 into New Zealand cash. (She was to be responsible for all the couple's 'housekeeping' arrangements in New Zealand.) Then they took a taxi to the Travelodge Hotel overlooking the Auckland wharves – a booking that had been made for them from France – where they would stay the next four nights. Within days they would be in touch with the *Ouvéa* crew, and with a more senior DGSE officer due to arrive in Auckland the following day.

On the morning of Sunday 23 June, the *Ouvéa* crew had their first opportunity to examine Te Hapua in clear daylight. If the Parengarenga heads conceal clues as to the nature of the harbour and its channel, then Te Hapua is even more decep-tive. It straggles along the shoreline in a series of weatherboard houses, caravans, tents and wrecked car bodies, interspersed with macrocarpa and pohutukawa trees. Wooden boats and battered aluminium dinghies lie anchored offshore or pulled up on the rocky breakwater below the dirt road. It looks for all the world like a depressed village in a Central American republic. The appearance is misleading.

The district is certainly depressed economically. But social security payments, fish in the harbour, home-grown vegetables and a community spirit that impels the 150-odd residents to share rather than hoard food ensure that nobody goes hungry. Some of the shacks are holiday homes; others seem derelict because the people who live in them do not place a high value on the suburban priorities of fresh paint and trimmed lawns. There is no keeping-up-with-the-Joneses in Te Hapua. Pride is expressed in the maintenance of public facilities, such as the church and the marae.

Above all else Te Hapua is a close community. The surmounting of a series of crises over the years – epidemics, rural depressions, natural disasters, drownings, the loss of some communal lands – has welded residents together tightly, protectively. No local person goes without physical or emotional support. Maori values dominate daily living and rites of passage. Wrongdoing tends to be dealt with within the group rather than by outside authority. And strangers are regarded with suspicion until they have proved their good faith by contribution to community activities and appearance over a long period of time.

In spite of the closeness and the isolation, the village has produced a larger number of national Maori leaders than any other community of comparable size: a cabinet minister, two presidents of the Maori Women's Welfare League, a beauty queen, prominent clergymen. Te Hapua *is* isolated. It is 104 kilometres from a doctor and 258 from the nearest city. But it none the less manages with a high degree of success to prepare those who want it for a career in the world outside; those who do not, the whanau or clan continues to sustain at home.

These things are not immediately apparent to strangers, especially to strangers from another country. To people raised in metropolitan France, Te Hapua would characterise New Zealand as a Third World country. It would seem redolent of poverty, graft and primitive systems of communication and law enforcement. The sight of it would lead European sophisticates to feel superior; and spies to feel secure.

Hec Crene is the kind of man to modify such an impression, though. He moves confidently and projects an air of authority. Nothing intimidates him and he is an example of proverbial New Zealand resourcefulness. Early on 23 June he donned his khaki ranger's uniform and drove down to Te Hapua, reaching the waterfront just before 10 a.m. It was a fine, sunny day.

He found the *Ouvéa* anchored about 50 metres off the wharf. She was a good-looking yacht, he thought, well shaped, fibreglass, red below the waterline and bright white above. An orange rubber dinghy lay strapped to the top of the cabin. A French flag hung over the stern, tied to the back stay. One crew member was visible in the cockpit and another was attending to something on deck. Crene waved for them to come in. The Frenchmen complied with such alacrity that they almost demolished the wharf as they motored in quickly and glanced off the old wooden piles.

Crene asked if the skipper was aboard. The man he later identified as Xavier Maniguet said yes, and the taller man with curly hair – Velche – appeared at his shoulder. 'Would you mind coming ashore to the post office with me and ringing Customs?' No, said Maniguet, they would not mind.

As they walked the few yards down the road to Sucichs' store the taller man asked, a little apprehensively, Crene thought, 'You are Customs?'

'No, no,' he explained. 'I'm just here on their behalf.'

In the shop Maniguet had a long conversation with Lew Sabin and both men seemed satisfied.

'They're going to Opua,' Sabin told Crene when he had taken the phone back. 'I've told them not to bring anything ashore, especially food. And not to drop anything overboard, like rubbish. Someone'll see them at Opua.'

On the way back to the wharf Maniguet seemed more relaxed. He asked again if there was somewhere the crew could take a shower. Crene suggested the school.

'No,' said Maniguet. 'We went up there yesterday. We did not get a good reception.' Then he looked at Crene and said,

'Would you like to come on board and see the boat?'

Crene said he would. So Maniguet introduced him to the others (the New Zealander would not remember the names) and showed him over the deck, the cockpit, the saloon, the galley and the sleeping quarters. He opened lockers to show where and how things were stored. Naturally, Crene would be able to say later – and this was the probable reason for the invitation – that he had noticed nothing remarkable or sinister: just the fact that everything was clean, stowed away and shipshape. They were very well organised for boaties, he thought. Especially for boaties who had just taken a hammering in a storm.

Then Maniguet offered him a beer and he sat down to drink it at the table in the saloon. The doctor talked fluently, Velche hesitantly. The others – one blonde, one dark – apparently unable to speak any English, simply sat in silence, drinking coffee.

Maniguet's conversation ranged over the All Blacks and their rugby battles with France, of which he had some knowledge, the extent of farming and sand mining around Parengarenga, how the *Ouvéa* got its name (from one of the Loyalty Islands north of New Caledonia), where it was built (in France in 1982) and its performance.

'How the hell did you get over the bar?' Crene asked, genuinely astonished.

'Oh, a bit bumpy,' said Maniguet, shortly.

'What made you come in here?'

'We had a rough day on Friday, needed shelter.'

'Where did you come from?'

'Straight from Noumea.'

Crene advised them to clear the bar the following day in company with a couple of tugs that were due to take out a bargeload of sand, and to keep in radio contact with them. Maniguet shrugged. Finally, Crene reminded them not go ashore or drop food overboard.

'Oh I know about that,' Maniguet said. 'I'm a physician. We'll stay on the boat.'

While Hec Crene was talking with the *Ouvéa* crew, yet another DGSE agent was clearing Customs at Auckland Airport. Lieutenant Colonel Louis-Pierre Dillais had, like the Turenges, entered New Zealand from Los Angeles. He had also been in Noumea at the same time as the *Ouvéa* crew and stayed until they were safely en route for Norfolk Island. He was, in fact, the commander of the DGSE's Rainbow Warrior operation.

It is a mark of Dillais' professionalism and competence that little is known about him outside the service for which he works. He was 38 years old in mid-1985, and his reputation among his colleagues was impeccable. Those who would speak of him did so only with respect and admiration. It *is* known that he had been in charge of the Aspretto combat school when Alain Mafart/Turenge had been deputy-commander. The two men had already worked together intimately and would do so again in New Zealand.

Witnesses who saw Dillais in New Zealand knew him as Jean Louis Dormand.* They describe him as tall (about 1.8 metres) and muscular, with a sharp-featured face and short brown hair. He kept an impressively low profile, especially in comparison with the *Ouvéa* crew, and spoke little; his English was poor. Most of his movements within New Zealand became a matter of conjecture: because he was not often sighted; or not often sighted doing anything that people would find memorable.

Dormand took a rental car from the airport and booked into the South Pacific Hotel in the centre of the city, minutes away from the Travelodge where his close colleague Alain Turenge was staying. It is probable that he contacted him within a short time of his arrival (the New Zealand Post Office logs international and long-distance calls but not local ones). Later in the day, Dormand rang Paris, the same DGSE number that Christine Cabon had called when she was in the city. The content of that conversation is unknown. It is likely that he

---

*Most of the agents chose an alias close to their actual names: it helped them to respond rapidly and to remember their cover-names; it raised the possibility of accusing other people of errors if their covers were blown; and it could add confusion to a subsequent investigation of an operation.

reported that three further agents had reached New Zealand; six, if the *Ouvéa* crew had found some means of contacting him or the Turenges. But there is no record of a phone call that day from Parengarenga.

At nine o'clock on the morning of Monday 24 June, the *Ouvéa* slipped out of Parengarenga with as little notice to locals as when she had arrived. Velche and Maniguet did not communicate by radio with the incoming tugs, as Hec Crene had suggested. The Frenchmen simply watched the tugs come in and then went straight out of the harbour themselves, following the same course as best they could. Again the tide was high, this time outgoing, and they appeared to encounter no difficulties.

In the course of the next ten hours the *Ouvéa* moved along more than 100 kilometres of coastline, making that day the lengthiest leg of its cruise in New Zealand waters. Precisely where the crew stopped is unknown, but later events made it probable that this was the day on which explosives were put ashore for later collection, along with the Zodiac inflatable and black Yamaha outboard motor bought by Audrenc in London. All this equipment had to be off the boat prior to Customs inspection at Opua in two days' time.

Wherever they hid the cache, the place had to be accessible by sea (so as to reach it in the first instance by yacht and rubber dinghy), and by road (for subsequent collection). It also had to be remote from the likelihood of inadvertent public observation. The exact site may never be found: but the weight of circumstantial evidence suggests somewhere in Rangaunu Harbour near Kaitaia; or in adjacent Doubtless Bay, possibly at Cable Bay. Much would have depended on the casual movements of people on shore on the day. Being the middle of winter there were few holiday-makers using the beaches in June.

By the evening of 24 June the *Ouvéa* was safely in Whangaroa Harbour. The precise location of their anchorage was uncertain for eight months: the *Ouvéa*'s log specified Kaouou Bay. Nobody investigating the ship's movements could find such a place in New Zealand geographic records or on coastal charts. One expert went so far as to say that there could be no such word in Maori, it had to be a French mis-transcription. In February 1986, however, a police officer spotted the name on a nineteenth-century whaler's chart: it was the old name for an inlet just inside the western head of Whangaroa Harbour, under high cliffs; but it had long since passed out of usage and off charts. As the Parengarenga episode had done, it raised intriguing possibilities as to what charts the *Ouvéa* might have been using in the area. An old French whaler's map? Or something archaic photocopied in a New Zealand library by Christine Cabon?

In Auckland, the other agents remained in their original accommodation, but emerged to make transport arrangements: Jean Louis Dormand to return the Toyota Corolla he had hired from the airport and replace it with a Holden Gemini station wagon; the Turenges meanwhile to rent the very make of car Dormand had rejected – a Toyota Corolla.

All three then virtually disappeared from the public record for the next four days. Dormand continued to sleep at the South Pacific and rang France twice more during the week; nothing is known about his daytime movements. The Turenges checked out of the Travelodge the following day and into the Hyatt Kingsgate, also overlooking the Auckland waterfront, but this time with a clear view of Marsden Wharf, where the *Rainbow Warrior* would berth in ten days' time. They continued their reconnaissance of the area, especially of likely places to launch and retrieve Zodiacs without attracting undue attention.* There were few daylight sightings of them over the next week. The *Ouvéa* crew, on the other hand, were to become increasingly visible. Too visible: it had to be part of their orders.

---

*One scenario in the Tricot report two months later was an almost exact description of the Turenges' role at this time. '[They] would have observed the layout of the Port of Auckland in detail, the habits of those who frequented it, the way in which the police do their work; then [they] would have reported their findings to other agents . . .'

At 10 a.m. on 25 June, shortly after they had cleared Whanga-roa Harbour, the *Ouvéa* crew went scuba diving off Flat Island. According to the boat's log it was the only such attempt they made in New Zealand waters. The sea was cold and murky; they saw little and caught nothing.

By 3.30 that afternoon the boat had reached the Bay of Islands, Mecca for yachtsmen cruising New Zealand's north-east coast. It is a wide, sheltered harbour with – as its name suggests – dozens of islands off which to anchor and lay up. It is also the cradle of New Zealand's colonial history. It was there that the Frenchmen's compatriot Marion du Fresne was killed by Maoris in 1772 when he breached local custom. The port of Russell (one-time 'hell-hole of the Pacific') had been a favourite destination for French and American sailors seeking grog and prostitution in the early nineteenth century. And in 1840, northern Maori leaders had signed the Treaty of Waitangi there, after which the sovereignty of their country was ceded to Britain; that subsequently controversial action was taken in part to prevent a declaration of sovereignty by France, who were about to establish a colony at Akaroa in the South Island.

The *Ouvéa* sailed up an arm of the harbour that took them past Waitangi, between the twin townships of Paihia and Russell, and eventually to Opua, the port where they were to clear Customs. The crew missed the public wharf, where they ought to have moored, and tied up instead at 4 p.m. at the privately owned Colensos' fuel jetty.

In the takeaways bar which is part of the Colensos' complex of shops, Maniguet asked how he could contact Customs. Pat Colenso, a 39-year-old English immigrant, warmed to the French doctor, as did most New Zealand women who were to encounter him. He was clean-cut, tidy and tanned, and looked as if he had just walked off a ski resort. 'I'll ring Whangarei for you,' she said. And did.

Meanwhile the Frenchmen bought packets of fish and chips to eat on the boat and took back with them every road map that the Colensos' service station had in stock. Feeling sorry

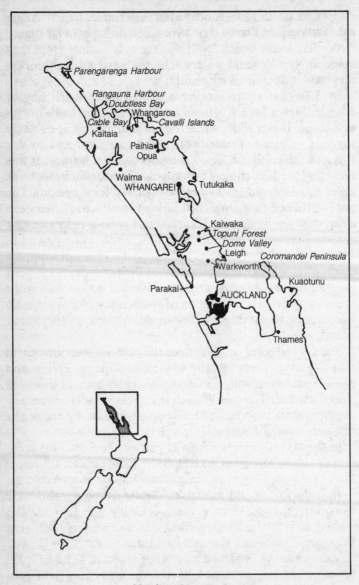

Northern New Zealand

for them – it was bitterly cold and already dark – Pat Colenso said they were welcome to stay the night at the fuel jetty.

Customs officer Frank MacLean and Ministry of Agriculture and Fisheries inspector Gordon Grant arrived from Whangarei – an hour's drive from Opua – at about 6.30 p.m. MacLean, a hearty ex-Australian, believes in taking his time over his duties and forming an instinct as he does so about whether a rummage of a vessel is required rather than an inspection. So he had a beer with the *Ouvéa* crew and chatted as he explained and filled in their entry forms. He directed most of his questions to skipper Velche, who answered with Maniguet's assistance. Jean-Michel Berthelo sat opposite MacLean at the saloon table and – while he was alert – appeared to understand nothing. Audrenc lay down on his bunk.

When MacLean commented that it was a poor time of the year to go sailing, Maniguet said, 'Ah yes. But a good time to go skiing.' And he revealed his plan to do so, asking the Customs officer about the relative merits of North and South Island ski slopes. MacLean recommended the South Island.

There were a couple of oddities. MacLean was surprised at how clean the boat was and the extent to which everything was stowed away – unusual in his experience of yachties. And they seemed to have no personal gear beyond Maniguet's briefcase and the crew's duffle bags.

'What about this guy who says he's a photographer and doesn't have any camera?' MacLean asked, referring to Audrenc.*

'He's on vacation,' said Maniguet quickly. 'He does not want to be bothered.'

'Fair enough,' said MacLean, a tolerant man.

He was also struck by the fact that while Maniguet's passport was so full of visas he had trouble finding room for another stamp, the others all had brand-new documents.

---

*Other crew members had cameras with them, but far less sophisticated models than would be used by a professional photographer.

In the end he decided that the boat was clean. They had already landed at Parengarenga, so any drugs would be long gone; they were not New Zealanders returning home, so there would be no videos under the sails. And there was nothing to declare to the agricultural officer. It never occurred to him that there might be explosives aboard. After an hour, MacLean and Grant wished the Frenchmen well and took their leave.

That night at the South Pacific Hotel in Auckland, Jean Louis Dormand recevied a telephone call from Opua. Later still he rang France. If they had not been told previously, the DGSE now knew that six agents were in place in New Zealand, that all had completed immigration formalities without arousing suspicion, and that equipment related to the forthcoming operation was safely concealed.

The *Ouvéa* crew spent most of 26 June at Opua. They brought their laundry to the machines at the Colensos' shop and washed and dried it there. They also stocked up with food from the grocery store and fuel from the wharf pump. Otherwise, they had a lazy day. Fifty metres opposite, at the head of the public wharf, they could not have missed seeing a building with a large sign across the verandah advertising Rainbow Yacht Charters, one of the largest boat hire companies in the Bay; the office also had notices in the window with rainbows arching across a coloured photograph of an anchored yacht.

Opua was a good place to rest but not to play. It is a quiet community with a minimum of port facilities: the Colensos' shops, a post office and a harbourmaster's office. Late in the afternoon the crew slipped their mooring and motored back up the channel to Paihia, tourist centre of the Bay of Islands, a cluster of shops, hotels and restaurants. They tied up at the pontoon attached to Fullers' Wharf. From there they had a clear view across the bay to Russell which – then known as Kororareka – had been the first European settlement in New Zealand; and they could see the promontory two kilometres away where the Treaty of Waitangi had been debated by Maori and Pakeha representatives 145 years earlier. In the past decade, on the anniversary of the treaty signing, that reserve had become an arena for annual confrontation between Maori activists and government authorities as the country attempted to grapple with emerging Maori nationalism.

There is no evidence that the *Ouvéa* crew displayed more than casual interest in the country's history (although they had been supplied with a book, the *Insight Guide to New Zealand*, published in Singapore, which included extensive historical background). They did not go sightseeing. They decided instead to go ashore that night and seek a little recreation. They had, after all, things to celebrate: a safe arrival in New Zealand after a perilous entry into their first harbour, successful concealment of some 20 kilograms of explosives, and clearing Customs.

The place the Frenchmen chose for their first meal ashore in New Zealand is part of a modern beachfront hotel, the Paihia Autolodge. The Reef Restaurant on the first floor has windows overlooking the harbour towards Russell. It is simply furnished with square tables seating four. There are dark beams overhead with colonial-style lamps, and bamboo-patterned wallpaper. Food is the usual New Zealand hotel fare: French and European dishes, some fresh seafood.

Xavier Maniguet, Raymond Velche and Jean-Michel Berthelo walked to the hotel shortly before 7.30 p.m. (it was within sight of the wharf). Eric Audrenc stayed behind to guard the yacht. Inside, they found their way upstairs to the Castaway Bar, adjacent to the restaurant. They were neatly but casually dressed, in faded denims. Maniguet and Berthelo wore dress shirts and Velche a black seaman's jersey. They drank in the bar before moving into the restaurant at about 8.30.

The thing apparent above all else to people who watched them that night was their determination to home in on local women. Led by the fluent Doctor Maniguet, they tried to make contact with every youngish female they sighted: the hotel receptionist, a waitress in the bar, the waitress who served them in the restaurant, and two unescorted women eating at an adjacent table.

The other diners, who were halfway through their meals when the Frenchmen entered the dining room, were an 18-year-old hairdresser from Canberra; and Carol Nash, 35, short, dark-eyed, a police constable's wife who owned a hair salon in Whangarei. The Australian woman was a guest in the hotel; Nash had escorted her round the Bay and was returning home that night. They did not notice the yachtsmen again until Nash was settling the bill at the cash desk near the door. The wine waiter approached them and said three French gentlemen had asked him to invite the women to have drinks with them in the bar after dinner.

'It's probably some Kiwi guys having us on,' Nash said to her friend. But she told the waiter they were going to have a drink anyway and would be there for about 15 minutes. Exactly 15 minutes later, the three men came into the bar and Xavier Maniguet asked if they might join them.

It was Maniguet, of course, who made the first and the most enduring impression. He looked like an aging film star: olive skin, blue eyes, wavy blond hair combed forward over his head. He was muscular and exuded energy and enforced charm. And he talked, practically non-stop.

Velche was about ten centimetres taller and skinny. He too was blond but had thicker, curlier hair than Maniguet. He also had a thin moustache and a scar over his left eye. He took part in the conversation mainly through cross-talk in French. But he also spoke English, hesitantly. Berthelo was shorter than Maniguet, with dark hair, Latin features and dark complexion. His cheeks too were dark, with five o'clock shadow. He was attentive but seemed to have no English; nor did he take much part in the conversation in French. He seemed serious-minded, watchful, even apprehensive.

Carol Nash asked what they were doing in Paihia and Maniguet explained they were on holiday, on a yacht.

'Have you cleared Customs?'

'Yes. At Opua. We rang from Parengarenga.'

'You didn't sail *into* Parengarenga?'

'Yes.' Maniguet and Velche nodded vigorously. 'It was bad,' Maniguet said. 'Only about one metre of water under the boat.' Recollecting the experience, the three men all looked as if they were reliving a near thing.

Well aware now of Maniguet's ease with English, Nash asked him what he did for a living.

'Physician. Specialising in tropical and diving medicine. I travel a great deal. I have recently spent six months in Abu Dhabi.'

'Did you like it?'

'No. I do not like Arabs.'

'What do you do?' Nash asked the others.

'Just skipper on boats,' Velche replied. Berthelo said nothing.

'Are you married?'

Only Maniguet responded. 'Oh no. I like women too much.'

After Nash had explained what she did and where she lived, the Frenchmen told her they would be sailing to Whangarei. She gave Maniguet her business card and told them to contact her there. She would help them find their way around the city. Maniguet thanked her and pocketed the card. Then he got up to pursue waitresses, who looked as if they were going off duty.

It was after 11 p.m. and the women decided to leave. Quietly, Nash told the younger woman not to let Maniguet see where her room was. It was obvious that he hoped for company for the night. So they went outside to say goodbye to each other and to the Frenchmen.

The Australian went back into the hotel, and Maniguet followed shortly afterwards. Alone with the less talkative pair, Nash asked if they would like a ride to the yacht. They thanked her and accepted, though it was less than a minute away by car. At the wharf, they in turn invited her onto the boat for coffee. Nash considered before she accepted: there *were* two of them; they were behaving like gentlemen; and she had an hour's drive ahead of her. 'If it's good French coffee,' she said.

They laughed. They seemed more at ease without Dr Maniguet. She walked with them to the end of the wharf, where they helped her down onto the boat.

On board, they roused Eric Audrenc, who swung off his bunk in a sleeping bag and seemed surprised that his shipmates had brought company. He was introduced to Nash, who quickly realised that he had only slightly more English than Berthelo.

The coffee turned out to be instant. As they began to drink it at the saloon table, Xavier Maniguet returned, rebuffed. While Nash glanced at a French magazine, he asked if she spoke French. 'None at all,' she told him. 'And I don't understand it.'

Finishing her coffee, she said she would see them in Whangarei and take them to a discotheque. They laughed again and seemed pleased. Maniguet offered to take her to the car.

'Are you married?' he asked her on the wharf. Nash considered how much she should say. People sometimes reacted peculiarly to the police connection. 'Yes, you have been,' he said, not waiting for a reply. And he begun to talk about something else.

'Drive carefully,' he told her as she wound down her car window. Was he genuinely concerned, she wondered? He seemed a little bantam cock of a man, on the make, too confident and optimistic to be upset by rejection. His good humour was excessive: he spoke and acted as if life was a game and he intended to get as much fun out of it as possible. While Nash had warmed to the other three men and their quiet politeness, she wanted to squelch Xavier Maniguet.

Driving home, Carol Nash remembered something that had happened two months before. A Whangarei clairvoyant, whom she had visited for entertainment, had told her she would have severe difficulties in the coming year. They would involve a boat, and Norfolk Island would be a factor. The troubles would continue until October. 'You are going to become terribly public and you won't like it, because you're a private person,' the woman had said. 'You'll come out of it: not bitter but stronger.'

Nash had been surprised at how specific and confident the woman had been. Playing along, she had assumed she was being told that a journey was in prospect. Now she had met people from a boat, who had come from Norfolk Island . . . She laughed and shook herself out of the reverie. Such things were not to be taken seriously.

The following morning the *Ouvéa* left Paihia some time after nine o'clock. The yacht continued to make its way down the east coat of Northland, the crew stopping and photographing other bays and coves as they went. They paid particular attention to places that were unpopulated but had road access. By nightfall they were at Tutukaka, a narrow harbour bounded by steep cliffs and high hills. Again, they filled fuel tanks. The following day at 2.30 p.m. they entered Whangarei Harbour, original home port for the Greenpeace yacht *Vega* and base for the DGSE agents for the next ten days. From here they would carry out instructions so bizarre that – once they were uncovered by a plague of journalists – local residents could scarcely believe such activities had occurred in and around their quiet provincial city.

The Whangarei town basin surrounds an estuary at the head of a deeply indented harbour. Bristling with masts, it is crammed with yachts and launches moored to jetties and piles on one side, and to a wharf on the other. It is also within minutes' walking distance of the city centre. The immediate neighbourhood is thick with marine supply shops.

The *Ouvéa* tied up to another pontoon. Then the crew was directed by the harbourmaster's office to a berth close to the town basin bridge, one of the piles off a small jetty. Here the Frenchmen did nothing to make themselves inconspicuous. They hung a tricolour over the stern. Maniguet and Audrenc hailed other boats and waved to passers-by who looked their way. Crew members were also seen urinating off the boat in public view in the course of the next ten days, something most yachtsmen refrain from doing in port.

On the other side of the bridge, clearly visible from the yacht's mooring, was a massive mural painted on the harbourside wall of a building. It depicted Maori and European visions of land and sky. 'You and I are born from the Skyfather and Earthmother,' the inscription stated in English and Maori. And the visions were linked and unified by an enormous rainbow.

Shortly after three that afternoon Carol Nash was working in her salon when one of her staff told her there were two men at the door. One was Xavier Maniguet, the other Jean-Michel Berthelo. She greeted them with a kiss on both cheeks. They had just arrived, Maniguet said. They would be grateful for local directions. He asked how to contact car hire firms and aero clubs. Nash gave him the car rental numbers and rang the Whangarei Aero Club for him. He found that he would not be able to pilot a plane in New Zealand without his log book, but he could be taken for a flight by a club member (which he was, two days later).

Nash also offered the men use of the salon's washing-machine and clothes-dryer, and they said they would bring laundry back later in the day. She asked if they would like their hair washed. Maniguet said yes. As she began to work shampoo into his scalp with her fingers, she found that the top of his head was corrugated with scar tissue. He also appeared to have had hair transplants.

'What happened to you?' she asked, alarmed at the extent of what must once have been horrific injuries.

'I go through the windshield of a plane,' he said. 'I was teaching somebody to fly and he took us into the side of a mountain.' He was lucky, he added, to be alive.

Afterwards, Nash asked the men if they would join her that night. She was going to a restaurant and nightclub with her staff and some of their friends. 'Yes,' Xavier said with his curious mixture of formality and enthusiasm. 'We are with you. We do not know here and we are happy for you to take us.' They agreed they would meet again at the salon at six.

'No jeans,' Nash warned them. 'They don't allow jeans at the nightclub.' 'No jeans,' they echoed as they walked back to the *Ouvéa*.

Pip's Nightclub in the centre of Whangarei is patronised largely by people in their twenties and thirties with money to spend. It demands what it defines as a respectable standard of dress and offers drinks, food, music and dancing. But it tends not to come alive until late at night.

When Maniguet, Velche and Audrenc arrived at the salon at 6 p.m., therefore, dressed in sports clothes and jackets, Nash suggested they go first to Reva Meredith's Pizza Parlour for a meal. She had already bought red wine to take with them. Her staff and their partners would make the party up to ten.

Meredith's small restaurant is a favourite gathering place for yachties staying over in Whangarei: 'the last pizza before Australia.' Californian, blonde, middle aged and lively, Meredith is a good hostess. Sister of film star Gene Barry, she had left the west coast of North America 15 years before to escape the pace, the tinsel and the pollution. Her parlour is intimate and homely: low lighting, red check tablecloths, a piano and a whale rib in one corner; old bottles, dried flowers and peacock feathers around the walls.

She knew Nash, who introduced the Frenchmen as visiting boaties; and she seated them at a window table, alongside a rainbow sticker on the glass. Next to the window – and directly above the Frenchmen's table – was a Greenpeace poster:

When the earth is sick,
and the animals disappear,
the Warriors of the Rainbow
will join together
to protect the wildlife
and heal the earth.

Rainbow Warrior, Pacific Peace Voyage, 1985.

Meredith, a conservationist and Greenpeace supporter, had been given the poster by a friend. She was happy to promote awareness of the Pacific Peace Voyage along with other ecological issues (there was a whale poster on another wall). She imagined that the Frenchmen, like other yachtsmen, would feel at home among evidence of such concerns.

Later, serving Nash's guests their three large pizza specials and being kidded by Maniguet ('You look like a French actress, you know?'), Meredith dropped a slice of pie on the floor – the first time she had done this. 'I'll give you 75 cents off the bill,' she told them. No one was offended.

Towards the end of the meal, Police Constable Digby Nash, Carol's husband, joined what remained of the group – several had already moved on to the Whangarei Hotel. He sat down and chatted with the Frenchmen. At that point, they did not know his identity or his occupation.

Before the party left, Meredith brought over her visitors' book for the Frenchmen to sign. It was sprinkled with messages and sketches from yachties of every nationality. Maniguet wrote: 'For a sailing initiation, Tasman Sea was a good one . . . The main interesting lesson is that a 40 horsepower Engine on a sail ship is very very useful, very convenient, very efficient and in fact why to get a mast??'

Underneath, Velche added: '(of course) Xavier n'est pas un pur yacht man.' Nash contributed 'Voilà France'; and Audrenc sketched a television screen with a stick figure lying on the floor watching it.* 'Peut-être y'a t'il autre chose en N.Z.' (Perhaps there is something more in New Zealand.)

There *was* more, at least for that night. Late on Fridays, Whangarei rouses itself uncharacteristically. Shops are open until 9 p.m. and thousands of people come into town to buy things, to eat in restaurants or outside takeaway bars, to haunt

---

*This drawing was the subject of endless speculation in the press and in books about the *Rainbow Warrior* affair. Several writers claimed it showed a frogman and a hole in the side of a ship, with water pouring in. As such, it was cited as evidence of the Frenchmen's recklessness. This interpretation is nonsense.

video parlours, to drink, or simply to wander in the streets among the crowd. The Frenchmen made their way with their New Zealand friends to the Whangarei Hotel, a short walk from the Pizza Parlour. There was standing room only in the public bar, which was noisy and smoke filled. They had one round of drinks – Velche and Audrenc a Steinlager, Maniguet a spirit – and told Nash they did not like the place. She explained they were not staying there, it was simply a pause on the way to Pip's, to allow them to sample New Zealand drinking habits. They remained unimpressed.

At the nightclub the group divided in two: the Frenchmen, the Nashes and Carol's older staff in a round cubicle against one wall; younger members of the group at a nearby table. The yachtsmen asked for the wine list and, after consultation in French, ordered French champagne. Then they waited and looked at their surroundings with something less than approval. Pip's has a warehouse-like appearance, softened only slightly by carpets, curtains and pot plants. Some guests were eating, some dancing to recorded music, most were drinking and talking.

Half an hour later the wine had still not arrived and Maniguet was upset. He asked Carol Nash what could be wrong. She called the waiter over and said it was unsatisfactory to have to wait so long for such an expensive purchase. Finally it came – a bottle of Pol Roger – and Maniguet paid by credit card. Things relaxed once the glasses were filled. Maniguet became animated again in conversation with the group; Velche asked Carol Nash to dance; Audrenc danced with one of the other women.

Later, after talking about other matters, Xavier Maniguet asked Digby Nash what he did for a living. Nash said he was a police-man. Maniguet did not comment directly, but Nash detected an immediate switching-off on the Frenchman's part, as if he had lost interest. He also found the crew's conversation amongst themselves more difficult to follow after his admis-sion, as if they were deliberately speaking faster or in some kind of patois. They seemed to have realised that he, unlike his wife, understood some French.

At about 1 a.m. the Frenchmen got to their feet and announced they were leaving. They said goodnight all round and thanked Nash profusely, but made no arrangement to meet her again.

Over the weekend the *Ouvéa* crew got to work in earnest, carrying out their instructions. They were not seen socialising for the next two days.

First thing on Saturday morning they hired a car from Avis. They asked for a station wagon, saying that they had some bulky gear coming which they needed to transport. But the company did not have any that day. So they took a red Ford Telstar and said they would exchange it for a larger vehicle when one became available. Curious about them, the local Avis manager wondered if they had a military background, because of the way they conducted themselves.

They also visited several marine suppliers to ask about diving gear, life-jackets and navigation lights. At one of these shops, they bought a small outboard motor; at another, a grapnel, saying they planned to fish in Whangarei Harbour. Told it was completely unsuitable for that purpose, they took it none the less. Over subsequent days they also purchased charts of the local coastline, a Zodiac repair kit and a drogue (a sea anchor). And they used the car to stock up on provisions for the boat.

On Sunday 30 June, Jean Louis Dorman is known to have been somewhere between Warkworth, where he had stayed two nights before, and the Bay of Islands. Early in the afternoon, Raymond Velche was in the same area in the Ford Telstar (he kept a lunch receipt from the Dome Valley Road House, only five kilometres from Warkworth). There is a strong possibility that the senior DGSE officer met the *Ouvéa* skipper and Jean-Michel Berthelo that day. A document recovered from the *Ouvéa* by New Zealand police noted the location of a remote side-road between Dome Valley and Warkworth. Dated 30 June, it carried an inscription which translated as 'Recce TV [presumably "rendezvous"] Car Ray + Michel.' The road in question crosses a one-way bridge then fades into a dirt track. There are no overlooking houses and no through-traffic. It is an ideal meeting place for people who do not wish to be observed. Apart from this evidence, it would seem odd if agents working for the same government should come 20,000 kilometres and then not meet when they were apparently within five kilometres of each other.*

The *Ouvéa* crew were back in Whangarei by 5 p.m., however, where Velche and Berthelo tried unsuccessfully to get rooms at the Grand Hotel (which was fully booked). Dormand was installed in Paihia Autolodge – where the yachtsmen had eaten the previous week – a little later in the evening.

Xavier Maniguet too was active on Sunday. He had arranged with the Whangarei Aero Club to make a 30-minute flight over the city and its environs, including the entrance to the harbour. In the air he made a peculiar remark to his pilot, James Shaw. He said that Leigh – a coastal fishing community about half way between Whangarei and Auckland – was a pretty place. He gave no indication how he knew this or why he made the comment. Subsequently, it was to perplex police investigators and generate a number of theories.†

Ouvéa documents indicated at least three further meetings with agents in the same area, one of whom was code-named 'Henry'; two appear to have been planned before the crew reached Whangarei and must therefore have been based on intelligence supplied by Cabon or Dormand; a third was indicated by the presence of the Turenges' receipt for $166 from a Pahia motel, which for some reason they had handed over to the *Ouvéa* crew, and by their fingerprints on road maps found on board the yacht.

†That the *Ouvéa* had sailed south from Tutukaka to Leigh before heading south again for Whangarei on 28 July, for example; or that Cabon had sent information about that part of the coast and the crew had discussed it. But why? Was it planned that the *Ouvéa* should lay up there after its supposed departure from Whangarei?

Once the scenic trip was over, Maniguet stayed at the airport to take a commercial flight from Whangarei to Auckland. In Auckland he hired his own car, a Mitsubishi Sigma, and checked in at the Sheraton Hotel. He stayed two nights, converting so much foreign currency into New Zealand cash that he 'broke' the hotel's bank. On Tuesday 2 July he left for the South Island for his skiing holiday. He flew to Christchurch, from there to Queenstown, and subsequently over the Fox Glacier in Westland.

On Monday 1 July, the couple known as Alain and Sophie Turenge followed Jean Louis Dormand out of Auckland. They too headed north but up the west coast, to the Kaipara Harbour, 35 kilometres from the city. They stopped at the resort town of Parakai, close to a spa complex. There, by extraordinary coincidence, they stayed two nights in a motel unit owned by the New Zealand Prime Minister, David Lange.*

It *was* coincidence. The unit – number 12 at the Hinemoa Motel – happened to be the only one vacant when the couple enquired at the office. They did not request it. It was convenient for them, however, being set back furthest from the road and therefore less subject to public scrutiny. When the Turenges returned to Parakai a week later, they asked to be booked back into the same unit, which had a spa pool fed by a natural hot spring.

That same day, Raymond Velche too was concerned about accommodation. He tried to reserve two rooms with double beds at the Grand Hotel at Whangarei. Only one was available for that night, however (with a Renoir print on the wall), and one single. After booking them, he drove around the city looking for somewhere that could provide future long-term

---

*The Lange family had bought it as a combined investment and holiday home. It is used by the motel when the Prime Minister does not require it. Lange was to say later that he received about $168 from the motel for a year's hireage; which meant he expected to earn about $1 from the DGSE for the Turenges's occupancy.

occupancy. At first he aproached the Aotea Motel, which had no vacancies. Then he found Motel Six in Bank Street, close to the centre of the city. It had rooms available.

The crew wanted to repeat the routine they had established at the Castaway Hotel on Norfolk Island: use shore-based accommodation as an antidote to the cramped conditions on the yacht, and possibly to create more privacy for the entertaining of female guests. Velche also had to be available for regular telephone contact with his commander, Dormand. The plan was that as skipper, he would sleep away from the boat each night and Audrenc and Berthelo would take turns at staying on board on guard duty. All three would breakfast together the following morning.

The unit Velche chose at Motel Six, 1A, was larger than the others (it had originally been the motel reception area) and furthest away from the office and the likelihood of observation by motel staff. It had a combined lounge-dining-room-kitchen, a bathroom, and two bedrooms, one with single beds and one with a large double. Velche was to occupy the double bed. He signed his address in the register as 'boat harbour'.

Proprietor Barry George had difficulty understanding the yachtsman's accent. He thought the crew intended to check in that day and grabbed a bottle of milk to put in the unit. 'No, no,' said Velche. 'Not tonight. Tomorrow night.' And he explained that there would be two of them in the unit at night and three for breakfast each morning, as the crew member on boat duty joined them to eat and shower. They would want breakfast around 8 a.m., and he opted for so-called continental fare: juice, toast, jam and coffee.

For reasons he could not articulate, Barry George thought there was something odd about the Frenchman and his booking. He did not expect him to return. As Velche left, George said to himself, 'Oh yes, I'll believe it when I see it.'

At six that evening, Carol Nash was at home preparing a meal for herself and husband Digby. The telephone rang. It was Brett Panoho, one of her assistants at the salon, saying that the

Frenchmen were looking for her. Carol said she would drive down to see what they wanted. When she reached the salon she found the crew sitting out the back drinking beer. They were planning to eat at a Chinese restaurant, the King Dragon, and wanted her to join them.

She could not. She had promised Digby she would not be away from the house long, and the Frenchmen still had to return to the hotel to shower and change. So she declined and went home.

That night, while the *Ouvéa* crew ate at the King Dragon, part of their satellite navigation equipment, some clothes and some toilet items were stolen from the Telstar.* It was parked back at the boat harbour and they had apparently considered it a more secure place to store gear than on the boat itself.

Back at the Grand Hotel, Velche put through a call to Noumea Yacht Charters. He said that Maniguet and the crew were unwilling to sail the *Ouvéa* back to Noumea because of the rough weather they had encountered on the voyage south (Maniguet in particular had been extremely seasick). He asked if a replacement crew could be found in New Zealand. Roger Chatelain thought not, but undertook to consult with the owners.

On the morning of 2 July, the Frenchmen were again mobile. Velche and Berthelo checked out of the Grand Hotel and headed south in the Telstar, ostensibly to visit Auckland. En route they had a major misunderstanding.

They stopped for lunch again at the Dome Valley Road House, midway between Wellsford and Warkworth. They were met there by another man who has not been identified, but was probably Dormand. Velche got into his vehicle for the

---

*Velche was to tell Carol Nash that their new outboard motor had been stolen too. But he did not report this to the police; and the second motor was sighted a week later when Velche and Maniguet were observed transferring gear needed for the bombing into a camper van at Kaiwaka.

remainder of the journey to Auckland and Berthelo was to
follow in the Telstar. Somehow the vehicles became separated
and Berthelo found himself in Auckland without his skipper.
He eventually turned around and drove back to Whangarei
alone. Xavier Maniguet, meanwhile, was flying to Christchurch
and Queenstown.

Only Eric Audrenc was inactive for the day, guarding the
Ouvéa.

That afternoon was Carol Nash's customary half-day off to
compensate for working extra hours, and she went home to
change. She intended to return to the salon at about 3.15 to
see how staff were managing. On the way, however, she decided
to drive via the town basin to check what was happening on
the *Ouvéa*. The crew had drawn a map for her on Friday,
indicating that it was four berths up from the bridge. At Paihia
she had seen it only at night; she was not certain she would
recognise it again.

She walked on to the jetty for berth number 5 and saw the
yacht tied to a pile beyond it, the French flag hanging over
the stern. Also near the stern, naked to the waist and sitting
in the sun, was Eric Audrenc. He waved and asked if she
wanted to come aboard. She said yes. So Audrenc got into
the orange dinghy moored to the yacht and rowed the few
metres to the jetty.

Eric Audrenc had put on a red and black checked swanndri
(bush shirt) and his English was poor. But he was excitable
and extroverted and keen to talk. On board, he and Nash con-
versed with the aid of a French-English dictionary and copious
sign language. He managed to explain that Maniguet had gone
to Queenstown and the others to Auckland, but that Velche
and Berthelo were expected back that afternoon. Nash found
their tourist guidebook in the cabin (the *Insight Guide to New
Zealand*) and began to browse through it as Audrenc made
coffee. She drew his attention to photographs of the All Blacks
playing France and of a couple of Bay of Islands marlin.

At about 4 p.m. a shout from the wharf revealed Jean-Michel Berthelo waving to be collected. He too was wearing a swann-dri, a blue and black one, looking every inch a New Zealand hunter. Eric fetched him in the dinghy and they both showed Nash the labels on their tops, which they said they had bought as New Zealand souvenirs. Nash found conversation with Berthelo even more difficult. Not only was his English non-existent, he seemed less confident than Audrenc. They too resorted frequently to the dictionary.

Berthelo indicated he had come straight from Auckland, a two-hour drive, and that the sun had hurt his eyes. 'Where's Raymond?' Nash asked, puzzled. Still there, Berthelo indicated. Coming back late afternoon.

As they relaxed, they moved on to talk about general matters. Berthelo and Audrenc wanted to know what religion New Zealanders were. Mostly Protestant, Nash told them. They nodded as if that proved something. Not to be at a disadvan-tage, she then said she had been to New Caledonia and found the French in Noumea arrogant.

'That's because they think you are English,' Audrenc told her. Both men then thumbed their dictionaries and showed her 'bastard' as a synonym for 'English'. Nash was aghast. Berthelo assured her that the British and the French had disliked each other from the days of the Second World War. This feeling had intensified as a result of the British war with Argentina, he said. The Argentinians had used French rockets and French guns to kill the British. French guns were very good, he said. Mrs Thatcher had not liked that.

One of the men mentioned Moruroa and the need to test nuclear weapons there and asked how she felt about it. 'It's too close to New Zealand,' she said. 'It is necessary' was their only response. 'Is François Mitterrand popular back home?' Nash wanted to know. Eric Audrenc only shrugged his shoulders. He had no comment to make about his socialist president or his government.

Talk turned to indigenous peoples: Maori in New Zealand, Kanaks in New Caledonia. The Frenchmen had a simple solution for the problems raised by the mixture of races and cultures. 'White men must rule,' they told Nash, it was the only way civilisation would work.

After skirting these potentially contentious political and philosophical matters, Audrenc invited Nash to have a drink. He would make them a Daquiri, he said, with white rum, lemon juice and sugar. 'But only one, or you fall off the boat.' Berthelo, still serious, declined anything alcoholic.

By 7.30 p.m. there was no sign of Raymond Velche. The others said they would like to eat and asked Carol Nash to recommend a restaurant. She said she would take them to Shaolin, run by French-speaking Vietnamese.

'But,' said Audrenc, 'we must leave message for Raymond.'

So Nash drew a map from the town basin to the restaurant marking in her salon as an additional point of reference. Audrenc then indicated north and south in entirely the wrong directions. They all laughed. 'I won't sail with *you*,' Carol told him. He agreed it might be dangerous.

The next hour turned into a madcap drive around Whangarei in Nash's car, looking for Velche, trying the Shaolin (which was closed), looking for Velche again (Audrenc and Berthelo were visibly worried about him), choosing another restaurant, leaving a new message and map at the yacht, and finally sitting down to an Italian meal at Amici, next to the city's massage parlour.

Amici is a spartan eating place – brick walls and plain wooden tables – that specialises in pasta dishes. Nash and the two Frenchmen had ordered their meals and were starting their minestrone by the time Velche found them. He walked in and sat next to Carol, opposite his crew mates, and launched at once into a long conversation in French, of which, of course, she understood nothing. He seemed to be reporting something.

Afterwards, he told Nash they had had part of their satellite navigation gear stolen from their car the previous night. She asked why the equipment had been there at all, but did not understand Velche's reply. He added that an outboard motor, a jacket, a pair of shoes and his shaving gear had also been taken. Nash suggested he report the theft to the police. He agreed to do so.*

Nash also asked Velche how he had returned to Whangarei. He said by bus. 'Why did you catch a bus when Jean-Michel was driving back?' He didn't answer. Later, when they were alone, he said, 'When you spent a lot of time in the same company it is good to be by yourself. Three weeks on the boat is a long time.'

After the meal, Nash and Velche drove back to the boat while the other two walked. He collected some gear and told her about the motel, suggesting she return there with him for coffee. So she followed the Telstar back to Motel Six, unit 1A.

Inside, he made instant coffee and told her he was expecting a telephone call from Auckland. He switched on television and they watched together for about a quarter of an hour while they drank coffee. Then the phone rang.

Nash could understand nothing of the conversation, which was actually Jean Louis Dormand ringing from Paihia. The only feature she could remember subsequently was that 'Nouvelle Calédonie' recurred with some frequency. Velche hung up after about seven minutes and said he would have to ring New Caledonia. But when he tried to raise the motel office there was no reply. He abandoned the call.†

Nash, thinking that the conversation could have related to the missing sat-nav component, said she was going to Auckland the following day and might be able to replace it. Velche said no. He thought it was worth about $NZ4,000. It was too big

---

*He did report it, but did not lay an official complaint; the Whangarei police did not date the report.

†The following morning he rang Roger Chatelain again, to find that Noumea Yacht Charters did not think there was any prospect of finding another crew to return the yacht. It was possibly this proposal that he was arguing about with Dormand the night before.

a responsibility for her to worry about.

He seemed on edge about that problem; or about something else. And he complained that he had bought a pair of running shoes in Auckland that had turned out to be too large. He was particularly cross because the man in the shop had assured him they were the right size. He would try to exchange them for another pair in Whangarei.

On Wednesday 3 July the Turenges completed their celibate stay in separate beds at the Prime Minister's motel unit at Parakai and checked out in the morning. They were spotted and remembered in Auckland in the course of the day, driving around the wharves and looking at ship berths. By late afternoon they were investigating accommodation in the suburb of Pakuranga, close to where they planned to hire a camper van two days later. They finally booked in at Waipuna Lodge Hotel in the eastern suburb of Mt Wellington.

Jean Louis Dormand was also back in Auckland that day. He took a room on the seventh floor of the Hyatt Kingsgate Hotel, which gave him a panoramic view of Marsden Wharf, where the *Rainbow Warrior* was to dock four days later.

Carol Nash too was in Auckland on the Wednesday, but returned to Whangarei at about 10.15 p.m. As she drove past Motel Six, she saw a light on in the Frenchmen's unit, which was on the roadside corner. She stopped to see if they had sorted out their sat-nav problem.

As she knocked she realised that whoever was inside might be entertaining female friends.* Raymond opened the door, dressed only in his underpants.

'Are you alone?' Nash asked before making a move to enter.

'Only my friend is here,' said Velche. 'Come in.'

He turned on another light and Eric Audrenc came out of one of the two interior bedrooms.

---

*In fact the crew managed to keep their female guests separate from one another, largely as a result of alternating use of the Grand Hotel, Motel Six and the yacht.

While Velche got dressed again, Audrenc made coffee and then they sat and talked. Nash asked about the missing gear. That was all right now, Velche told her. They had been to a marine suppliers that day and had been promised the part. He assured her that they were no longer worried about it.

At 11 p.m. Nash finished her coffee and went home.

Late on Thursday afternoon, the three Frenchmen returned to Nash's salon. Their red Telstar was coated in thick dust. They had driven a considerable distance that day on unsealed roads. They asked directions to the nearest car-wash.

They had further questions too. Where could they play squash? Nash suggested the Otaika squash courts and told them how to get there. Where could they buy more shirts? She thought the Farmers Trading Company or War Assets Store would offer the best range. Finally, they agreed to meet for dinner at seven o'clock the following evening, when Xavier Maniguet would be back from the South Island.

The *Ouvéa* crew had stayed at Paihia in the Bay of Islands; Jean Louis Dormand followed them there three days later (staying for four days); and now Sophie and Alain Turenge were to head there too, three days behind Dormand.

They left their Mt Wellington hotel on the morning of Friday 5 July and hired a white Toyota Hiace camper van from Newmans' Mt Wellington depot. After what must have been a meandering drive, which took them through Whangarei, they reached Paihia six hours later. There are no records of daytime sightings of the *Ouvéa* crew that day. They appear to have been out of town. Again, they could easily have intercepted the Turenges en route for Paihia, possibly on the deserted road that they had selected for their previous rendezvous.

At Paihia, the Turenges booked into the Beachcomber Motel, one of the few with gardens and a view across the bay, and asked for a unit facing the sea. They were given a double room. Alain registered as 'Turenge, 105 Avenue du Général Bizot, Paris' – an address that turned out to be false.

Motel staff noticed two things about the French 'married' couple. They seemed to have very little luggage when they checked into the motel. And – as they had done in previous accommodation – they slept in separate beds.

After work on Friday evening, Carol Nash was having her customary end-of-week drink with staff at the back of the salon. Somebody came in and said a Frenchman was waiting to see her. She was surprised, having arranged to meet the crew at seven. She went into the salon to find Xavier there, looking uncharacteristically lost.

'So, you're back.'

'Yes. I've been to Queenstown. Where are my crew?'

'What makes you think I'd know,' Nash asked, teasing him. He laughed. 'Actually, they're playing squash and I'm meeting them at seven.'

'They are not at the Grand Hotel,' said Xavier. 'I have looked.' This was the first Nash knew that they had stayed there.

'No, they're at Motel Six.'

'Where is that?' Maniguet looked puzzled and seemed cross that no message had been left for him.

'If you wait while I change my clothes, I'll take you there,' said Nash. Maniguet agreed, but still appeared angry.

At Motel Six, proprietor Joan George was yet another New Zealand woman charmed by Xavier Maniguet. She found him handsome, courtly, and – she said later – 'sexy'. The man had a rank maleness so appealing to some women that it amounted to an almost aphrodisiac quality. Checking in, he gave his address as 'Ouvéa boat'.

'Are you with the Frenchmen in 1A?' she asked.

'Yes,' he said. 'They are my friends.'

'Do you want to go into the same unit?'

'No. I prefer my own.' He was given unit 15, well away from the rest of the crew.

Carol Nash then drove the Frenchman to the Otaika squash courts, where she thought the crew would be playing before dinner. But they had left. Maniguet suggested they go to the Grand, where he had reserved a room and left his rental car. Nash parked in the hotel carpark while Xavier cancelled his booking, then suggested a drink. They still had half an hour before she was to meet the others. They went into the private bar, where Maniguet bought Steinlagers.

Sitting at one of the small bar tables Nash mentioned that part of the sat-nav gear had been stolen from the Telstar. Maniguet's mood changed instantly. His face flushed and he glared. 'What was it doing in the car?' Nash said she had no idea; but getting upset would not rectify the problem. Maniguet recovered at once. 'Of course,' he said. 'Of course. You are quite right.'

He changed the subject and pointed to his leather case, as long as a briefcase but twice as wide. 'Look, Carol,' he said. 'I've travelled the world with this. I need no more. In it I have five shirts, two pair of trousers, and two of shoes.' He pulled out a red swanndri. 'Look. A souvenir of New Zealand.'

Nash laughed, because of the other swanndris. They must have conferred. She asked about Queenstown.

'Queenstown! Queenstown was very good. I enjoyed it. But I lost all my credit cards there.'

'Did you get them back?'

'No. But I just telexed to have them replaced. It was no problem.'

'How about Auckland?'

'Ah! Auckland.' He gave Nash a quick résumé. He had stayed at the Sheraton. He had looked over the Regent and had a drink there, but said he had not liked it. He had met an Englishwoman and spent the night with her. And he had eaten at two restaurants: Melba and Number Five. 'Number Five was excellent.'

'You sure get around, Xavier.'

'Yes, I do. First class all the way.' This, Nash felt, was said boastfully rather than tongue-in-cheek.

They finished their beers and returned to the motel in separate cars.

This time the light was on in unit 1A. Maniguet strode in and had a heated and rapid discussion with Velche. Nash presumed it was about the sat-nav equipment, and sat down to wait for them to finish. As they talked, Nash became conscious of how different the atmosphere tended to be when Maniguet was present. Without him, the crew were relaxed, communicative; with him, there was an element of tension. She put it down to his being the leader of the group. Later, when she knew who they were, Nash felt that there had been a major difference of opinion that night between Maniguet and the crew as to how their part of the operation was to be carried out.

When the protagonists had settled whatever was at issue, they all had a laugh over the fact that Velche had beaten the other two at squash, but strained a muscle for his pains.

Maniguet announced he was hungry and impatient to get to a restaurant. Nash suggested they go again to Shaolin, where Velche, Audrenc and Berthelo had eaten two nights before and enjoyed the food. Maniguet and Audrenc set off in advance in the doctor's Mitsubishi. Nash waited while the others changed out of their squash gear and shared a couple of Steinlagers with her.

At the Shaolin an hour later, Maniguet and Audrenc had already ordered when the rest of the party arrived. While the others waited for their food, Truc Piotrovska, three-year-old son of the Vietnamese cook, ran round their table shooting at each one of them in turn with a toy pistol. As it was pointed at her, Carol Nash grimaced.

'What is the matter, Carol, you do not like guns?' Maniguet asked her.

'No,' said Nash. 'They kill people, don't they?'

'Yes, yes,' said Maniguet impatiently. 'But it is absolutely necessary that children play this way. It is part of growing up.'

Late that night at the motel, Carol Nash was able to talk to Velche alone in the privacy of his unit (the others had gone to Maniguet's room). He told her he had an older brother and a younger one. He had owned a yacht in the West Indies, he said, and spent a great deal of time sailing it through the Caribbean, on charter work and taking tourists diving.* 'But it gets too expensive, Carol, to slip it twice a year. So I sell it.'

Later still, she asked why he had not left any message for Maniguet at the yacht or the hotel. He shrugged his shoulders and said nothing.

The following morning, Saturday, was frenetically busy. It began with Velche and Maniguet both making calls to Dormand at the Hyatt Kingsgate in Auckland, possibly because they needed an arbiter for their quarrel the night before. An hour later Alain Turenge rang Motel Six from Paihia, apparently to arrange a meeting with the crew.

Outside, when Maniguet tried to start his car, he could not get the engine to fire. Agitated, apparently worried about being late for something, he burst into the motel office and asked if he could call the rental company.

'Which one?' asked Barry George, but did not understand the reply. 'Have you got a problem?'

'Oh,' said Maniguet. 'I didn't close the door properly last night. So the inside light was on and now the battery is flat.'

Barry George went outside with the Frenchman to investigate. The car, a silver Mitsubishi Sigma, was parked in front of unit 1, next to the space for Velche's unit. The battery was indeed flat. The vehicle had automatic transmission and could not be push-started.

'Hang on,' said George. Being the good motelier he was, he fetched a battery and jumper leads and within minutes he had the car going again. Maniguet expressed surprise, admiration and relief, and drove off in a hurry. The occupants of 1A had already disappeared for the day.

---

*In fact he was there on undercover assignments for the DGSE.

There was to be a discredited claim that a Newmans camper
van was seen on the forecourt of Motel Six at about 9.30 that
morning. It could not have been the Turenges. They were taking
their breakfast at Paihia at 8.30 a.m. And they were seen in
the van driving through Paihia close to 10 a.m. To have
appeared at 9.30 in Whangarei, one hour's drive away, they
would have had to move at supersonic speed.

The Turenges *were* spotted again on Saturday morning, however, in interesting company.

Some time before 11.30, a resident of the Hokianga village
of Waima – about an hour's drive from Whangarei and 45
minutes from Paihia – was walking from her home to the
general store. About 800 metres from the shop she came across
a Newmans camper van parked in a metal storage area on the
right-hand side of the road. There were three people in the
vehicle and they appeared to be a having a hot drink and study-
ing maps. 'How far is it to Hokianga Harbour?' one of the
men asked her. She told them, about ten minutes. They thanked
her and she walked on. Later she was positive about identifi-
cations of Alain and Sophie Turenge. Her description of the
third person matched that of Xavier Maniguet.

Maniguet was almost certainly meeting the Turenges – well
away from the agents' previous routes and places where they
might be recognised – to brief them on rendezvous points and
pick-up places to be used over the coming three days. Specifically, it could have been to arrange a meeting with *Ouvéa*
crew members to collect the concealed Zodiac and outboard
motor; and to explain to them where the explosives were hidden
in a separate location so that the Turenges could move them
once the *Ouvéa* was ready to leave New Zealand and was
therefore less likely to be associated with them. Such a briefing
could not be carried out by telephone; it required close study
of map references and sketches. The question about Hokianga
Harbour to the passer-by was simply a cover; or yet another
false trail in the unlikely event of the meeting being reported
to the police.

By late afternoon that same day, Maniguet had driven to
Auckland and checked in again at the Sheraton Hotel. The
Turenges had returned to Paihia. The *Ouvéa* crew had taken
the Telstar back to Avis. It had clocked up an astonishing 1,400
kilometres. Now they exchanged it for a silver Commodore
station wagon. 'Our gear has arrived,' Velche told the Avis
staff. 'We need the space.' Another crew member spent much
of the morning trying out, drying out or running in a Yamaha
outboard motor (which was not functioning well). Then all
three played squash in the afternoon at the Kensington Squash
and Fitness Centre, their third successive day on the courts.

Sunday 7 July was the day the *Rainbow Warrior* reached
Auckland. It was also the day on which two further DGSE
agents arrived in the country – the men entrusted with the actual
sabotage of the boat. And it was probably the nearest the *Ouvéa*
crew came in New Zealand to a day of rest.

It began with a fright for a middle-aged Whangarei man –
wandering along the town wharf with a 35 mm camera around
his neck – and possibly for the Frenchmen staying there.

The amateur photographer often strolled around the town
basin, filming yachts, trawlers, birds, or anything that took
his fancy. On this morning, looking over the edge of the concrete wharf, he spotted the *Ouvéa* with its French flag hanging
over the stern. There was a young woman sitting on the deck
in the sun reading a book, and he waited for her to look up
so that he could greet her and ask exactly where the boat was
from: New Zealand was a long way from France.

The longer he stood there, however, the more motionless
the woman became, concentrating on her book. He became
convinced that she was aware of him and was determined not
to raise her eyes. He became annoyed. He was accustomed to
greeting people in a friendly fashion and scarcely ever
encountered rudeness among the yachting fraternity.

When he finally turned away from the yacht the woman got
up quickly and disappeared into the cabin. Within minutes two
men in their thirties – both of them of medium height – climbed

up a ladder and on to the wharf. They were talking in a language he recognised as French (which he had studied at school), but he was unable to understand them. They walked quickly past him, also apparently making a deliberate effort to ignore him and the camera.

Beyond the sheds at the end of the wharf, they met another man getting out of a station wagon. He was taller than the first two. As they conferred, the Whangarei man considered filming them. He began to bring his camera up to his eyes. As he did so the tall man – the leader, he thought – detached himself from the group and began to walk towards him. He seemed fit, sturdy and purposeful. The older man felt suddenly vulnerable. There was nobody else in sight.

When the tall man was within metres of him, the photographer angled his camera away towards yacht masts, and then followed a shag which came winging low up the harbour and skidded on the surface of the water beyond the boats. The Frenchman, who had seemed to be about to speak to him, let out a long breath, turned and walked away.

The photographer too walked off, in the opposite direction, cross that he had allowed himself to feel menaced by strangers on his home ground. He considered going to the police; then decided that he really had nothing of any substance to tell them.

Another local who wanted to find the *Ouvéa* that morning could not. Carol Nash crossed the town basin bridge to discover that the yacht was no longer in berth number 5 where she had last seen it. She felt let down. The crew had spoken on Friday night of leaving within days. But she had imagined they would find time to say goodbye. She had come to know them well enough to expect that, she felt.

In fact, the yacht had been told by a harbour board official to change berths. It had moved some days earlier to the town wharf, official mooring for boats in transit, on the opposite side of the estuary to its original berth. This was to facilitate Customs formalities. Curiously, the yacht the Frenchmen initially tied up next to was the trimaran *Kliss II*, owned by

Greenpeace members and scheduled to sail in the Peace Flotilla to Moruroa with the *Rainbow Warrior*.* The two crews did not communicate with one another and *Kliss II* left Whangarei on 6 July.

While the *Ouvéa* crew was worrying about being filmed and Auckland Greenpeace members were preparing for the appearance of their flagship, Jean Louis Dormand was organising a discreet welcome of his own. The previous night he had checked into the Gateway Lodge, a hotel close to Auckland Airport. On Sunday morning two more of his agents disembarked there, at 8.15 a.m.

One, who identified himself as Alain Tonel, aged 33, was short, slim, fit-looking, with a dark complexion and prominent nose. He spoke English fluently. The other, whose English was poor, gave his name as Jacques Camurier. He was taller (1.75 metres), older (35), with sandy hair. Both men claimed to be physical education instructors at a girls' college in Tahiti, where they had booked and boarded their flight. They originally had open tickets for the return journey, but at Auckland Airport, possibly after consultations with Dormand, they arranged to leave New Zealand on 24 July.

After they left the airport there were to be no confirmed sightings of the men for the next two days. Evidence involving them in the *Rainbow Warrior* bombing is circumstantial, but compelling. Their passports turned out to be false. No real persons of those names and occupations were found in Papeete. They were of a similar age and build to the other DGSE agents already in the country. Dormand had moved to the Gateway Lodge to be close to the airport the night before they arrived. And they were in his company for a lengthy period after the bombing.

These were the circumstances that gradually swung the

---

*In the event, *Kliss II* stayed at home. The bombing of the *Rainbow Warrior* and consequent absence of a large support ship on the voyage from New Zealand forced her to abandon the Moruroa voyage.

attention of the New Zealand Police away from the activities of the *Ouvéa* crew and towards Tonel and Camurier. Further, the fact that they succeeded in dropping out of sight immediately after their arrival suggests a degree of professionalism; they were behaving like agents who – unlike the *Ouvéa* crew – were actually going to carry out the sabotage of the Greenpeace vessel and hence they took considerable care not to be seen in its vicinity.

Where they stayed is not known. But Dormand hired a red-and-blue-striped Toyota camper van in Auckland the morning after their arrival. Then he too disappeared for the next two days.

Velche, Audrenc and Berthelo apparently spent most of Sunday morning cleaning the *Ouvéa*, checking gear, and generally getting the yacht ready for sea. In the afternoon they played squash again and visited the Golden Palace Massage Parlour. They lazed and drowsed away the end of the day in a glow of saunas and relief massages, and one of them took one of the parlour girls back to the boat that night.

Back in Auckland, Xavier Maniguet too was having a comparatively lazy day for a normally active man. He spent the morning in bed at the Sheraton with a New Zealand woman he had met the night before. In the afternoon, he took his friend for a drive along the Auckland waterfront, past the wharves and out along Tamaki Drive to Okahu Bay and Mission Bay, where they had a late lunch. It is not clear whether he saw the *Rainbow Warrior* come in, nor whether he was looking for it – nor whether his waterfront drive was a reconnaissance for events that were to take place there in three days' time. That night he rang Motel Six: possibly to pass on information about the arrival of the additional agents. Their presence ensured that the *Ouvéa* crew would not have to carry out the bombing; and that equipment for the sabotage could now be assembled and delivered.

The Turenges had a more stressful day. Prior to leaving the Beachcomber Motel in Paihia, Alain had ordered an unusually large breakfast: lots of bacon, eggs and toast. It seemed more than one person could eat. Then, when manageress Jill Couch brought it to the unit, Turenge met her at the door and blocked her way. She got the strong impression that he did not want her to enter and wondered if an additional person was visiting the unit.

There was a further incident when the French couple checked out at mid-morning. While they were loading what the manageress thought had become a larger amount of luggage than that with which they had arrived, Jill Couch's small dog jumped into the camper van through the back door. Both Alain (who had previously been excessively relaxed and gentlemanly) and Sophie became extremely agitated. Alain retrieved the animal himself before it got beyond arm's reach of the door. He interposed his body between the van and motel staff, preventing anyone else from looking inside the vehicle.*

They took a long time to get to Auckland, via Whangarei and Warkworth, and their exact route is not known. They had no motel booking in the city and it was only the fact that they broke their windscreen and needed to replace the vehicle that forced them to return that night. The accident, they said, had occurred on a coastal road near Warkworth. By 7.30 p.m. they had again booked into Waipuna Lodge in Mt Wellington, distressed to find that they would be unable to exchange the van for another until the following day.

Thus Jean Louis Dormand, Alain Tonel, Jacques Camurier, Alain and Sophie Turenge and Xavier Maniguet all appear to have spent the night in Auckland on the day that the *Rainbow Warrior* arrived there.

---

*Police later believed that the additional gear with which the Turenges left Paihia, and which they wanted to prevent others from seeing, may have been diving equipment delivered to them by an *Ouvéa* crew member.

Monday 8 July seems to have been a hectic and full day for most of the agents. Velche, Audrenc and Berthelo came to Carol Nash's salon at ten in the morning to ask her out that night. She was pleased to see them both and said she thought they had gone. They explained about shifting berths.

Out in the street, Velche said that the following day was his birthday and they planned to leave the same morning.* Before he got any further Carol interrupted. In that case, she said, she would take *them* out to dinner – to say goodbye and to celebrate the birthday. 'I have to go first to Auckland to pick up Xavier,' said Velche, 'at noon.'

'Will you definitely be back in time for dinner?' Nash asked. 'I don't want to book and find you're not here.'

'We shall be back. Meet us at the boat at eight.'

At 12.15 p.m. yet another French agent arrived at Auckland Airport – this time from Tokyo – bringing the number in the country to ten. He was François Régis Verlet, the Singapore-based computer technician in his early twenties who was also the son of the man who had employed Xavier Maniguet at Abu Dhabi. At the time of his arrival in New Zealand he had been away from Singapore for 11 weeks (he left only days before Christine Cabon reached New Zealand); he was to disappear from his job after the *Rainbow Warrior* bombing.

In Auckland he stayed at the same youth hostel that Cabon had used. He was to tell police that he spent his first full day in the city walking. But it was to be his movements on the second day – the day the *Rainbow Warrior* was sunk – that were to have special significance for those charged with investigating the bombing.

Maniguet drove himself back from Auckland on Monday 8 July and arrived in Whangarei at about one in the afternoon. He handed the Sigma to Audrenc and Berthelo, who spent the

---

*His birthday was actually two days later, the day of the *Rainbow Warrior* bombing, by which time the *Ouvéa* would ostensibly be at sea.

afternoon in Whangarei shopping for supplies for the return voyage. Maniguet and Velche drove to an unknown place to collect some bulky gear, which they loaded into the back of the station wagon. Then they headed south.

Nearly 70 kilometres from Whangarei, on the main road to Auckland, forestry workers Brendon Walton and Murray Hoyle were spending the afternoon felling and trimming trees. They were working on the edge of the Topuni State Forest, alongside a lay-by used to store road metal. Shortly after 2.30 p.m. they saw a camper van with a pop-top swing off the road, do a circuit of the metal dump, then drive off again north, towards Whangarei.

Ten minutes later the silver Commodore station wagon arrived, driven by Velche. At first it parked on the forest side of the dump, close to where Walton and Hoyle were bringing down trees. Then – to avoid being observed closely or to escape the possibility of being hit by falling pines – Velche drove to the far side, away from the workers. He stopped the station wagon again but left the engine running.

Hoyle and Walton were suspicious. There had been allegations of marijuana growing and dealing in the district – under cover of the forest – and responsible citizens were on the lookout for clandestine meetings (both men belonged to a Closed Brethren church). So they strolled over to speak to the occupants of the Commodore, who were looking at their watches and seemed anxious.

Peering into the back of the station wagon as they approached, Hoyle and Walton saw two outboard motors (one dark and one silver), two large blue bags with handles, similar to those in which Zodiac dinghies were packaged, and some red plastic petrol tanks.

'What's the trouble?' Hoyle asked.

'We're looking for some friends in a camper van,' answered the man they later identified as Maniguet. They noticed he was wearing a large diving watch.

'Have you seen them?'

'There *was* a camper van here. It took off about ten minutes ago. Heading north.'

Maniguet and Velche consulted, heads together. Then Velche accelerated suddenly, swinging the Commodore back on to the road and almost colliding with an oncoming car. He drove off at high speed. Suspicions heightened, Brendon Walton wrote the registration of the vehicle in the dust on the tailgate of his forestry truck: just in case.

Velche and Maniguet found the camper van about eight kilometres further north, parked in a tree-shaded roadside rest area just beyond Kaiwaka.

When a middle-aged Auckland couple returning from Whangarei pulled into the same parking area shortly after 3 p.m., they drew up about four metres behind the agents' vehicles, which were parked alongside a picnic table. As they watched, they saw two men transfer an outboard motor from the car to the van. One they identified subsequently as Alain Turenge. They also saw a second engine lying in the back of the Commodore, and the New Zealand man was surprised that there was nothing around it to stop it rolling or to prevent oil seepage into the upholstery. 'I bet that motor's stolen,' he said to his companion.

Whatever they had stumbled upon, it was the end of the transaction. One of the men outside threw a can into a rubbish bin and waved to the Auckland couple. Then the camper van drove off, followed by the station wagon, heading south.*

---

*Alain Mafart and Dominique Prieur, alias the Turenges, were to be adamant later that it was not *their* camper van that met the Commodore that day; in which case it could only have been Jean Louis Dormand's. In the light of subsequent evidence, however, the New Zealand police believed that the meeting *was* with the Turenges, and would have prepared evidence to this effect for court proceedings. Under interrogation in France, Xavier Maniguet also conceded that this meeting had taken place. But he claimed it was for the purpose of procuring women, and that the man he and Velche spoke to was the pimp. An unlikely explanation in view of the way such assignations are arranged in New Zealand and in the light of the engagement already arranged for the coming evening with Carol Nash.

That evening, while the crew showered, shaved and dressed
in preparation for dinner, Raymond Velche made his way alone
to the motel office.

'Please, I would like an extra room for tonight,' he said.

Barry George told him the motel was fully booked and that
the unit they had was the only one available.

'Okay,' said Velche, shrugging. 'I stay there then.'

At 7.55 p.m. Carol Nash drove down to the town wharf. She
got out of her car and waited by the harbour board sheds. It
was too dark to see where the *Ouvéa* was moored. After about
five minutes she heard a car tooting from the road. When the
sound persisted she realised it must be the crew and went to
investigate.

It was Raymond Velche in the Commodore, parked in the
middle of the road to make himself conspicuous. He wound
down a window and told her to jump in. They then drove round
to the *Ouvéa*, tied up a short distance away behind the Navy
League Hall. Only the mast was visible from the wharf.

Velche called down to the others, who swarmed up a ladder.
Maniguet was carrying a plastic bag full of wine bottles. They
were all well dressed, well groomed, and excited. Maniguet,
wearing a close-fitting navy jersey, was the smartest. 'You
won't need the wine, Xavier,' Nash told him. 'The restaurant's
licensed.'

'Ah, but will they have French champagne?' said Maniguet.
'We'll take it just in case.'

They piled into the Commodore and Velche drove to Nash's
car. He and Carol changed vehicles and led the way to the restaurant while the others followed in the station wagon.

The Forum is the most expensive restaurant in Whangarei. Its
advertising promises 'elegant dining with an international standard of menu and service' and 'a wide selection of local and
imported wines to appeal to the most discerning patron . . .'
It is in a high-ceilinged entertainment complex with rafters,
dark wood panels and plush decorations: very much the kind

of restaurant favoured by middle New Zealand for nights out on special occasions.

Nash and her guests began with aperitifs in the velvet-lined bar in the foyer. She and Raymond drank vodka and orange, Xavier and Eric brandy Alexanders, and Jean-Michel a port. Again, she noticed their palpable good humour. Their excitement was of the relaxed variety, the kind people feel when an examination is over. Was it because they were leaving, she wondered?

In the dining room they happily crushed around a circular table and ordered: two bottles of French wine (one white, one red), and scallops for an entrée. Velche was going to try New Zealand oysters but the waitress warned that they might not be fresh.

'Carol,' said Xavier, looking pleased with himself, 'I have learned a new expression. What can it mean? "Wham, bam, thank you, Ma'am."'*

Nash laughed. 'Yes,' she said, 'we Kiwi girls have cause to use it a lot. You're a wicked Frenchman.'

Maniguet showed a flash of concern. 'Wicked? What do you mean wicked?'

'I mean wicked-naughty.'

Maniguet relaxed and laughed.

The crew gave Velche a French-English dictionary and phrase book for a present and everybody made use of it throughout the meal, raising the level of comunication and hilarity. A local family at an adjacent table assumed the crew were wealthy businessmen from Tahiti having a night on the town.

For mains they all ordered chateaubriand, and they asked for their desserts in French, causing confusion and exposing the thinness of the Gallic veneer which characterises New Zealand menus, wine lists and restaurant service. After dessert, Maniguet suggested a return to Motel Six for coffee and champagne. 'For the birthday,' he said. 'For the birthday.'

---

*Maniguet was alleged subsequently by an Australian journalist to have seduced eight different women in seven days.

Nash insisted on paying for the meal by cheque, having determined that it was her shout. But after she had left with Velche, Berthelo returned, told the staff to rip up her cheque and paid again in cash.

Back at the motel Audrenc and Berthelo brewed up coffee and Velche laid the unit's thick glasses on the table.

'Do you know how the French open champagne?' Maniguet asked Carol, keeping up the role of ringmaster.

'No.'

'Well, in France we would put the champagne on the table and cut off the neck with a sabre, without touching the bottle with our hands. Here is our sabre.'

He handed Velche the bottle and the bread knife from the kitchen. Raymond loosened the wire, scraped the foil up the neck and, with a flick of the wrist, took off the head of the cork with the knife. The remainder popped out and he filled the glasses as the bottle overflowed. Everybody toasted Raymond. Nash was unable to understand the nature of some of the French compliments, but Velche was delighted. The atmosphere was distinctly celebratory.

After coffee, Audrenc and Berthelo returned to the boat. It was well past midnight. Nash and Velche shared the double bedroom; Maniguet took one of the single beds in the other room.

High spirits carried over to the following morning. When Nash awoke, Maniguet was shaving and showering. Audrenc and Berthelo burst into the unit, fighting puppyishly to get to the toilet first. Maniguet was bundled out of the bathroom and the joking – all in French – continued.

Velche got up, ordered breakfast from the office and tidied away the relics of the night's revelry. He too seemed happy, though he was never as demonstrative as Maniguet and Audrenc. When Barry George carried in the breakfast tray he was surprised at the number of people waiting at the table (usually they remained out of sight until he had deposited the food). 'Five loaves and fishes for five thousand,' he announced to a polite but uncomprehending audience, then left them to it.

Over breakfast – fruit juice, piles of toast, jam and coffee – Audrenc found the weather forecast in the morning paper, whooped, and then swished it rapidly in front of everybody's eyes, far too rapidly for them to read it.

Raymond and Carol left the motel first while the others were packing before they returned the rental cars. She, now feeling dejected, was to deliver the skipper to the boat. She gave Velche her business card and said, 'Send me a card from Norfolk Island. So I know you're safe.' He said he would. Half-seriously, they undertook to meet in Paris under the Eiffel Tower on 9 July 1986. At 8.30 she dropped him off at the town wharf.

At 10 a.m. on 9 July the *Ouvéa* cleared Customs and at 11.30 cast off into the river and left Whangarei for Norfolk Island and Noumea, sailing with a stiff breeze. The crew had been in New Zealand for seventeen days. They had done few of the things they had told people they were there for – little diving, no fishing, and no sailing to Auckland or Tauranga. But they *had* been busy. Their rental cars had run up phenomenal distances – a total of 1,657 kilometres, sufficient to have driven the length of the country.

Six days later, the morning after a night trip home from Auckland, Carol Nash was late leaving for work. She was cross when the telephone rang at 9.30, delaying her further. The operator said she had Norfolk Island on the line.

'Raymond, is that you?'

'Yes.'

'You arrived safely?'

'Yes. We arrive yesterday, Sunday. Had very strong wind.* You are not at work?'

'No, I went to Auckland yesterday. I was tired. You know it's silly, Raymond, but I don't even know your last name.'

*In fact the *Ouvéa* had reached Norfolk Island two days earlier.

'I don't understand.'

'Your last name. Your surname. I don't know it.'

'I understand. It is Velche. V-E-L-C-H-E,' said the man soon to be identified as Roland Verge.

Carol Nash, not hearing properly, wrote down 'E-L-C-H-E'. Raymond said he would call her from Noumea and they said goodbye. She never heard from him again.

THREE

The Bombers

August 1973

The French military had first revealed the full extent of its
animosity towards Greenpeace and Pacific anti-nuclear voyages
in 1973. The previous year, David McTaggart's yacht *Vega*
had been rammed by a French Navy corvette off Moruroa while
conducting the first Greenpeace protest near the atoll.
McTaggart and his crew of three were taken into genteel
custody, which included a civilised lunch with Admiral
Christian Claverie, commander of the nuclear test force on
Moruroa, alongside the atoll's lagoon. In 1973, however, the
navy signalled that its patience and its gentility were at an end.

McTaggart, a moustached Canadian, was an unusual pro-
tester. Aged 40, three times married and a millionaire who had
gone bust, he was fanatically competitive. In addition to
clawing his way to the top of the construction industry in
California and Colorado, he had been a Canadian and world-
champion badminton player. His entrepreneurial flair was
typified by the poster he devised to promote his lodge in
California's Bear Valley: it showed his third wife schussing
naked and was captioned 'Ski Bear'. His preoccupations at
that time, he noted later, were 'sex and work and sports, booze
and cigarettes'. All that changed in 1969 when a propane gas
explosion destroyed the California lodge and maimed two
employees; the litigation that followed absorbed almost all his
assets. As an antidote to grief and anger, he bought the
12-metre ketch *Vega* in New Zealand and spent two and a half
years cruising the Pacific.

On the sea he felt as near to home as he ever had. His Scottish father and American mother had taken him to an island off British Columbia for three months of each year from the time he was three months old until he was 14. He was comfortable in boats and his longest affair was with the ocean. A favourite quotation from Hugo Grotius, the seventeenth-century Dutch statesman and jurist, encapsulated his feeling about being on the water:

> . . . the father of created things and bounded only by the heavens: the Ocean whose never failing waters feed not only upon the springs and rivers and seas, according to the ancient belief, but upon the clouds, also, and in certain measure upon the stars themselves; in fine, that Ocean which encompasses the terrestial home of mankind with the ebb and flow of its tides, and which cannot be held or enclosed, being itself the possessor rather than the possessed.

In spite of the fact that Vancouver was his home town, McTaggart had not heard of Greenpeace, originally based there, until 1972. That year he saw and answered an advertisement by the conservation organisation calling for volunteers to sail to Moruroa to protest against French nuclear testing, which had been taking place in the Pacific for seven years.

Greenpeace agreed to sponsor him and he set sail from Auckland in *Vega* in April, originally with a crew of four. He was driven primarily by anger that the French government had declared a 260,000 square kilometre area of international waters around Moruroa off-limits to all shipping. They had no basis in international law for such a proclamation; it was an arbitrary consequence of their determination to test nuclear weaponry in the atmosphere, as far from France as possible.

McTaggart and his reduced crew of three reached the exclusion zone at the beginning of June 1972. The French Navy then attempted to scare him off by employing a cruiser, minesweepers and tug boats to play 'chicken' with *Vega*, charging and crowding it on the high seas. Finally, on 1 August, the yacht was rammed and disabled by a minesweeper and the protest was at an end.

In 1973, as a consequence of publicity given to *Vega*'s first voyage, the French had to confront a plague of protest vessels off the atoll. Worse, in addition to yachts such as *Tamure*, *Spirit of Peace* and *Magic Isle* and the large ketch *Fri*, these vessels included the frigates *Otago* and *Canterbury* sent by the new Labour government in New Zealand to draw attention to atmospheric nuclear testing and help mobilise world opinion against it. 'We are a small nation, but we will not abjectly surrender to injustice,' Prime Minister Norman Kirk had said as the first frigate left Auckland.

McTaggart and Greenpeace were determined to add *Vega*'s presence to the flotilla. In fact, by the time he reached the exclusion zone in August, the other vessels had either departed or been taken into custody. This time the French Navy was ready for *Vega* and dealt with the ketch and its skipper with gloves off.

On 15 August, the minesweeper *La Dunkerquoise* launched a Zodiac inflatable with seven commandos to board *Vega*. McTaggart later recorded what followed:

These were no ordinary French sailors. Their faces were contorted with savagery and I could see that they were struggling to be the first to reach me. I saw the knives sheathed at their sides and I had a brief flicker of relief that they didn't have them in their hands. Then I saw the long black truncheons.

'This is private property,' I said. 'You can't come aboard.' And then, because I knew they intended to beat me whatever I did, I brought my arms up in a blocking motion level with the neck of the soldier who was now halfway over the railing and with all my strength I checked him hard. It was enough to stop him in his tracks and for a second we were frozen face-to-face with snarls in our throats. Then there were two others coming over the side fast and before I could make any other move, the commando in front of me had grabbed my T-shirt and jerked it over my head. I felt each of my arms being grabbed in vice-like grips so that I was pinioned.

The first truncheon came down with a weight and force unlike anything I had ever felt on the back of my head and the second came down across my shoulders and the next blow landed on the back of my neck and the next on my head again and the next on my spine and the next on my shoulder-blade and the next against my kidney and I was suddenly in the air being flipped over the railing and being yanked furiously into the inflatable, unable to catch a single breath or even find a way to make a sound. Two hands grabbed my right arm and jerked it down over my left hip and two other hands had my left arm, holding me as though I were in a straightjacket unable to try to cover myself. With scarcely a pause, the truncheons were flailing again, each blow rattling my teeth so that it seemed they would be shattered and that my spine and ribs and skull would cave in any second. Back. Neck. Head. Kidneys. I writhed and thrashed but was so expertly pinned there was absolutely nothing I could do, not even duck, and that was somehow the worst part as the truncheons continued to land at random, two truncheons smashing against me at once, three landing almost simultaneously, as though they all had gone mad and were simply trying to smash me to death, stamp me out of existence like some loathsome bug. Through the wild ringing in my head, I could hear their grunts. I could not believe I was still conscious.

Then, with one man still pinning each arm, I was yanked upright and jammed in a sitting position against the side of the inflatable. Something crashed into my right eye with such incredible force that it seemed to come right into the middle of my brain in an explosion so that I thought that half my head had been torn off. And then everything went black.

When McTaggart regained consciousness, he saw with his one functioning eye that the Frenchmen were beating his companion, Nigel Ingram. The other crew members, Ann-Marie Horne and Mary Cornie, were filming and photographing the action.

Minutes later the commandos tossed the *Vega*'s video camera overboard together with one 35 mm camera, which they thought had been taking the photographs. They were wrong. The still camera was a decoy and the one Ann-Marie Horne had used was hidden.

Later, when McTaggart had been flown to hospital in Tahiti (with permanent damage to his right eye) and *Vega* again towed into the Moruroa lagoon, Horne smuggled the remaining film past French guards by hiding it in her vagina.

While McTaggart was in hospital the French authorities – military and political – denied that he had been beaten. He had ducked away from the boarding party, they said, slipped and hurt his eye on one of *Vega*'s cleats. Another story published in the French press claimed that the Canadian skipper had taken to unarmed French sailors with a spinnaker pole (which in fact took two men to lift). The French ambassador to Canada assured Prime Minister Pierre Trudeau that the allegation that the commandos were armed was a lie.

When Nigel Ingram got back to Canada with Ann-Marie Horne's film and handed it to Greenpeace for processing, the result was sensational. Thirteen photographs were developed successfully. They showed clearly the boarding of *Vega*, the weapons carried by the commandos, the brutality of McTaggart's and Ingram's beating and the video camera being thrown overboard. Greenpeace released them to the news media and they were published worldwide. The French government spokesmen who had denied the allegations were silenced and furious.

There was more. On 1 November that same year the French government announced that it planned to halt all atmospheric testing and detonate future bombs underground at Moruroa, a decision which a French court said later may have been precipitated by McTaggart's protests and the reactions they produced. And after long-running litigation against the French authorities, the French government was ordered by the court in May 1975 to pay 2,000 francs to assess damage to *Vega*, at that stage owned by Greenpeace. The court also ruled, however, that it was not competent to deal with matters arising from the boarding of the yacht and the attack on McTaggart and Ingram. McTaggart contested this and continued to press further charges.

As a result of these actions, no individual came to be so

actively disliked by the French military as David McTaggart. When the Canadian government agreed to support his claims, an external affairs official in Ottawa called him and said, 'You can't believe it, just how mad they are at you over there . . .' From 1981, one of the maddest was Charles Hernu, French Minister of Defence. 'Every time your name was mentioned,' contacts told McTaggart, 'he couldn't come down off the ceiling.'

In 1985, when the *Rainbow Warrior* made its Pacific Peace Voyage, McTaggart was chairman of Greenpeace International, having spent much of the previous ten years building it into a worldwide organisation. And Charles Hernu was still in power, the longest serving Minister of Defence in the Fifth Republic and the only member of François Mitterrand's cabinet to hold his position continuously for four years. He was also the minister responsible for authorising the DGSE's operation against Greenpeace and the bombing of the *Rainbow Warrior*.

In retrospect, it is not possible to construct an explanation for all the extraordinary number of car trips which French agents made around rural roads in northern New Zealand in June and July 1985. In particular, it is difficult to account for the 1,600 kilometres which the *Ouvéa* crew ran up from their Whangarei base over 11 days. According to the Tricot report, their mission was to survey the northern coastline, to continue their 'observation of the seaboard, the harbour and of ships at anchor' which they had begun at sea. And the purpose of that exercise, allegedly, was to become familiar with the area and to become known in it, so that they would have sufficient expertise and credibility to join a future Greenpeace protest flotilla. These explanations can be dismissed: they were part of the smokescreen put up by the DGSE before the French admitted responsibility for the *Rainbow Warrior* bombing; they were implausible explanations for the agents' determination to be so noticeable.

Some trips *have* been accounted for, however. At least five led to meetings with other agents, Dormand and the Turenges. Another would have permitted the collection of the grey Zodiac and blue Yamaha outboard motor concealed before the *Ouvéa* reached Opua. Still another resulted in the transferral to Dormand or the Turenges at Kaiwaka of the dinghy and motor, along with fuel tanks and the additional outboard motor bought in Whangarei.

Once this last transaction was completed, it was possible for other agents to use the Zodiac to retrieve the explosives, which had apparently been hidden in a more remote location than the dinghy and the engine (the chance of the *Ouvéa* crew being found with explosives presented a greater threat to the operation than their possession of an outboard motor and rubber dinghy). The equipment had been handed over mid-afternoon on 8 July. Evidence suggests that the Turenges then headed north to recover the explosives in the early hours of 9 July, the morning the *Ouvéa* sailed out of Whangarei Harbour. This timing was crucial. It made it less likely that those responsible for bringing the explosives into New Zealand – the *Ouvéa* crew – would be associated with them should those explosives be discovered in the course of transportation. Their recovery only one day before the bombing also decreased the likelihood that *any* French agent would be found with incriminating evidence.

This hypothesis, and the likelihood that the *Ouvéa* crew had hidden the explosives in the vicinity of Rangaunu Harbour or Doubtless Bay on 24 June, are given weight by the appearance of the Turenges – complete with Zodiac – at a dairy on the outskirts of Kaitaia early on the morning of 9 July.

Sophie and Alain Turenge could not have been more of a contrast with the *Ouvéa* crew. They displayed no warmth or friendliness, either between themselves or towards others. They spoke to other people only when they had to, to make arrangements for travel, accommodation or withdrawing money, or to ask directions. While Alain was polite, he was never extroverted in his behaviour in New Zealand; Sophie was remembered as someone perpetually solemn and preoccupied, her most frequent expression a frown. Several people who dealt with her found her eyes – magnified by large round glasses – inexpressibly sad. Both Turenges acted one step short of furtiveness, as if they did not want to be remembered; but they *were* remembered for their very solemnity and abruptness, unusual in tourists.

Two New Zealanders who were to remember them for these traits were Trevor and Erna Rogers, who own a dairy and general store just north of Kaitaia on the road to Parengarenga and Cape Reinga. Most New Zealand shops do not begin trading until between 8.30 and 9 a.m. Coffee shops and restaurants start even later in the day. Exceptionally, however, some dairies open before 7, to catch the early-morning business provided by people on their way to work or families who have forgotten to stock up on breakfast foods.

Trevor Rogers unlocked his doors at 6.30 a.m. on 9 July. He was outside checking his coolstore when he saw a Newmans camper van pull over on the gravel in front of the shop. Surprisingly, it had a gleaming Zodiac dinghy with a blue outboard hitched to the back at an angle. Surprisingly, because it was still dark and cold, an odd time of day and year for anyone other than a professional fisherman to be heading towards the sea or coming back from it. Rogers was also puzzled by the angle of the Zodiac. The boat and engine did not look secure. If the owners were travelling any distance, he would have expected them to carry the dinghy deflated and inside the van. Its disposition suggested they had not come far.*

The Rogers subsequently identified the couple who got out

---

*Certainly not as far as Parengarenga. It would have been unsafe to carry the Zodiac in that manner for more than 100 kilometres; and the camper van's mileage made it impossible for them to have travelled an additional 200 kilometres. All this adds to the likelihood that the explosives had been hidden within easy distance of Kaitaia at Doubtless Bay or Rangaunu Harbour, both of which had suitably private locations accessible by road and water. While the Rogers were uncertain as to whether this sighting occurred on 8 or 9 July, it had to be the ninth, because the Turenges could not have collected the Zodiac – from Velche or Dormand – until the previous afternoon.

of the van as Alain and Sophie Turenge. They were dressed in heavy clothes and looked tired and dishevelled, as if they had been up all night. Alain was unshaven. Inside, Sophie asked in a heavily accented voice if there was a coffee shop open nearby. The Rogers suppressed a laugh and said no. The visitors had obviously learnt little about New Zealand trading hours. And so Sophie peered at the shelves and into the freezer and bought yoghurt and instant coffee.

'Are you having a holiday?' Erna Rogers asked politely.

'No,' said the woman shortly. Then, as if that seemed too abrupt, she added: 'Just travelling around.'

The couple themselves exchanged few words. They seemed as unfriendly and uncommunicative with each other as they were with the Rogers. They gave an impression of being fatigued and stressed; having made their purchases they climbed back into the van and headed into Kaitaia. By lunchtime they were again at Parakai and had once more checked into the motel unit owned by the New Zealand Prime Minister.

The Turenges may have taken the explosives with them to Parakai (in which case they could have carried them into David Lange's motel unit); or they may have made a rendezvous with Jean Louis Dormand and handed them over to him, Tonel and Camurier. More probably, they concealed them en route. The most likely spot is a valley on a back road between Puhoi and Parakai, which the Turenges had photographed half a dozen times on or after 7 July, after they had left Paihia (the preceding pictures on the film are of the Beachcomber Motel). Subsequently they had no explanation for the existence of these photographs: they were not tourist-type shots of New Zealand scenery, just views of a very ordinary-looking piece of New Zealand farmland – a valley with pasture, fences, some trees and hayshed. The pictures could have been taken as a guide for somebody else, in case the Turenges themselves were unable to recover the explosives or in case changed circumstances prevented them from doing so for some time. It is difficult to think of any other explanation.

Wednesday 10 July was the day the *Rainbow Warrior* was bombed. It is also one of the days on which it is difficult to reconstruct the locations and movements of the DGSE agents known to be in New Zealand to sink the vessel. The *Ouvéa* was somewhere off the New Zealand coast. Alain and Sophie Turenge left Parakai early in the morning and headed for Auckland – they were sighted on several occasions on the waterfront and in the vicinity of the Auckland wharves in the early afternoon. (Later, they claimed, they lunched in the Auckland Domain and shopped in Parnell.) François Verlet began and ended the day in Auckland. And the precise whereabouts of Jean Louis Dormand, Alain Tonel and Jacques Camurier are unknown until early evening.

Short of a participant confessing (improbable) or a further leak from the DGSE (possible, but decreasingly so with the passage of time and the service's determination to recover from the débâcle), it may never be possible to establish with precision who did what on that day, nor to prove judicially who actually placed the explosives on the *Rainbow Warrior*. But the known facts favour one hypothesis above all others; and it is one that has not been publicly suggested previously.

The involvement of Christine Cabon, the Turenges and the *Ouvéa* crew in the conspiracy to sink the Greenpeace vessel was established by hard and connecting evidence within a relatively short time after the bombing: sightings of significant meetings, records of telephone calls, the recovery of incriminating documents, observed behaviour consistent with involvement. What could *not* be established, however, was that any of these agents carried out the bombing itself.

It was not Cabon; she left New Zealand six weeks before. It was not the Turenges. In spite of Alain Mafart's extensive experience as a combat frogman, it is widely accepted (by the New Zealand police among others) that his and Prieur's role was, as they eventually admitted, logistical and supportive; that is why murder charges against them were subsequently reduced to those of manslaughter. Nor is there any evidence that a member of the *Ouvéa* crew attached explosives to the *Rainbow*

Warrior, in spite of *their* expertise as combat divers. Early police speculation that the bomber may have been Berthelo – based on two compelling pieces of evidence – turned out to be misplaced and was quietly abandoned. There is no evidence that the *Ouvéa* was close enough to Auckland to provide frogmen for the sabotage, nor was there any need for it to be, given the proximity of another group of divers, the so-called 'third team'. And the footprint left in the Zodiac abandoned by the bomber did not match shoes known to have been bought or worn by the *Ouvéa* crew, nor the foot size of Berthelo.

The next pertinent consideration is whether there *was* a third team responsible for placing the bombs, as the newspaper *Le Monde* claimed late in 1985, quoting DGSE sources; and whether the then-director of the DGSE, Admiral Pierre Lacoste, resigned rather than reveal details about the composition of that third team as (again) *Le Monde* claimed. If he were to answer questions about the bombing put to him by Defence Minister Charles Hernu, Lacoste said in September, 'I would endanger the lives of certain officers and warrant officers who have carried out particularly dangerous missions . . .' Of whom was he speaking? Not of Cabon, Mafart, Prieur, Verge, Barcelo and Andries, all of whose identities had already been revealed in the Tricot report and in the press. He could only have been speaking of the men known to the New Zealand police as Jean Louis Dormand (but already identified as Lieutenant Colonel Louis-Pierre Dillais), Alain Tonel, Jacques Camurier and François Verlet.

Dormand's involvement in the planning and direction of the bombing operation has already been established; François Verlet's is also apparent, and becomes more so as the operation nears its culmination. What of Tonel and Camurier? Why were they in the country?

An initial answer is to be found in the wide pattern of dates and events that links them to the operation as a whole. Once the *Rainbow Warrior*'s detailed itinerary was known, it was apparent that the vessel would remain in Auckland from 7 July to 21 July. Given that the DGSE had decided previously to incapacitate it in a New Zealand port rather than at sea, the boat had to be sunk within that fortnight, 7–21 July.

How do the French agents' known movements relate to this itinerary? Interestingly, the *Ouvéa* was on hire until 28 July. Which means it could have remained in New Zealand for the crew to perform their logistic role right up until the last day possible for the sinking (21 July) and still return to Noumea on schedule.

The Turenges were originally booked to leave New Zealand on 22 July, as was Jean Louis Dormand. Tonel and Camurier were due to depart on 24 July. Had circumstances made it difficult or impossible to bomb the *Rainbow Warrior* on 10 July, therefore, all the agents involved could still have been in New Zealand and available to carry out their roles in the operation up to 21 July, the day of the vessel's departure. Such a pattern may not constitute evidence in a judicial sense; but it is utterly consistent with involvement on the part of all the parties named.

The location of Tonel and Camurier within this pattern; their high degree of physical fitness apparent to those who skiied with them in the South Island; their established close association in New Zealand with Dormand, former director of the Aspretto Combat Diving School; the refusal of the French authorities to release any information about them after the bombing – all these factors point to their presence as either a team of back-up frogmen, or as the saboteurs themselves. Given the exclusion of the Turenges and the *Ouvéa* crew from the latter role, the weight of suspicion has to fall on them.

Such suspicion is increased by the fact that Tonel and Camurier took great pains not to be seen in Auckland after they disembarked on 7 July. It makes sense that the *actual* bombers should not be seen to be associated with the scene of the crime; just as it makes sense to suggest that the Turenges, Dormand, Velche, Berthelo and Maniguet – all of whom *were* seen in Auckland – can by that very fact be disqualified from the roles of actual saboteurs. The whole emphasis in training for such operations is to make it as difficult as possible for

subsequent investigators to establish the links of evidence that
might lead to apprehension of those directly responsible and
to their conviction in a court of law.

If Tonel and Camurier took immense care not to be seen
in Auckland on the day of the bombing – in contrast to their
subsequent behaviour as tourists in the South Island (where
they were as visible as the *Ouvéa* crew had been in Whangarei),
where were they on 10 July and how did they get to the scene
of the bombing?

There are at least two possibilities. One is that they remained
concealed in Dormand's camper van – in effect his mobile command post – somewhere in the Auckland environs. Another
is that they were hidden well away from Auckland until the
time of the bombing.

An otherwise obtrusively peculiar set of facts points to the
latter alternative. On the one day he travelled outside of
Auckland, the day of the bombing, François Verlet drove a
rental car to Thames, an old goldmining town at the base of
the Coromandel Peninsula. He *did* go to Thames: he claimed
he did and answers to questions from the New Zealand detective who interviewed him convinced police that he did. Why
did he admit the visit? Because he believed he had been seen
and would be remembered there by a witness. He did what
agents are trained to do in such circumstances. The standard
practice in interrogation is to admit what has already been
established – or can be established from other sources – but
to place an entirely different interpretation on the evidence from
that of the interrogators. In other words, the best lie to tell
is that which is closest to the truth. Verlet's explanation for
visiting Thames was that he had simply planned a drive 'in
the country'. He said he had intended to go as far as Hamilton
but got sidetracked on other roads and finished up in the goldmining town. He returned to Auckland at about seven o'clock
that night.

The next part of a curious juxtaposition is that Sophie
Turenge claimed she and her husband drove to Thames that
same night, after the bombing, before going on to Hamilton

the next morning. She said they slept in their camper van next to the airstrip known euphemistically as Thames Airport.

Why should three French agents visit Thames – not favoured as a tourist destination – on one day, within 12 hours of their being involved in the blowing up of a ship in Auckland Harbour? Short of a coincidence too extraordinary to be believed, there can only be one explanation: Dormand, Tonel and Camurier had driven there in their hired camper van to lie low on 9 July. The district abounds with little-used side roads, concealed rest areas and bush cover close to the roads. They were quite possibly in a hidden location selected and notified by Christine Cabon, who had reconnoitred the area on the weekend of 11 and 12 May.

Verlet's journey to Thames on 10 July, therefore, was for the purpose of liaising with Dormand, Tonel and Camurier, possibly even to bring one or other of them back to Auckland in his own rental car. The Turenges' journey back there on the night of the same day, with the third person seen to board their camper van, could have been to deliver the saboteur to a rendezvous with Dormand, allowing the senior officer to then drive south with Tonel and Camurier. By the afternoon of 11 July, all three Frenchmen were safely on board the inter-island ferry crossing Cook Strait, safely distanced from the scene of the crime and from any subsequent enquiry. Why should they have moved south when they did – as rapidly as they did – if they were not participants in the bombing? They were to remain safely distant; an initial lack of direct evidence linking them with the bombing – a situation they had engineered – meant that the attention of investigators would be focused for a long time on those who had been identified near the scene, or on those who had left a trail of clues so unsubtle that they came to police attention within days.

Linking this hypothesis to verifiable facts, the bombing of the *Rainbow Warrior* is likely to have been carried out in the following manner.

Early on the evening of 10 July, at about 7 p.m., two men

whose descriptions match those of Tonel and Camurier were noticed carrying an inflated Zodiac into the water down a private right of way at Stanley Point on Auckland's north shore. One man, seen only from behind (Tonel) had dark hair. The other, wearing a wetsuit, was fair and balding: this was Jacques Camurier.

The witnesses, the mayor of Devonport and his wife, did not see a motor, nor any sign of other equipment. But these could have been carried down the same path after they had turned back to their meal, from which they had been momentarily distracted; or picked up elsewhere. The delivery vehicle was Dormand's camper van, which could not be seen because of the distance of the right of way from the road.

Within half an hour of this sighting, François Verlet had driven down to Marsden Wharf after having a meal in the city. He claimed to the New Zealand police that it was sheer coincidence that he parked near the *Rainbow Warrior*'s berth. But his conversation with Greenpeace members Rien Achterberg and Chris Robinson indicates otherwise: he told them he knew about the Pacific Peace Voyage and had come to wish them luck.

Verlet was, in fact, carrying out further reconnaissance. He was on board the vessel about an hour before the explosives were attached to it. The Turenges' lawyer was to claim in court that his clients knew that a party was expected to be in progress when the bombs went off: 'It [was] confidently expected that both because of the celebrations and the hour, no one would be in the engine-room . . .' It was one of the reasons the Turenges believed that nobody would be killed. They believed this, and expected it, because Verlet had delivered information to them about the meeting of skippers in the ship's hold and the birthday party that was expected to resume at around 11 p.m.

The penultimate phase of Operation Rainbow Warrior, the bombing, began near Teal Park, a grassed area alongside Auckland's container terminal. Just around the corner from

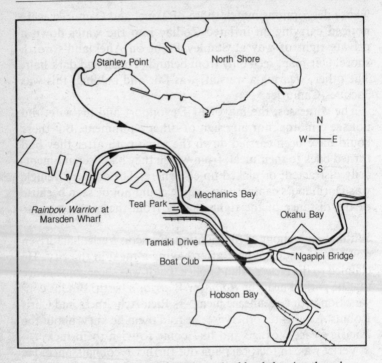

Waitemata Harbour and downtown Auckland showing the solo bomber's route in the Zodiac on the evening of 10 July 1985

the park itself, concealed by a large aircraft hangar, is a slipway belonging to Sea Bee Air, a company that offers amphibious scenic flights over Auckland. It is an ideal place to retrieve a Zodiac. Vehicles can be driven onto the slipway itself; there is dim but adequate lighting from the adjacent container terminal; and the immediate area is generally deserted at night.

Around 7.50 p.m. on 10 July, Verlet, the Turenges and Camurier in the Zodiac met at the Sea Bee Air slipway. The Turenges had been prowling around the area since 7.30, when they had been spotted driving the camper van nervously in and out of Teal Park. Verlet had driven from Marsden Wharf in his rental car. And Camurier had made his way across the harbour from Stanley Point (the amount of petrol left in the abandoned Yamaha motor suggests he had carried fuel tanks with him).

At this meeting, held under the subdued lighting of the container wharf and away from public gaze, the agents changed plans that had been carefully laid and approved by Dormand some days before. Instead of attaching the explosives to the hull of the *Rainbow Warrior* later in the evening, and setting them to explode several hours afterwards, the agents would take immediate advantage of the skippers' meeting, which made it likely that most people on board would be preoccupied with things happening below decks. Camurier would lay the bombs at once and set them to explode once the meeting was over and everybody was back in the mess, a relatively easy place from which to leave the boat after the first explosion occurred. In the agents' estimation, this would minimise the chance of loss of life.

This decision made, Verlet climbed into his rental car and drove to Auckland Airport to catch his flight to Tahiti. The Turenges began to prowl around nervously, filling in time before Camurier's return. The frogman himself set off in the dinghy through the dark and mist for Marsden Wharf, carrying two packets of explosives encased in plastic, a clamp, a rope, and his scuba gear – mask, flippers, and two rebreather oxygen tanks, which would not release bubbles under water.

There was a certain irony in the choice of a Zodiac for the mission. Greenpeace strategists had become aware of the range of tactical opportunities offered by inflatables – because of their speed under power, their manoeuvrability and ease of storage – since the French commandos had chased and boarded *Vega* (and beaten David McTaggart) from a Zodiac in 1973. Subsequently Greenpeace's own activists, the so-called 'commandos of conservation', had used the rubber dinghies to block the dumping of nuclear and chemical waste and to obstruct the hunting operations of whalers and sealers. Now Greenpeace's favourite weapon for non-violent protest was to be turned against it again by a violent French initiative.

Sometime between 8 and 8.30 p.m., Camurier motored and paddled two kilometres from Mechanics Bay to a point near Marsden Wharf, tethering his dinghy to a sheltered pile close to the *Rainbow Warrior*'s berth. He strapped two white oxygen cylinders to his back, a mask to his face, the breathing apparatus to his mouth and flippers to his feet. Then he slipped over the side into the icy winter water, protected by his wetsuit. Reaching back into the Zodiac, he located the packages of explosives, the clamp, and the rope to calculate their placement.

In spite of extensive searching and research after the sinking of the vessel, nothing is known about the shape or size of the bombs used. They destroyed themselves – and hence the evidence – when they detonated. Experts estimate that each package probably held five to ten kilograms of high explosives.

Camurier then swam underwater to the Greenpeace boat, his rebreather tanks ensuring that no bubbles escaped to the surface. This precaution was probably unnecessary. The Peace Flotilla meeting was still the focus of attention deep inside the hull and it was too cold for anybody to be on deck looking casually over the side of the vessel.

The first bomb was simply tied to the propeller shaft. Then, attaching the F-clamp to the protruding bilge keel below the waterline, the frogman used his knotted rope to measure the location of the engine-room wall. When he found the spot, he attached the second bomb, probably to the protruding ridge. He adjusted the timing devices on each package, setting the bomb on the hull to explode minutes before the deeper one attached to the propulsion system. Returning to the Zodiac, he started the motor and headed back to Mechanics Bay.

At about 8.30 p.m., the Auckland couple who had seen the Newmans camper van drive in and out of Teal Park an hour earlier encountered it again. When they returned from their walk on Tamaki Drive the vehicle was stopped behind their car. Curtains in the back of the van were drawn; they could not see who was inside, but there were sounds of movements and the van was rocking slightly, as if several people were shifting things around. When the couple drove off at about 8.45 the van was still there, waiting.

Over the next hour a series of accidents occurred that was to expose Operation Rainbow Warrior and sabotage its final phase, the recovery operation.

When Camurier got back to the container wharf he found that the tide was too low to get the Zodiac and motor out of the water at the pre-arranged pick-up point (dead low water had been at 7.34 p.m.). This unforeseen circumstance was a consequence of placing the bombs several hours earlier than originally planned. So he veered away from the wharf and headed for Okahu Bay, hoping to find an easier landing place along the waterfront.

The Turenges, confused and angry, lost sight of him as he moved out of the area illuminated by the container wharf lights. They got back into the van and tried to track the sound of the outboard along Tamaki Drive.

What followed was a string of sightings and 'hearings' of the rogue craft and its disoriented boatsman.

A man fishing from a bridge on Tamaki Drive about a kilometre east of Teal Park heard an outboard motor coming towards him in the dark at around 8.50 p.m. When the craft came into view, he saw it was an inflatable driven by a man in dark clothing and a woollen hat that appeared to be red. As soon as the helmsman saw the fisherman, he did a U-turn and headed back towards Mechanics Bay. Then the motor stopped. After a pause it restarted, and the movement of the sound suggested it was now heading in the opposite direction, towards Okahu Bay.

Two kilometres away, another fisherman saw the Zodiac and its sole occupant in a wetsuit and bare feet motor under Ngapipi Bridge and into Hobson Bay. A third man, a cyclist on the city end of the bridge, heard a splash underneath him and then saw the Zodiac emerge on the Hobson Bay side. Still another witness watched the inflatable being propelled hand over hand along the breakwater rocks by a man with a weatherproof jacket over his wetsuit. He appeared to be pulling the dinghy around a corner and in the direction of the Auckland Outboard Boating Club headquarters.

By this time Camurier had jettisoned the Yamaha outboard (causing the splash that the cyclist had heard) and the oxygen tanks. There was to be considerable argument among investigators as to whether this was deliberate or accidental. On balance, the action was probably deliberate. Camurier was aware that he had been seen, and that the longer it took him to get ashore, the greater the chance that he would be seen again. In the circumstances, the less visible evidence linking him to his actual mission the better.

The Yamaha lay concealed underwater beneath the bridge. Had it not been for the coincidence of the cyclist passing at that very moment, there would have been no reason for the police to look there and recover it as rapidly as they did. It was this recovery that was to lead them back to Barnet Marine in London and Eric Andries' purchases there on 29 May (the outboard motor had a serial number, whereas the Zodiac bought at the same time was unmarked).

The disposal of the oxygen bottles is more difficult to account for. One was recovered from the Hobson Bay shoreline six days later, suggesting it had been thrown away at the same time as the Yamaha; the other, as a result of tidal action, was picked up at Pollen Island near the head of the harbour on 28 July. Both had markings describing their French manufacture. They represented such an obvious link with the French military that for some time police were inclined to reject that theory, or to suspect that they had been planted to ensure that the operation would be traced back to the French and thus be exposed and publicly branded a failure.

One bottle was completely empty of oxygen, the other almost so. The mission itself would not have used up anything like this quantity, so the oxygen must have been expelled deliberately; possibly in the belief that this would cause the bottles to fill with water and sink and thus never be found. It was an erroneous assumption, but an understandable one made on the part of a man who could have been close to panic. Had the Zodiac been removed from the water at the scheduled time and place, of course, none of the gear would have had to be jettisoned.

By the time Camurier was hauling the dinghy around the rocks in Hobson Bay, he had only three nylon bags with him, one small and the others large. At least one of these would have concealed his diving gear, which he had no plans to discard.

The next sighting was made from the Auckland Outboard Boating Club headquarters overlooking Hobson Bay on the inner side of Tamaki Drive. Burglaries from members' boats moored on both sides of the Tamaki Drive causeway and from the clubhouse itself had led to the formation of a club vigilante group. Members were now rostered to guard the headquarters and to patrol the surrounding area at night. The scheme was an elaboration of the 'neighbourhood watch' programme which had evolved in the Auckland suburbs over the previous year, with police encouragement. The vigilantes would not arrest anybody, but if they spotted anything suspicious they were to ring the police, who would send a patrol car to investigate.

At about 9.30 p.m., one of the two patrol members stationed in the clubhouse heard a splash somewhere in front of him. He turned his binoculars towards Tamaki Drive and saw a Zodiac being hauled out of the water and then carried by two men up some steps towards the roadway. They placed the dinghy upside down next to a tree, then began to pile gear alongside it. Next, one of the men left the scene and began to run along Tamaki Drive in the direction of Teal Park. Some minutes later he was back, in the back of a camper van. Both men began to load bags into the van.

The watching boat club members were convinced that they

were witnessing the aftermath of a burglary. While one rang for the police, the other got into his own car and drove to where the unidentified men had just completed loading the van. As he wrote down the registration number, the van did a U-turn and headed off along Tamaki Drive, away from the city. The Zodiac, which had been chained to a small pohutukawa tree on the roadside, was abandoned.

A police patrol did arrive to investigate, but not for another 18 minutes – by which time the camper van had long gone. But the police were given the registration number, LB8945. And they had the Zodiac which, mysteriously, had been stripped of its metal plate and serial number, and of its wooden transom, which should also have been numbered.

Alain Turenge had followed the movement of the Zodiac with difficulty. Eventually, somewhere past the first concrete bridge on Tamaki Drive, he abandoned the camper van and ran along the roadside, trying to hail his fellow agent. He eventually caught up with Camurier after the frogman had turned under the Ngapipi Bridge and begun to manoeuvre his dinghy towards the boathouse. As soon as he reached some steps, Turenge ran down them and called to Camurier to hurry.

Both men carried the Zodiac up to the road and Camurier reported that he had been seen. One of the agents also noticed the flash of binoculars from the clubhouse. Realising that they appeared to be acting suspiciously and that the police might be called they decided to remove themselves as quickly as possible. Turenge sprinted along Tamaki Drive for the van and drove back at speed. After they had loaded Camurier's gear and the frogman had climbed into the front, Sophie Turenge accelerated away just as the boat club member stopped opposite to record the van's registration. They left the dinghy because Dormand was supposed to collect it.*

---

*Dormand never did collect the Zodiac, however. He may have been warned shortly afterwards that it was now under observation, and he knew that without markings and stripped of gear there was nothing to link it to a French government sabotage operation. It was probably safe to leave it there.

And so the Turenges fled Hobson Bay with the recovery part of Operation Rainbow Warrior a shambles in their wake. The evidence left behind would be sufficient to ensure their arrest, their conviction on charges of manslaughter and arson, the eventual establishment of a link between the bombing of the *Rainbow Warrior* and the highest echelons of the French government, and the near-collapse of that government, which would continue to deny responsibility for the operation until the evidence indicting it was overwhelming. A short hour of mishaps bungled an operation that had taken half a year to plan and three months to carry out. Without those mishaps, it could well have succeeded: all the agents involved might have escaped from New Zealand and the evidence linking the bombing to the DGSE would have remained circumstantial.

The movements of the agents after ten o'clock on the night of 10 July are shadowy. At some point, possibly back at Thames but more likely close to Auckland, Camurier would have been delivered to Dormand and Tonel. They then headed south in their chief's camper van and boarded the Cook Strait ferry *Arahura* at Wellington at 4 p.m. the following day, to cross to the South Island.

While the trip to Wellington must have been rushed, the agents showed no sign of panic or tension once they reached the South Island. It was as if the geographical distance between the two islands had become a psychological one, insulating them from anxiety and responsibility. From 12 July, the three agents travelled leisurely. Were they waiting to see what would happen to the Turenges? Did they remain in the country in case orders were given for Mafart and Prieur to be sprung from custody? Or were they simply so confident that they had covered their tracks – and that the police would become wholly preoccupied with the Turenges and with the *Ouvéa*'s false trails – that they felt they could see out their allotted time in New Zealand as tourists?

Whatever the reason, they drove first to Methven, a Canterbury town at the foot of the Southern Alps, and stayed there for the next three days – although not quite together. Dormand slept at the A. & P. camping ground, Tonel and Camurier at the local youth hostel. For two of those days they all skied at the nearby Mount Hutt resort.

On 15 July the agents separated. Dormand headed south to Queenstown, where he stayed at the Travelodge for the next six days and nights. He joined many tourist excursions from this base, including rafting on the Shotover River (where, to his visible annoyance, he was photographed – a picture later circulated by the police).

Tonel and Camurier stayed at Methven until 18 July, when they transferred to the Mount Cook National Park and stayed in the youth hostel there. Then followed a curious pattern of recreation. During the day the agents chose expensive activities, such as heli-skiing (where parties hire helicopters to fly them to the upper slopes of the mountain away from established ski fields, allowing them to ski down virgin slopes). In the evenings they ate at expensive restaurants, such as the one in the Hermitage Hotel. At nights, however, they continued to sleep in the youth hostel, usually shelter for travellers with little money to spend. They kept their fronts as Tahitian physical education instructors, although on occasions they swapped Christian names on introductions. Unlike Dormand, they did not seem to mind being photographed by fellow tourists. They must have felt entirely safe. And they had as much success forming relationships with the opposite sex (fellow youth hostellers) as their compatriots had had in Whangarei.

While the third team headed south to enjoy a pleasant after-math to what had been (for them) a successful operation, Alain and Sophie Turenge seem to have spent what remained of the night of 10 July at Thames. The following morning they drove to Hamilton. Their previous plan had been to continue on to Wellington, where they were scheduled to return the camper van. But several factors made them change their mind. They had heard on the radio that a man had been killed when the *Rainbow Warrior* was sunk. And they knew they had been observed in suspicious circumstances the night before.

At Te Rapa in Hamilton, therefore, they rang a DGSE number in Paris and obtained permission to change their plans. They went to the Air New Zealand office in the provincial city and altered their bookings to allow them to leave New Zealand from Auckland the following morning. Then they returned to Auckland to spend a nervous night in the Gold Star Auckland Airport Motel in Mangere, where they tried to dispose of evidence that would later be of considerable interest to the New Zealand police (muddy clothing and some liferaft stickers).* The following morning they would return the van to Newmans, because they were certain that the police would be watching all New Zealand airports for a foreign couple in a Newmans camper van. Then they would take a taxi to the airport and – if everything went according to this revised plan – they would leave the country where they were now major suspects in a terrorist bombing enquiry.

One of the unsolved mysteries arising from the events of the night of 10 July is the precise whereabouts of the *Ouvéa*. According to the yacht's return log, it was 120 kilometres north-east of North Cape at the time of the bombing. But the log's description of weather and wind conditions for that night are inconsistent with those recorded by the New Zealand Weather Office. This discrepancy (and others in the log) led police to conclude that the *Ouvéa* was *not* where it claimed to be that night; and then to ask, if not, why not? Where was the boat, and what was its role in the whole operation?

Contrary to the claim of the subsequent Tricot report, the crew had clearly not come to New Zealand 'to train in navigation . . . to inform the [DGSE] on the gathering of the Greenpeace flotilla', or 'to study the possibility of joining a

---

*The origin and significance of the Plastimo liferaft stickers remains a mystery. They suggest either that a second, smaller craft may have been used on the night of the bombing, possibly by Alain Tonel; or that Camurier may have used it as a pontoon to help transport the heavy packages of explosives from the Zodiac to a position closer to the *Rainbow Warrior*.

boat for the future campaigns'. The only one of these instructions they might have carried out was that of training in navigation. There is no evidence that they made any attempt to gather information on the Greenpeace flotilla, let alone to take steps that would allow them to join up with such a fleet. When they were in a position to act in accordance with these alleged instructions (alongside *Kliss II*, for example, or among Greenpeace supporters such as Reva Meredith), they made no attempt to do so. They did not cultivate Greenpeace associations nor talk with people about the organisation. The instructions quoted by Tricot were obviously devised to 'sanitise' the whole operation once it came under public scrutiny.

In fact, the movements and behaviour of the crew, and the nature of forensic samples taken from the hold of the *Ouvéa* by the New Zealand police in Norfolk Island, make it clear that the yacht's primary role was that of bringing to New Zealand the explosives that would sink the *Rainbow Warrior*. In addition, they brought the Zodiac dinghy used in the operation, outboard motors (one of which was recovered) and fuel and diving gear. All this meant that the agents deputed to carry out the actual sabotage, Tonel and Camurier, could enter the country unencumbered and hence be less likely to attract suspicion.

Secondly, the *Ouvéa*'s role was a diversionary one. The crew, with their almost recklessly high-profile activities in Whangarei (including consorting with Carol Nash, a policeman's wife), ensured that *they* would attract suspicion and be investigated after the bombing. They were, in effect, laying a false trail that would make it easier for the actual saboteurs to leave the country before they became objects of suspicion. Indeed, so successful was this tactic that Dormand, Tonel and Camurier were able to remain in New Zealand for a further fortnight after the bombing – to have their holiday in the South Island – without running the risk of being associated with Operation Rainbow Warrior. And all this while the police had the Turenges in custody and were already interrogating the *Ouvéa* crew in Norfolk Island.

The only thing that took the crew of the *Ouvéa* by surprise was the fact that they came under investigation as early as they did, which almost prevented their safe return to and subsequent escape from New Caledonia. Further, the alacrity with which the police reached Norfolk Island meant that dozens of documents revealing their involvement in the operation and linking their activities to those of the Turenges and Dormand fell into the hands of New Zealand investigators. That cannot have been sought nor anticipated.

Thirdly, it is inconceivable that the *Ouvéa* was not also in New Zealand in a back-up role. The crew was highly trained in combat diving; Maniguet was experienced in diving medicine. These attributes cannot have been irrelevant to their selection for this particular operation. It may have been the original intention to keep the *Ouvéa* crew in New Zealand on standby: in case Tonel and Camurier did not arrive for some reason or were apprehended, or in case something went wrong in the course of the operation. Maniguet could attend to any injuries and Velche, Berthelo or Audrenc could replace Tonel and Camurier in the role of saboteurs. The *Ouvéa* might also have figured in Dormand's plans for getting other agents out of the country, particularly if things became difficult and airports were placed under surveillance.

In the event, such plans seem to have been abandoned. Once Dormand was in the country and had looked over the field of operation, he may have concluded that he, Camurier, Tonel, Verlet and the Turenges could carry out the actual sinking of the *Rainbow Warrior* without need for further assistance from the *Ouvéa* crew. The *joie de vivre* that crew members displayed in Whangarei on the night of 8 July could have related as much to confirmation that they would *not* after all have to carry out a role on the night of the bombing – with all the risks attendant upon such involvement – as to anticipation of their imminent departure.

Xavier Maniguet's precise role is more difficult to define. He *was* involved in the whole operation. His associations and his behaviour in New Zealand make that clear, even though his time away from Auckland and especially his skiing in the South Island gave him an alibi, a plausible excuse for saying he was a lone tourist. Was he simply there to give the crew one fluent English speaker and thus ensure that they negotiated the hazards of officialdom and made necessary arrangements and purchases? Was he in fact a more senior officer in the operation (bearing in mind his status as a naval reservist) than Velche? Certainly many people who had experience of the crew – especially Carol Nash, who observed them more closely than anybody else – deduced that Maniguet was the 'boss'; his demeanour and that of the crew in relation to him seemed to support such a belief.

Then there is his expertise in treating diving accidents. For this to have played a relevant part in the *Ouvéa*'s back-up role, Maniguet would have had to have been within travelling distance of Auckland on the night of the bombing. The likelihood that he might have been is increased when one considers that Camurier used rebreather equipment, which is more dangerous and more prone to accident than conventional scuba gear.

Is it possible, as some police investigators believed, that the *Ouvéa* was hove to off the New Zealand coast on the night of 10 July, in some location that would have enabled Maniguet or back-up frogmen to have returned to Auckland by road in the event of an emergency? It *is* possible, and Maniguet's discussion about Leigh (50 kilometres north of Auckland) with the Whangarei Aero Club pilot on 30 June added weight to this suspicion.* If the yacht received the all-clear on the evening of 10 July, it would still have reached Norfolk Island on 13 July, its actual day of arrival.

It is not known how much fuel the *Ouvéa* used in the Whangarei to Norfolk leg of its voyage, because it is not known how much was in its tank when it left New Zealand. But before

---

*If the crew knew about Leigh, and favoured anchoring off or near it, it could only be because they sailed that far south from Tutukaka on 26 June, then doubled back to Whangarei Harbour (they had time to do this); or because Christine Cabon had provided them with highly specific information about that part of the coast.

departing from Whangarei, the crew bought 200 litres of diesel in plastic containers (the tank itself held 145 litres); and then obtained a further 240 litres in Norfolk. All of which suggests that the yacht was simultaneously motoring and sailing to increase its speed. It did not need to do this if it had made the Whangarei–Norfolk run, as the crew claimed, in 46 hours.

This in turn suggests that the *Ouvéa* was not as far from the New Zealand coast on the night of 10 July as its crew members alleged. They may not have taken part in the bombing of the *Rainbow Warrior*, but they may well have been within recall range if something had gone seriously wrong.

Another interesting source of speculation is whether or not loss of life as a result of the *Rainbow Warrior* bombing was planned or accidental. A subsequent leak to the French press revealed that the DGSE had vetoed a plan to blow up the vessel at sea, because of the likelihood that the crew would be lost with the boat. The Turenges themselves were to claim privately that the timing of the bombing was altered so as to reduce the possibility of people being injured. Further, when they were in the custody of the New Zealand police and (unknown to them) under surveillance by a French-speaking constable, Sophie Turenge commented to Alain: 'It's a pity somebody had to die, even a child.' He replied, 'That's the way it has to be.'

It is true that the agents apparently consciously refrained from blowing up the *Rainbow Warrior* when the peace flotilla meeting was in session, an action that would have destroyed a considerable part of Greenpeace's leadership. It is equally true, however, that no phone call was made to evacuate the boat before the explosions. At best, the agents concerned showed a callous disregard for human life: the effects of explosives of the power they used, detonated on a ship's hull, could neither be controlled nor predicted.

Jean Louis Dormand planned and supervised the operation and delivered the frogman, Zodiac and explosives on the night of the bombing; Jacques Camurier placed the bombs on the *Rainbow Warrior* with Alain Tonel standing by; François Verlet boarded the *Rainbow Warrior* for further reconnaissance within hours of the bombing; the Turenges collected Camurier afterwards. The irony in this is that the agents actually caught and charged with the bombing were the ones most peripherally involved on the night iself; they may in fact have *been* caught – as they claim – because of measures that were taken to minimise the likelihood of loss of life.

The New Zealand police investigation of the *Rainbow Warrior* bombing was in motion on the morning of 11 July. Police and Navy divers, clawing their way through darkness, debris, and diesel-clogged water, had found the body of Fernando Pereira at about 4 a.m. Although there was no proof at that stage that the explosions which sunk the ship had been deliberate acts of sabotage, the circumstances were such as to justify the setting up of a homicide enquiry as soon as detectives began to come on duty that day.

The first briefing was held in the presence of a dozen members of the Auckland CIB squad at 8.15 a.m. on the fourth floor of Auckland Central Police Station – an ugly institutional-looking building on the southern side of the city centre. The crime co-ordinator for the CIB night patrol, Detective Sergeant Tim Smith, gave a run-down on what was known to have happened: the *Rainbow Warrior* had been sunk by unknown means; one crew member was dead; names, addresses and brief statements had been taken from other members of the crew. It might be sabotage and homicide, but that was yet to be established.

The 12 Auckland detectives present perched on desks and chairs and took notes. François Verlet's name was mentioned as a possible suspect: the coincidence of a Frenchman on board the vessel within hours of the explosion had seemed sinister to some Greenpeace members. But there was nothing else to go on at that point. There were a few desultory questions before the meeting broke up after about 20 minutes.

During the day, further staff were directed to the squad from throughout the Auckland district. Detective Inspectors Bert

White and Maurice Witham assigned duties, drew up organisation charts and called in ancillary staff. Detectives were
dispatched to conduct further interviews with the *Warrior* crew,
other Greenpeace members and wharf staff. Specialists were
called in: photographers, fingerprint experts, DSIR staff. By
late afternoon those immediately involved with Operation
Rainbow had increased to 22. By that time too the divers had
established that the explosions were external ones and that
therefore the boat had been deliberately sunk. Police now
realised that the investigation was likely to be of considerably
greater magnitude than a conventional homicide enquiry. So
Detective Superintendent Allan Galbraith, a dour 48-year-old
former Glaswegian running the Auckland CIB, was appointed
officer in charge. (Galbraith had also studied terrorist sabotage with Scotland Yard's bomb squad.)

At the end of the day some specific leads had been established
in addition to suspicions about François Verlet. Names of about
half a dozen other French nationals who had been seen in
Auckland were being checked. And the sighting of the Newmans camper van on Tamaki Drive and the noting of its registration led police to ask all Newmans depots to report the return
of the vehicle, scheduled for delivery in Wellington on 15 July.
By the end of the week the investigating team would grow to
56, and then to over 100 at the height of the enquiry. Over
the next four months, members would inteview over 6,000
people, a record for a New Zealand police operation.

The first major breakthrough came on the morning of 12 July.
At 8.30, Detective Sergeant Terry Batchelor, officer in charge
of suspects, was staring at the empty basket on his desk marked
'Incoming Information' and wondering when he would have
something to put in it, if ever. He was also thinking about the
drawer full of other files he was supposed to be working on
– a couple of armed robberies and a particularly vicious rape
– and speculating about when he might be able to get back
to them. His desk telephone rang. It was Control telling him
that the foreign couple had just brought the camper van into

the Newmans depot in Mt Wellington, in Auckland's eastern
suburb. The staff would attempt to delay them.

Batchelor slammed down the phone and called to three colleagues to accompany him, including a female detective, Robyn
Borrie. Aware that suspects could not be relied upon to wait,
38-year-old Batchelor was tense and anxious to be on the road
as soon as possible. In the basement carpark he was furious
to find that their vehicle was hopelessly hemmed in by other
cars. It would take some time to free it. Then Batchelor noticed
that the Chinese cleaner had a new Ford Falcon out the front,
belonging to a member of the police hierarchy. The detective
rushed over and grabbed the keys from the cleaner's hand.
'What you do, what you do?' the man asked in astonish-
ment. By this time the other detectives had opened the doors
and were piling in. Batchelor expained rapidly that he needed
the vehicle to catch some suspects in a big crime. 'Big crime,
big crime,' he repeated loudly. The cleaner seemed not to understand a word and took a couple of swipes at the keys, trying
to retrieve them. Deciding that the only way to solve the
problem was to leave, Batchelor swung the driver's door open,
jumped in and drove straight out of the carpark. The cleaner
had by this time stepped back and was holding his head wailing,
'That boss's car, that boss's car.'

At Mt Wellington, 12 kilometres away, the staff at Newmans
Motor Caravans were detaining the two Turenges, but with
difficulty. The office had been warned the previous night to
look out for the couple. Police had also telephoned 22-year-
old Becky Hayter, the receptionist who had hired out the second
van to the Turenges after they had broken their windscreen,
for a description.

When Hayter arrived at work shortly before 8.30 a.m. on
12 July, she was at first unaware of the Turenges' presence
at the counter. They had already presented themselves to
another receptionist and said they had to cut short their stay.
They were to fly out of Auckland that morning.

'How was the holiday?' Glenys Dyson asked them.

'Fantastic,' said Alain.

'Awful,' said Sophie.

The Turenges estimated that they were entitled to a refund of $130, and it was as a staff member was arranging this that Hayter recognised the couple. She asked another woman in the office to call the police, who told them to stall the Turenges. The staff pretended they had to check the paper work for the refund and that this would take some time; then, when the Turenges became visibly restive, said that their refund cheque would have to be signed by one of the managers, none of whom had yet arrived at work.

Alain showed his irritation in a controlled manner, drumming his fingers on the public counter. Sophie kept going to the automatic tea and coffee machine, taking drinks, then visiting the toilet. After about 20 minutes a plainclothes detective, David McSweeney, walked into the office and up to the counter.

'Where are they?'

'Right behind you,' said Becky Hayter. McSweeney jumped. He turned to the Turenges, identified himself, and asked if he might search them. (This was for firearms.) They agreed, and he frisked them rapidly.

'We have a plane to catch at 11 o'clock,' said Alain Turenge, looking annoyed.

'I know,' said McSweeney. 'There'll be no problems.'

Detective Sergeant Batchelor arrived minutes later. He too introduced himself politely and showed the couple his identification card. 'I would like to speak to you at the Auckland Central Police Station, sir, and I will require the lady with you to accompany us.'

'My wife and I are flying out of New Zealand this morning,' Turenge countered. 'We have to be at the airport.' Batchelor was relieved that he spoke English, and intrigued by the American accent.

The Turenges spoke with one another in French for several seconds, then appeared to reach a verdict. 'Yes. We will go with you. But we do wish to catch our flight.'

'That's perfectly all right,' said Batchelor. 'If we are satisfied with your answers to our questions, we will have you taken to the airport.'

The couple nodded and moved outside with their police escort. At the cars, however, they balked when they realised they were to be separated. Batchelor explained that they would be travelling in vehicles one behind the other, and that they would be able to see each other all the way. Sophie would be accompanied by the female detective, Robyn Borrie. After further consultation the couple agreed, and the cars made the 20-minute trip back to Auckland in convoy.

The New Zealand detectives now had the Turenges in custody. But they were not especially comfortable about their position. Batchelor had realised on the way back to Auckland Central that they ought to have been armed: they were dealing with suspected terrorists. They would have been at a distinct disadvantage had the Turenges been carrying weapons.

Then there is no law in New Zealand allowing police to hold people on suspicion of terrorism. Unless or until specific charges can be laid, suspects can only be detained for questioning if they agree. Had the Turenges known this, or had immediate access to a New Zealand lawyer, they could have declined to accompany the detectives to the police station; they could not have been taken there against their will. It would still have been possible to catch their 11 a.m. flight out of the country. The Turenges, however, were ignorant of New Zealand law. For the time being, they co-operated.

Back at Auckland Central, the second in command of Operation Rainbow, Detective Inspector Bert White, spoke to Batchelor on the radio telephone. Then he prepared to receive the Swiss couple. They were processed quickly; their names were taken and they were searched, then they were escorted to separate interview rooms. Superintendent Allan Galbraith decided that the more robust Batchelor would interview Alain

Turenge. Sophie would be spoken to by a quieter detective with a record of being able to establish rapport with female suspects, 35-year-old Neil Morris.

The rooms, one on the fifth floor of the ten-storey police building, one on the sixth, were small, bleak and sparsely furnished. They had blue lino on the floor, flecked grey walls, a formica table and three chairs. In each case one detective would ask questions while another wrote down questions and answers in a hard-cover notebook.

Batchelor began with the mandatory caution to Alain Turenge, that he did not have to answer any questions put to him. If he did consent to being interviewed, however, then anything he said would be recorded and might be used in evidence in any subsequent legal proceedings. Turenge said he understood, had nothing to hide, and wanted to co-operate. And so the interview began.

Batchelor: 'Why do you think we wish to speak to you?'
Turenge: 'Because of the ship in the harbour that blew up.'
Batchelor: 'Which ship?'
Turenge: 'Greenpeace.'
Batchelor: 'Have you seen the ship?'
Turenge: 'Yes, on the TV.'
Batchelor: 'Why else might we want to speak to you?'
Turenge: 'Because we had lunch down by the ship and met someone.'

This last was news to Batchelor. But he did not wish to say so. Part of the art of interrogation is to extract information by suggesting that you know more than your suspect. He paused and had a good look at the man sitting across the table from him.

Alain Turenge was French in appearance, in his mid-thirties, and about 1.7 metres in height. He seemed fit and would have weighed about 64 kilograms. That morning he wore a dark brown tweed jacket, viyella shirt and brown corduroy trousers.

Round his neck was a green cotton scarf, which he twisted from time to time as he spoke.

His face was his most arresting feature. It was handsome in a rugged way. The eyes were alert and looked directly at Batchelor's the whole time they were together. His flaw was a scar on his nose, running from the left side, across the bridge and almost to the forehead. It was very noticeable and came close to deforming the nose. His lips were thin and often pursed as he listened. The dominant impression Batchelor had was a novel one for a New Zealand detective: he felt he was talking to a clever, analytical man; possibly one who was cleverer than he. This could make it difficult for the detective to establish and retain authority. At the outset, however, Turenge was showing no reluctance to answer questions. He did so without hesitation, politely and with apparent sincerity.

Batchelor was ready to resume. He told the Frenchman that his camper van had been seen on the waterfront the night that the *Rainbow Warrior* was bombed, and that the New Zealand police believed the Turenges were involved in the bombing. Then he continued questions.

Batchelor: 'What is your full name?'
Turenge: 'Turenge, Alain Jacques.'*
Batchelor: 'How old are you?'
Turenge: '34, 16/8/51.'
Batchelor: 'What is your country of birth?'
Turenge: 'Switzerland, Genève.'
Batchelor: 'What do you do for a living?'
Turenge: 'Trading manager for Thompson and Company.'
Batchelor: 'Where are they based?'
Turenge: 'Paris, 45 Quai le Gallo.'
Batchelor: 'What phone number?'
Turenge: '555 32 14, perhaps.'
Batchelor: 'How long have you worked for them?'

---

*The same first names adopted by Tonel and Camurier as part of their aliases. Among the other agents' false names were two Frédériques and two Jeans.

Turenge: 'Two years.'
Batchelor: 'Are you currently on a paid holiday?'
Turenge: 'Yes, that's how they do it in France.'
Batchelor: 'When are you due back at work?'
Turenge: '25 July.'
Batchelor: 'What is your address and phone number?'
Turenge: '105 Avenue Général Bizot – 13 42 43 87.'
Batchelor: 'Do you live at this address with your wife?'
Turenge: 'Yes.'
Batchelor: 'Do you have children?'
Turenge: 'No.'
Batchelor: 'What is your wife's name?'
Turenge: 'Sophie Clair Frédérique Turenge.'
Batchelor: 'When was she born?'
Turenge: '24/5/49.'
Batchelor: 'What is her occupation?'
Turenge: 'Lecturer in sociology at Nanterre.'
Batchelor: 'How long have you been married?'
Turenge: 'Ten years.'

Curious about Turenge's unmistakable American accent, Batchelor asked how he acquired it. The Frenchman said he had gone to Minnesota at the age of 18 to work as a petrol station attendant for a month. Since then, he claimed, he had listened to a great deal of country and western music and so retained his vocabulary and accent. It did not seem a likely explanation for one so fluent in American-English and Batchelor told him so; it was far more likely that he had lived and worked there for a longer period. Turenge simply made a Gallic gesture whose constant repetition Batchelor was to find annoying: he shrugged his shoulders, turned the palms of hands upright, cocked his head to one side, and blew a puff of air through pouted lips.

The detective also asked about Turenge's facial scar. The Frenchman told him it was the result of a cancer operation. He had had a mole on his face which he scratched continuously, he said, and this became cancerous. Eventually it was operated on and the growth removed. Batchelor, not wholly convinced, asked Turenge if he had any other marks and the Frenchman pulled up his shirt. A second scar, jagged, ran from his sternum down to the top of his groin. It looked like the result of a bad wound, or of a major accident. Turenge claimed it was simply the consequence of an appendix operation that had 'gone bad'. That too seemed an unconvincing story. The mark ran nowhere near his appendix. Turenge gave Batchelor details of the alleged places and dates of both operations, all of which turned out subsequently to be false. Batchelor felt from the outset that both scars were souvenirs of combat.

Batchelor turned then to the Turenge's movements after their arrival in New Zealand on 22 June. His suspect became more careful, more circumspect in his release of information. He frequently said, 'I don't remember.' He conceded that his wife made all the travel arrangements, that they had taken the camper van so as to travel more flexibly, but that they also stayed in hotels because Sophie did not like sleeping in the van. He claimed they had travelled as far north as Cape Reinga and as far south as Hamilton. Then Batchelor steered him back to the matter of immediate concern.*

Batchelor: 'Did you know the Greenpeace boat was in Auckland before you came here?'
Turenge: 'No.'
Batchelor: 'Are you certain?'
Turenge: 'No, not exactly — I might have seen it in the newspapers.'
Batchelor: 'Did you know it was here or not?'
Turenge: 'I can't understand your meaning.'
Batchelor: 'When you arrived in Auckland, did you know the *Rainbow Warrior*, the Greenpeace boat, was here?'

---

*Both interrogators continued to go back over travel arrangements and other mundanities with the Turenges. This was in part an attempt to establish their movements in New Zealand; and in part to find and probe discrepancies in their respective stories.

Turenge: 'No, I did not.'

Batchelor: 'Are you aware of the boat's significance to the Peace Movement?'

Turenge: 'Yes, everybody is.'

Batchelor: 'What are your feelings about it?'

Turenge: 'I have no strong feelings about it.'

Batchelor: 'What is your opinion regarding nuclear power and weapons?'

Turenge: 'I don't agree with them but I have no strong feelings. I wouldn't go out on to the streets about it.'

Batchelor: 'Do you know your wife's opinion on this matter?'

Turenge: 'No, we don't discuss it.'

Batchelor: 'Do you know what else they do?'

Turenge: 'Oh yeah, the baby seals and the whales.'

Batchelor: 'What did you do the day the ship was sunk?'

Turenge: 'We were in a motel at Helensville at Parakai, where you can go for a swim in big pools.'

Batchelor: 'What else did you do?'

Turenge: 'We came south. It was our plan to go south. We came down to Auckland, we ate in the Auckland Domain by the rugby ground, by the grandstand.'

Batchelor: 'What time was it?'

Turenge: 'About four in the afternoon.'

Batchelor: 'What then?'

Turenge: 'We went and looked at the shops in Parnell.'

Batchelor: 'After that?'

Turenge: 'We went down to the waterfront to the park where the seaplanes are. We parked in the park.'

Batchelor: 'Was it light or dark?'

Turenge: 'It was completely dark.'

Batchelor: 'What happened then?'

Turenge: 'I had an argument with my wife.'

Batchelor: 'What about?'

Turenge: 'I don't wish to say, it's personal.'

Batchelor: 'Was it something to do with staying in the van?'

Turenge: 'Yes.'

Batchelor: 'What did you do?'

Turenge: 'I went for a walk to calm down.'

Batchelor: 'You left the van?'

Turenge: 'Yes.'

Batchelor: 'Which way did you walk?'

Turenge: 'Towards the place where I helped the man.'

Batchelor: 'What were you wearing?'

Turenge: 'Blue jeans, red shoes, a blue sweat shirt.'

Batchelor: 'Which side of the road were you on?'

Turenge: 'On the side where the sea is.'

Batchelor: 'How far did you walk?'

Turenge: 'To the second bridge.'

Batchelor: 'Where and when did you see the man you helped?'

Turenge: 'On the other side of the road while I was walking back to the van. He was down by the side of the rocks rowing his boat.'

Batchelor: 'Did you speak to him?'

Turenge: 'He spoke to me because I was looking at him.'

Batchelor: 'What did he say?'

Turenge: 'He said for me to help him pull his dinghy out of the water.'

Batchelor: 'How far from the bridge did you first see him?'

Turenge: 'About 50 metres, I think.'

Batchelor: 'Did he appear to be shocked when he noticed you looking at him?'

Turenge: 'I would say no, but I couldn't say.'

Batchelor: 'Did you see a motor on the boat or did you hear one?'

Turenge: 'No, it didn't have one, there was no engine, he was rowing.'

Batchelor: 'So you helped him with his boat?'

Turenge: 'Yeah.'

Batchelor: 'What else did you do?'

Turenge: 'It was by some steps, he gave me the bags and then we pulled the boat up and turned it over. We chained it to the bank.'

Batchelor: 'What did you do then? What did you say to each other?'

Turenge: 'I asked him where he had come from.'

Batchelor: 'What did he say?'

Turenge: 'He told me he had come from a boat out in the sea. He indicated out towards the sea.'

Batchelor: 'What did he have with him?'

Turenge: 'Some bags.'

Batchelor: 'How many?'

Turenge: 'Three.'

Batchelor: 'What did they look like?'

Turenge: 'Nylon ones, two big and one small.'

Batchelor: 'What colour?'

Turenge: 'Green or blue, I think.'

Batchelor: 'What happened then?'

Turenge: 'I helped him pull the boat from the water and I asked him where he was going.'

Batchelor: 'Why?'

Turenge: 'I don't know.'

Batchelor: 'What did he say?'

Turenge: 'He said he had his car near there and he was going to it.'

Batchelor: 'What then?'

Turenge: 'I offered to take him.'

Batchelor: 'You offered him, a complete stranger, you in a foreign land – that was very good of you.'

Turenge: 'Yes.'

Batchelor: 'Why?'

Turenge: 'I don't know. I can't say.'

Batchelor: 'What did he say?'

Turenge: 'He said yes. I told him my van was near and that I could get it and take him.'

Batchelor: 'You had just had an argument with your wife, which made you leave the van, and you offered to give a complete stranger a lift to his car, not knowing where you are, or who you are talking to?'

Turenge: 'Yes.'

Batchelor: 'I am not satisfied with that answer. Did it not occur to you that your wife would not be happy? One would think your major concern would be making up with your wife. It does not make sense that you would be so concerned about a stranger's plight.'

Turenge: 'I do not understand.'

Batchelor: 'What I am saying is that if you are telling me the truth about the argument with your wife, you would have been too concerned about it to worry about helping a complete stranger.'

Turenge: 'That is what you say.'

Batchelor: 'Am I not speaking the truth?'

Turenge: 'Let me explain. It was good to help that man, my wife would calm down.'

Batchelor: 'Explain that further.'

Turenge: 'It would take her mind off what we were saying.'

Batchelor: 'Are you saying that it was a sort of diversion, one which may have helped quell the argument?'

Alain Turenge shrugged and pouted.

Batchelor: 'I am perhaps using words you do not understand.'

Turenge: 'I understand when you speak slowly, not fast.'

Batchelor: 'Tell me about the man.'

Turenge: 'He said his name was Peter.'

Batchelor: 'Can you describe him?'

Turenge: 'Yes, he was white, maybe 35 years.'*

Batchelor: 'And dressed?'

Turenge: 'He had a waterproof coat on, coloured red. It was nylon.'

Batchelor: 'It was night. How can you be sure he was white, I mean European?'

Turenge: 'He looked white and didn't speak with an accent.'

Batchelor: 'Describe his accent.'

Turenge: 'He didn't have one.'

Batchelor: 'You live in France, persons to whom you speak there would have no noticeable accent. But you are in New

---

*Camurier was, according to the information on his passport, 35 years old; in interrogation the best lie to tell is that closest to the truth.

Zealand speaking to a person in English. How can you say
he didn't have an accent?'

Turenge: 'It's difficult to say, I'm not sure.'

Batchelor: 'After you left the man, what happened then?'

Turenge: 'I ran back to the van. Sophie was at the back resting.'

Batchelor: 'What did you say to her?'

Turenge: 'I told her about the fisherman and how we could
help him.'

Batchelor: 'What did she say?'

Turenge: 'Nothing really. She agreed.'

Batchelor: 'Why should she agree to help a stranger? Wouldn't
she be more concerned about the argument?'

Turenge shrugged again.

Batchelor: 'What happened then?'

Turenge: 'We drove along the waterfront.'

Batchelor: 'Who drove?'

Turenge: 'Sophie.'

Batchelor: 'Why didn't you drive?'

Turenge: 'No reason, I got in the back and I was going to help
the man with the bags.'

Batchelor: 'Why didn't you sit in the front with your wife?'

Turenge: 'I just didn't.'

Batchelor: 'Where did you go then?'

Turenge: 'We stopped close to where the man was. I helped
him with his bags and we drove him to his vehicle.'

Batchelor: 'Where did he sit in the van?'

Turenge: 'Up the front.'

Batchelor: 'Why not at the back?'

Turenge: 'I do not know.'

Batchelor: 'Perhaps you knew him, Alain, that would explain
it.'

Turenge: 'No.'

Batchelor: 'Where did you take him?'

Turenge: 'Not very far. We turned off the waterfront road and
took him to a Toyota Landcruiser.'

Batchelor: 'Are you sure it was a Landcruiser?'

Turenge: 'Yes, I know what they look like. It was a Toyota.'
Batchelor: 'What colour was it?'
Turenge: 'Yellow.'
Batchelor: 'How could you tell? It was night.'
Turenge: 'I could tell from the distance we were.'
Batchelor: 'What did you talk about with Peter?'
Turenge: 'Not anything.'
Batchelor: 'I find that hard to believe. Surely he would have asked you where you had come from, things like that?'
Turenge: 'Maybe.'
Batchelor: 'If you're sincere, you must remember what conversation you had, or at least some of it.'
Turenge: 'We didn't speak much. I was still thinking about the argument.'
Batchelor: 'If you were so concerned about that, I suggest to you that you would have hardly picked him up in the first place.'
Turenge: 'What do you want me to say?'
Batchelor: 'How about the truth?'
Turenge: 'You are getting it.'

Batchelor stopped at this point. He was to go over this story again and again for the next three days, probing for weaknesses and inconsistencies, trying to throw Turenge off balance. The account simply did not ring true to the detective. You did not pick up a stranger in a strange country and then have no conversation with him. If the van had not been sighted by the boat club vigilantes, who had observed Alain behaving as he had, then the overall story would have seemed more acceptable. But knowing what he did, Batchelor was inclined to disbelieve the details the Frenchman supplied.

He asked for Turenge's passport to begin enquiries into its authenticity and Alain handed it over. Batchelor noticed there was no mention of scars under the heading 'distinguishing characteristics'. Then Detective McSweeney brought in drinks and sandwiches from the police cafeteria. Without their passports, taken for a plausible reason ('When we find they are in order you will be free to go'), the Turenges would find it difficult to leave the country.

Downstairs, going over the same ground with Sophie Turenge, Neil Morris was making even less progress. The suspect was polite and answered questions with apparent sincerity. But her emotions seemed closer to the surface than Alain's. She cried frequently, saying it was because she was worried about her sick mother (their ostensible reason for leaving New Zealand earlier than planned). There was also a language difficulty. Although Morris did not feel he needed to use an interpreter, he had to make an effort to speak in slow, simple English. Several times Sophie said she did not understand questions and he had to reword and repeat them. When she answered it was in a measured way, as if she was calculating the effect of what she said as she spoke.

Unlike Alain, she seemed physically fragile, thin to the point of emaciation. She wore corduroy slacks and a blouse, sensible but unspectacular clothes for travel. She was not made up and did not attempt to look attractive. She had none of her husband's chic, and this too was a factor that cast doubt on their story. Could they really be husband and wife?

Most important, by the time the detectives broke for refreshments and the removal of passports, they had uncovered a major inconsistency in the Turenges' respective versions of events: Alain said that Peter the fisherman was sitting in the front of the van when they drove him to his vehicle; Sophie claimed he was in the back. Both were adamant; both could not be right. It was not the kind of detail that they could be expected to get wrong only two days after the event.

In an effort to jog the Turenges' memories and prise further details (or inconsistencies) from them, the suspects were invited to take separate drives along the waterfront with their interrogators in the late afternoon. Neil Morris deliberately drove Sophie past the wreck of the *Rainbow Warrior* at Marsden Wharf. He watched her reaction in the rear-view mirror. She

stared fixedly ahead, showing no curiosity or interest. That
in itself was significant.

Terry Batchelor retraced Alain's movements with him. The
Frenchman's confidence waned only when they tried to find
where Peter the fisherman had allegedly been delivered to his
vehicle. This evidence was too specific for Turenge to fabricate.
A quick check in any specified street would reveal whether or
not a Toyota Landcruiser had been parked there. And so Alain
said simply that he was unable to find the location.

In the police car, Batchelor became a little tougher. He put
it to Turenge that there had been no fisherman, and that the
whole story was a lie. He went further and said that only Alain
and Sophie had been on Tamaki Drive on the occasion in question, and that he, Alain, had been the man in the Zodiac.

Turenge remained coolly controlled: 'It is obvious that you
do not believe me and I have no way of proving to you that
I am telling the truth.'

Batchelor said they would advertise for Peter the fisherman
to come forward and confirm the story. If he failed to do so,
the alibi would be shown to be false.

'You do not have anything to worry about,' said Turenge.
'That man will come forward. I know.'

Back at the station, the detective asked Turenge to make a statement setting out the answers he had given to questions put to
him so far. The Frenchman agreed. David McSweeney prepared
a typewritten document and Turenge signed it. Sophie was
asked to do the same, and an interpreter was called so that
the statement could be made in English and French. But she
declined.

Both suspects were photographed separately and then re-
united, sitting together in the CIB's general office. Sophie was
cold and borrowed a policewoman's mufti jacket. Batchelor
fetched them filled rolls and canned juice from the cafeteria
(the kind of food Sophie had told Neil Morris she abhored
in New Zealand). While they were eating, Alain said he needed

to visit the toilet. Batchelor put his own milkshake in a cardboard cup on the desk and rose to escort Turenge. As the Frenchman passed the desk he brushed the drink and it fell to the floor. Some ice-cream and milk splattered on to the bottom of one of his trouser legs. Turenge was furious. When he got to the bathroom he wet several pieces of tissue and began wiping vigorously to remove the small stain. Bachelor was impressed by his fastidiousness, but it put him in mind of a military person, not a civilian on holiday. Alain Turenge, he realised, acted and carried himself as if he was always about to go on parade.

In the office again, Alain Turenge asked the detectives if they were free to go.

Batchelor replied that they were, provided enquiries by Interpol confirmed that their passports were genuine. 'If your documents are in order, then you will have no objection to our checking them out,' Batchelor said bluntly.

'You are only doing your job,' said Turenge. 'If that is what you must do, then I agree.'

By this time, other law enforcement agencies were interested in the Turenges. The New Zealand government's committee on terrorism had met in Wellington that same afternoon, convened by the Prime Minister. This group existed to co-ordinate the flow of intelligence information among relevant arms of government and to advise the Prime Minister on what action government ought to take, or authorise others to take, to combat terrorism. In addition to David Lange, its members were the head of his department (as chairman), the Commissioner of Police, the Director of the Security Intelligence Service, the Secretary of Defence, the Chief of Defence Staff, and the Secretary of Foreign Affairs.

A decision was taken at this first meeting to seek further information about the Turenges: from the Western intelligence community, of which New Zealand was a contributing member, and from the Turenges themselves, by placing them under electronic surveillance. A warrant was issued immediately under an Act which allows bugging in New Zealand for the gathering of information on activities prejudicial to security and which is not likely to be obtained by other means.

That decision taken, the Commissioner of Police had to arrange for the Turenges to be placed in a suitable location; the SIS made preparations to fly one of its electronic experts to Auckland.

It was left to the policemen who had been interrogating the Turenges to nudge them into accommodation where the surveillance could be carried out. While the SIS man was planting his devices to pick up spoken and telephone conversations at a motel in Herne Bay, one of the detectives asked the Turenges if they would like him to arrange somewhere for them to stay. He had to be careful not to risk a refusal.

'It's too late to get you into a city motel now, on a Friday night. But we do know the management of one place that I'm sure would let you have a room if we asked on your behalf. Would that be acceptable?'

Fortunately for the police, it was. The detective was then required to keep the couple occupied with small talk until the unit was ready, which took several hours. At one point he left them for several minutes to visit another part of the office. When he returned they seemed asleep, heads together, hers on his shoulder. This was the first time they had acted like husband and wife. As the detective walked in, however, he saw one of Alain's eyes open, survey the whole room, then close again; even dozing, he was still alert.

At last the all-clear was telephoned through and the Turenges were delivered to the Unicorn Motel at around 11.30 p.m. They had had a long and stressful day. But they still found the time and stamina to ring one of the DGSE numbers in Paris for instructions, the first of their conversations overheard by the New Zealand Security Intelligence Service. Outside, the police surveillance team, the Red Squad, was mounting its own 24-hour watch on the motel.

Next morning the police still had no information from Interpol about the results of the passport enquiries. Knowing that the Turenges would be waiting anxiously, Terry Batchelor went to the Unicorn Motel with David McSweeney at 10.30 to report on the lack of progress and to check on the couple's state of mind.

Batchelor was concerned that their fear and their consideration of the previous day's interviews might lead them to withdraw the considerable degree of co-operation they had given police up to that time.

Sophie assured him that her husband had simply gone to the Air New Zealand booking office in the city to arrange another flight to France. 'Are we free to leave now?' she asked with obvious anxiety. 'Could you please explain the law to me. Do we have to remain here?'

Batchelor replied that she was not under arrest and was free to leave at any time. However, because their activities had been viewed with suspicion, they would have to wait until the New Zealand police were satisfied that their passports were genuine. He added that if they did try to leave the country before then, the police would be obliged to warn the airline that they were suspected terrorists, and no airline would allow them to board a plane in that circumstance.

'I understand what you say, but my husband and I are anxious to leave,' Sophie said. 'My mother is very sick in France and I wish to go home to see her.'

Batchelor said he sympathised. But there was nothing he could do to expedite the process until the police received confirmation of the validity of the passports. Then he and McSweeney left to look for her husband.

Alain Turenge had left by the time the detectives arrived at the booking office in Quay Street. But staff there told them an interesting story. A man by the name of Turenge had come in and asked for an immediate booking to France for his wife and himself. He produced a British Airways round-the-world ticket. When the woman at the counter told him it would take

about 20 minutes to reprocess the ticket, Turenge said he could
not wait. He slapped down $6,000 cash in American currency
on the counter and asked for new tickets. The person serving
him was astonished: she had never encountered someone prepared to dispense with a pre-paid ticket, nor seen anyone carrying that amount of cash. Nevertheless the new tickets were
issued and he left with them immediately.

Arriving back at the motel, Batchelor saw Alain Turenge pacing
the first-floor balcony, looking tense. When they met inside,
however, the Frenchman was courteous and in complete control of himself. Batchelor asked if his wife had explained the
situation, 'Yes,' said Turenge, 'she has told me we cannot
leave.'
   Batchelor said it was correct that they could not at that point
leave New Zealand. But they were free to travel within the
country until the passport checks were completed. All he asked
was that they let the police know where they could be contacted.* The Turenges communicated in French for several
minutes. Then Alain said, 'No, we want to return home. So
we will stay here until you receive the information you require.'
At which point Batchelor and McSweeney left them to the
unobtrusive care of the Red Squad.

Without alternative transport already arranged, it would have
been difficult for the Turenges to leave New Zealand. But it
would have been a simple matter to give their tails the slip.
Batchelor could think of several scenarios, and all made him
nervous. They could stroll down Queen Street among the Saturday shopping crowd, slip into a clothing store, buy new outfits,
and walk out with them wrapped. Then they only had to go
to a film, change in the theatre, and leave unrecognisable in
the stream of exiting patrons.
   In fact, the Turenges went out only once. On Saturday

---

*Had the Turenges taken up this offer, they would of course have been kept under
police surveillance.

evening, followed by two members of the Red Squad, they walked a kilometre up the hill to Jervois Road to eat at Papillon,* one of Auckland's better French-style restaurants. As an eating guide published about the time of their visit noted, Papillon is 'a very elegant BYO [bring your own wine], with dark walls with framed butterflies and excellent prints, ritz palms, peach-coloured tablecloths, tons of greenery and a small fountain in the courtyard'.

The night the Turenges ate there, the menu included pâtés, terrines, seafood and turkey mousse. It was good food, well prepared and presented – the kind they had found little enough of in the previous three weeks. It was not only one of their best meals in New Zealand; it was also to be their last night of freedom for a long time.

The police obtained no direct information as a result of the bugging of the Turenges' motel unit. This intelligence was collected, transcribed and made use of by the Security Intelligence Service. But the exercise was of immediate indirect assistance in confirming suspicions that the couple were agents, and specifically agents of the French government.

Firstly, there was the fact that the Turenges took the kind of precautions that were characteristic of trained operatives. They spoke to one another very little when they were inside the unit, but a great deal and with considerable intensity when they were outside – on the motel balcony, and walking up to Jervois Road on Saturday evening.

Secondly, there were the telephone calls, five of them made to Paris between Friday night and Sunday morning. The number was eventually (but not immediately) found to be a DGSE one. But the content of the calls had already indicated as much to the Security Intelligence Service. At the same time, making its own enquiries, the SIS received co-operation from other allied intelligence services and none from France. The

---

*'Papillon!' one of the senior detectives on the case said when he heard where the Turenges had eaten. 'Next they'll be heading for Devil's Island.'

negative inference to be drawn from that was that the agents were French.

Members of the government's committee on terrorism, drawing on information supplied by the police and by the SIS, thus knew that their worst fear was unfounded: the possibility that a team of terrorists from an unknown country was in New Zealand to blow up a number of targets, and that they might strike again. The SIS had had no prior intelligence about the presence or movements of French agents in New Zealand. But by the end of the weekend they had a reasonably clear idea of what they were now dealing with: a project on the part of French agents, presumably working with the backing of their government, to sink a Greenpeace vessel.

Members of the committee, especially the Prime Minister, were kept informed of developments throughout the weekend. They met again on the afternoon of Monday 15 July. After the meeting, choosing his words with great care, David Lange was able to tell journalists that there was 'an emerging pattern of evidence which the police believe is helpful for the solution of the question of who caused [the] destruction and death. It was a criminal act, there was more than one person involved, and there is a strong suggestion that it is an external operation.' He added that the most likely motives behind the bombing were a hatred of Greenpeace and an intention to stop the Peace Flotilla voyage to Moruroa.

This statement avoided specific accusations. And by speaking of police enquiries only, it necessarily concealed the contribution of the SIS to 'the emerging pattern of evidence'. But it made possible an intelligent deduction about the direction in which the evidence was already pointing.

Information and advice from the SIS was not relayed directly to police working on Operation Rainbow. But it conditioned the policy decisions about the investigation made by police at National Headquarters in Wellington (the Commissioner was a member of the committee on terrorism), and these decisions in turn influenced the advice and instructions given to senior police in Auckland, particularly Chief Superintendent Ian Mills and the officer in charge of the investigation, Superintendent Galbraith. They for their part kept the terrorism committee informed on a daily basis of the unfolding results of the Turenge interrogation and the gathering of other evidence.

Detectives at the work face knew little about the merging results of the total investigation. By ten o'clock on Sunday morning, however, they had received word from Interpol Switzerland that the Turenges' passports were forgeries. This was the first hard evidence that the couple were not who they claimed to be, and it increased the probability of their involvement in the sabotage of the ship to near certainty.

By Sunday morning too other evidence had come to hand that further linked the Turenges with the bombing. As a result of widely publicised requests for information from the public about the movements of the Newmans camper van, registration LB 8945, the Topuni forest workers Brendan Walton and Murray Hoyle had reported their sighting of a van and the Commodore station wagon on 8 July. Even more usefully, they had been able to provide the Commodore's registration number, which connected it with the *Ouvéa* crew. The previous day, the Whangarei Customs officer Frank MacLean had communicated his growing suspicions about the French yachtsmen to the police.

Another potential witness had come forward. Jill Couch, manageress of the Beachcomber Motel, had informed the police about the Turenges sleeping in separate beds, and about Alain's apparent unwillingness to let her into the unit the morning she brought him the larger-than-usual breakfast. Finally, searching rubbish from the unit that the Turenges had occupied at the Goldstar Auckland Airport Motel the night before they were taken into custody, the police found a discarded muddy pair of jeans, a muddy towel, and two adhesive labels off a Plastimo liferaft.

All this evidence added to the police's growing conviction that the Turenges were covering up involvement in a serious crime. Now the investigators had more specific information on which to base further interrogation, in addition to the water-front sighting on the night of 10 July.

Consequently Detectives Morris and Batchelor returned to the Unicorn Motel late on the morning of Sunday 15 July. They explained to the Turenges that they had new information which they were required to discuss with them at Auckland Central Police Station. Again, the couple were prepared to co-operate, but Alain pointed out that they had arranged to meet a lawyer at three o'clock that afternoon. Batchelor said that was no problem. The police would ring the firm of solicitors and tell them where the Turenges were; if they did not manage to reach them by phone, they would post a man at the motel at 3 p.m. to pass on the message.*

The legal firm of Russell McVeagh McKenzie Bartleet & Company is the most prestigious (and reputedly the most expensive) in Auckland. They had been engaged by the DGSE as a consequence of the Turenges' telephone calls to Paris. The arrangement had not, of course, been made by the DGSE itself, as part of the agents' mutual defence would be that they were *not* working for the French government. For this reason too the French Embassy in New Zealand had not involved itself in the case (a spokesman had, in fact, denied French collusion in the bombing). The contact with Russell McVeagh was made via a circuitous route of Paris lawyers, with instructions that every effort be made to have the Turenges released and that they continue to deny any connection with an agency of the French state. The corollary of this was that the freedom of one could not be negotiated by any admission of involvement in the *Rainbow Warrior* bombing, nor of membership of the DGSE.

---

*This was subsequently a source of contention. The police were unable to reach the solicitor by telephone; and the police officer left at the motel did not succeed in intercepting anybody. The lawyers suspected that the detectives had engineered keeping the Turenges in isolation from legal advice until after the next interrogation session. Police contested this vigorously.

Alain and Sophie Turenge were protected from such counsel
for a further day, however. They allowed the police to search
their personal luggage at the motel, and they returned to the
police station with Detectives Batchelor and Morris. The new
round of interviews began at about 1 p.m. on Sunday. This
time, of course, the interrogators had the advantage of new
information that the Turenges did not know they possessed.
After cautioning Alain Turenge, Batchelor canvassed ground
he had covered before.

Batchelor: 'You still say your full name is Alain Jacques
  Turenge?'
Turenge: 'Yes.'
Batchelor: 'Do you use any other name?'
Turenge: 'No.'
Batchelor: 'What is your date of birth?'
Turenge: '16/8/51.'
Batchelor: 'You were born in Switzerland?'
Turenge: 'Yes, Genève.'
Batchelor: 'Your parents are deceased?'
Turenge: 'Yes.'
Batchelor: 'What were their names?'
Turenge: 'Turenge, Jean Yves, father; Naldier Micheline,
  mother.'
Batchelor: 'How did they die?'
Turenge: 'In a motor accident.'

Batchelor paused, then said he wanted to ask about Turenge's
passport.

Batchelor: 'Where did you apply for it?'
Turenge: 'Geneva.'
Batchelor: 'Which year?'
Turenge: '1978, in Geneva or Lyon.'
Batchelor (pausing further for effect): 'We have checked your
  passport with the Swiss authorites. They say it belongs to
  a person named L...., J... P......., born on 24/6/52.
  What do you have to say about this?'

Turenge (shrugging): 'I do not understand.'

Batchelor: 'You don't seem shocked or surprised.'

Turenge: 'What do you want me to say?'

Batchelor: 'What do you think?'

Turenge: 'There has been a mistake.'

Batchelor: 'Do you know this man?'

Turenge: 'No.'

Batchelor: 'Did you supply a new photograph of yourself when you renewed your passport in 1982?'

Turenge: 'No.'

Batchelor: 'So the photo of you in the passport is the original one?'

Turenge: 'Yes.'

Batchelor: 'It doesn't show the scar on your face.'

Turenge: 'Yes.'

Batchelor: 'There is no record at the Geneva Records Office that Alain Jacques Turenge has ever existed. What do you say to that?'

Turenge: 'My answer is that I am stopping my co-operation with you.'

Batchelor: 'Why?'

Turenge: 'Because you say I am not existing. I am astonished.'

Batchelor: 'On all the passports that are issued, all physical identifying marks are recorded. Why aren't your two scars listed?'

Turenge: 'I didn't tell them. It's a personal thing.'

Batchelor: 'In some of the places you have stayed, you have not shared the same bed as your wife.'

Turenge: 'That is right.'

Batchelor: 'Why?'

Turenge: 'Personal problems.'

Batchelor: 'Your wife says that on the night of 10 July you were next to her in the front of the van and the man you helped was in the back. Which is it?'

Turenge: 'I am sure I was in the back.'

Batchelor then changed tack and confronted Turenge with some of the new evidence that had come to hand since the previous interrogation. He asked about Jill Couch's conviction that he had stopped her coming into the motel unit in Paihia.

Turenge: 'That may be true about not wanting her in there. I cannot say.'

Batchelor: 'Was there another person in your motel room?'

Turenge: 'No.'

Batchelor: 'The labels for the liferaft that we found in your Mangere motel room in the rubbish. Do you remember these?'

Turenge: 'Yes.'

Batchelor: 'We have spoken to the previous occupant of your room about this. He didn't leave them there. The writing on the labels was French. They were wrapped around a used tampon belonging to your wife. How did these labels get there?'

Turenge: 'I cleaned out the van, perhaps it fell from one of the fisherman's bags.'

Batchelor: 'What would a label be doing on the outside of one of the bags?'

Turenge: 'Perhaps it was in his hand and he dropped it when he put them in.'

After questioning Turenge about other matters, still seeking inconsistencies in his answers or admissions of error, Batchelor paused and looked hard at the Frenchman.

Batchelor: 'I am going to put it to you that you, along with other French people, are part of conspiracy and homicide involving the blowing up of the *Rainbow Warrior*.'

Turenge: 'All I can say is that it is your job to suspect. It is a big accusation.'

Batchelor: 'The facts that we know and the evidence we have so far gathered are a clear indication to me that you are directly involved or indirectly involved with the sabotage of the *Rainbow Warrior*. What is your reply to this accusation?'

Turenge: 'It is not true.'

Batchelor: 'Can you explain to me all these so-called coinci-
     dences we have discussed?'

Turenge: 'No, I don't understand the coincidences.'

Batchelor: 'Will you agree then that there are too many coinci-
     dences and that that is unusual?'

Turenge shrugged and pouted.

This round of interviews ended at 5 p.m. It had lasted four
hours. The Turenges were hungry (having missed lunch) and
David McSweeney fetched chow mein from a nearby Chinese
takeaway bar. The couple ate together voraciously in one of
the interview rooms.

Meanwhile Batchelor and Morris conferred. It was time for
further assistance. They had mentioned previously to Superintendent Galbraith that Alain and Sophie communicated
rapidly in French with one another when they were together.
The New Zealand detectives felt at a disadvantage not being
able to understand these exchanges. They had suggested to
Galbraith that a French-speaking officer supervise the suspects
between interviews. At six-o'clock that night, as a result of
their request, they were given the services of Nick Hall, a
22-year-old constable only three months out of police college.
He sat with the Turenges in the interview room for 35 minutes,
pretending to read a newspaper but paying close attention to
every word they spoke. Later in the evening he sat with them
again. Immediately after these sessions, he wrote an account
of what he had overheard.*

Three of the exchanges Constable Hall noted were of particular interest to the police. One of these has already been
noted: Sophie saying, 'It was a pity someone had to die, even
a child,' to which Alain replied, 'That's the way it had to be.'
Later, Sophie said, 'I wonder if they will pay Berthelo?' The

---

*The virtual absence of fluent French speakers in New Zealand police ranks was
to handicap inquiries at the outset. Subsequently a young French-New Zealand
constable, Jacques Legros, was to join the Rainbow team.

other comment was a recurring one, Alain saying to Sophie, 'Remember the mountain.'*

Neither detective revealed in subsequent interrogation that these exchanges had been overheard and understood. The police might wish to use the tactic again and they wanted the Turenges to remain off guard on such occasions. But they confirmed in the minds of the interviewers and police chiefs that they were dealing with French agents who had participated in the *Rainbow Warrior* bombing.

Interrogations continued laboriously throughout the night of Sunday 14 July and the early hours of Monday morning. Both detectives took the suspects over and over previous territory, pointing up inconsistencies, confronting them with evidence of involvement in the *Rainbow Warrior* sinking, pressing them to reveal their true identities. The Turenges stuck to their rehearsed stories, although Alain seemed stronger and more determined than Sophie.

Batchelor: 'There are a great many things about you that are not right. You give me a story that you helped this fisherman, a total stranger in a strange land, that you took him in your car to a place you can't remember. You say you did not talk with him. And all of this after having an argument with the lady you call your wife, which has caused you to leave the van?'
Turenge: 'It is what happened.'
Batchelor: 'It is lies.'

Turenge shrugged.

Batchelor: 'You will find that [mimicking the gesture] is not

---

*This last appears to be part of a technique used in training agents to endure interrogation. Asked about the expression subsequently, Alain Turenge said it was an image to fix in the mind and referred to two things: the need to be strong, like a mountain; and the fact that you had to walk up a mountain slowly, and, although this was difficult, you eventually came to the top and saw freedom on the other side.

enough. You will have to explain these things to a judge
and jury.'

Turenge: 'If this is how it will be.'

Batchelor: 'Your attitude is amazing. Do you really not care
about this?'

Turenge: 'I think you will put me in prison for a long time,
maybe 15 to 20 years.'

McSweeney: 'Murder is a life sentence in this country. Do you
accept this as your fate?'

Turenge: 'Yes.'

McSweeney: 'How can you do this when you can help us?'

Turenge: 'No one can help.'

McSweeney: 'We could.'

Turenge: 'No, it is too late. There is no help.'

Batchelor: 'Your country could help you.'

Turenge: 'I have no country, as you have said, for me all is
lost.'

Batchelor: 'And for the lady you call your wife?'

Turenge: 'She must take her chance. She knows how it is.'

Although Alain Turenge remained outwardly calm, there was
occasional evidence of his considerable inner tension. In the
early hours of Monday morning when he was sitting with both
the Turenges between interviews, Detective Batchelor noticed
that Alain's hand, held between his crossed legs, had gone
purple. As he stared, Sophie saw it too and said, 'Alain! Your
hand!' He glanced down, said, 'Oh,' uncrossed his legs, then
shook the hand until circulation was restored and normal colour
returned.

Shortly afterwards, Alain asked to speak with Batchelor
alone. Morris and Batchelor had said to both suspects that if
they co-operated it might be possible to let Sophie return to
France. It was simply a proposition at that stage and had not
been approved by the police hierarchy. Batchelor took the
Frenchman into his office and asked what he wanted.

'I do not want you to make false promises to my wife.
Promises you do not intend to keep.'

'I don't know what you mean,' said Batchelor.

Turenge leaned across the desk and, for the first time, looked menacing. 'I mean you have told her that if she answers questions she will be able to return to France. Do not make promises that you do not mean.'

This time Batchelor's mood changed. Up to that point he had been relentlessly friendly throughout the interrogation process. But now he felt his manner was being mistaken for weakness. He too leaned forward over the desk.

'Monsieur,' he said, 'if I have sympathy for anybody, it's for the little children who no longer have a daddy because you killed him. I don't care *that* much [he snapped his biro and flung both pieces in opposite directions] for the woman you call your wife.'

Turenge backed off and did not raise the matter again.

Neil Morris, meanwhile, felt that Sophie Turenge was close to folding. She was crying more often, and she had admitted that Alain Turenge was not her husband. She said she wished to ring her Uncle Emile in Paris about the passports being false. He would tell her what to do, she said.

Morris: 'Who is Uncle Emile?'

S. Turenge: 'I cannot say.'

Morris: 'Do you work for your government?'

S. Turenge: 'I cannot say.'

Morris: 'What would happen if the police in your country caught someone who was spying for the government of another country?'

S. Turenge: 'Big trouble.'

Morris: 'Who for?'

S. Turenge: 'The one who was caught.'

There was a moment of relief among these torrid sessions. Grasping for a topic of small talk between interrogations, Neil Morris reached for the previous Saturday's *New Zealand Herald* which lay on the table in the interview room. 'What is your star sign?' he asked Sophie.

'Leo,' she said.

Morris read out her horoscope for the days ahead:

As this week progresses, you will find yourself becoming more and more involved in someone else's problems and by the middle of the week you will be so entangled there will be no escaping the situation which will restrict your freedom. Hold out the olive branch to those who have recently offended you, as it is better to have friends than enemies.

There was a moment's silence. Neither could believe it. It could have been planted to persuade her to co-operate.

Then they laughed.

In the final hours of interrogation on Monday morning, Sophie hinted to Morris that she was after all ready to talk.

S. Turenge: 'I want to speak to a lawyer about being a parrot.'
Morris: 'You mean about talking? Telling the truth?'
S. Turenge: 'Of course.'

Later in the week, when she had an opportunity to discuss this proposal with her lawyer, Sophie changed her mind. She and the lawyer were to claim subsequently that the comment had been misunderstood; that she mentioned the parrot because of saying the same thing over and over again. Morris remained convinced that she had been prepared to co-operate with the police in some measure, if it meant that she could return to France.

Apart from Sophie Turenge's admission that she was not Alain's wife, the couple made no major concessions in interrogation and stuck with their pre-arranged story to explain their presence and movements on the Auckland waterfront on 10 July. At 11.30 a.m. on Monday 15 July, they were arrested in the presence of their solicitor on charges of entering New Zealand on false passports and refusing to provide evidence of identification. Sophie Turenge faced the additional charge of making a false declaration, namely that she was married. They were taken under escort to Mt Eden Prison.

The Turenges' court appearances caused the police considerable anxiety. First there was the question of security. It was possible that other French agents were still in the country and might try to release them.* Then there were the initial charges. They were not of themselves serious; it was probable that the pair would be released on bail, which would give them an opportunity to disappear if their employer had made plans for such an eventuality.

After their first lower court appearance on Tuesday 16 July, at which they pleaded not guilty and had their names suppressed, they *were* granted bail. But it was on bonds of $2,000 each with a surety of $2,000 each. They said they were unable to find sureties – the French government could hardly come forward with the money when the couple were still denying any connection with them.

Following a subsequent hearing initiated by their lawyer the next day, however, the surety provision was waived and they were granted $4,500 self-bail each. This meant they could be released until the charges were heard in court on 27 July. The police agonised over the next step. Should they take the risk, allow the Turenges to be released and try to tail them for ten days? Or should they contrive additional charges to keep them in custody? After consultation with police headquarters in Wellington, they finally agreed to lay new charges. But the decision was not made until the Turenges had been released from Mt Eden at 5.45 p.m. and collected by their lawyer, Gerard Curry.

What followed was a chase sequence worthy of the Keystone Cops: Gerard Curry and the Turenges leading in the lawyer's Alfa Romeo, a congregation of radio, television and newspaper journalists behind and sometimes around them, a Red Squad car, and Detective Sergeant Terry Batchelor trying to penetrate the journalists' ranks to re-arrest the French couple. This unruly convoy made its way in to Auckland at high speed. The city had never before seen anything like it.

*They were.

Everybody in the relevant positions of responsibility – police, defence counsel, politicians – had underestimated the degree of media interest that the *Rainbow Warrior* bombing would generate, and not simply in New Zealand but on the international scene. In the minds of journalists, however – and probably those of the public at large – the situation had irresistible ingredients: it appeared to constitute New Zealand's first instance of international terrorism; it seemed that the act of violence had been carried out by a government officially 'friendly' to New Zealand; it had been directed against a pacifist target. Most newsworthy of all, however, the story seemed likely to focus on real-life spies, to throw open to public gaze the normally obscure workings of a major Western intelligence agency. Further, if rumours about the Turenges' identity proved correct and journalists were able to establish their own links in a chain of evidence, the story might result in the fall of a major Western government. Intimations of Watergate, Woodward and Bernstein reverberated through newspaper offices in Auckland. These last elements too made the story a target for the attention of foreign journalists on a scale that New Zealand had never before experienced.

The whole situation had consequences that none of the parties foresaw. It provided a degree of competition unprecedented among Auckland journalists – particularly between the two daily newspapers, the *New Zealand Herald* and the *Auckland Star* – to be the first with news breaks. This was to lead Police Commissioner Ken Thompson to speak exasperatedly of 'a new aggressive attitude to reporting never before encountered in this country'. It also brought to some local journalists strings of 'rats' (other media outlets, especially overseas), again on a scale previously unknown. Several journalists, particularly those in radio, were rumoured to have earned fabulous sums of money in their employers' time.

The police were unprepared for this scenario and initially did not handle it well. They did appreciate that there would be a vast appetite for news about the enquiry, and that the public had a right to know what was going on. But in their

view that right was subject to the police's own need to conduct and conclude a successful enquiry. At the beginning of
the investigation they were holding two press conferences daily,
at 9.15 a.m. and 4.15 p.m. After three weeks this reduced to
one conference. In addition, Superintendent Galbraith frequently spent up to two hours a day speaking with journalists
individually.

The conferences were usually held in Senior Sergeant Trevor
Tozer's office, on the eighth floor of Auckland Central Police
Station (and two floors above the rooms where the Turenges
were being interrogated). The officer relaying information was
usually Superintendent Galbraith, who looked as if he found
the whole experience uncomfortable. He always greeted journalists politely, but then seemed tense and fidgeted with his
glasses while the spotlight was (literally) on him. He generally
read a statement from his own notes, updating the results of
police enquiries. Then he answered questions, formally and
nervously. On television, he looked besieged.

The *Herald* and the *Star* reporters were the only ones who
pressed questions emphatically, usually with an eye on one
another (each had assigned a team of reporters to the investigation, and the *Herald* often had two or three at the conferences). Where questions seemed out of line – because they
might prejudice investigations or seemed impolite – Sergeant
Tozer would butt in and say Superintendent Galbraith could
not or would not answer. The sessions lasted about 20 minutes.

The major worry of the police about the media centred on
early release of stories that might alert suspects still to be seen
or confuse witnesses yet to be interviewed; and stories that
might release evidence and be used subsequently by the defence
to claim that the possibility of a fair trial had been prejudiced.
Early in the investigation they tried to prevent the *Herald* running two stories: on the detention of the Turenges at the
Newmans depot on 12 July; and one which announced that
nine detectives were heading for Noumea in search of the *Ouvéa*
crew on 16 July. The *Herald* refused to co-operate and printed
the stories, apparently claiming that if they did not use them

other media would do so the following day.

These incidents and one other late in July (a story about Christine Cabon, broken by the *Star* when she was believed to be still in Israel) raised the possibility of news blackouts in the wake of acts of terrorism. The Commissioner of Police complained that problems had arisen 'because of a reluctance of editors to restrict publication of details . . . It is hard enough in the 80s to conduct a criminal investigation without people making statements to us fearful of the fact that information will become public knowledge immediately thereafter.' Some commentators proposed the establishment of a D notice system in New Zealand, similar to that in Britain, by which a committee of military and media representatives had the power to ban publication of stories affecting defence or national security. The D notice proposal was not taken further, however, and the media stuck steadfastly to their objective of disclosure in the public interest. The chairman of the New Zealand Editors' Committee of the Commonwealth Press Union spoke for newspapers when he said that any code preventing the publishing of news openly and reasonably sought was unthinkable. He received unexpected support from the New Zealand Prime Minister, who added that the insights shown by some newspapers into the *Rainbow Warrior* investigation were consistent with a vigorous press.

The preoccupations of the Turenges' lawyer, Gerard Curry, were related to those of the police. He wanted to ensure that his clients got a fair trial, and in particular that they were not publicly prejudged by media identification and speculation. He was carrying an additional burden. He had to work hard to persuade his principals in Paris that the Turenges would indeed receive a fair trial under the New Zealand justice system. Increasingly, his doubts on this matter were enlarged by the performance of the media rather than by those of the police or the justice system itself. He simply had not realised at the outset that he and the Turenges would be at the centre of an international news story; nor that this would provoke the unprecedentedly aggressive approach to reporting referred to

by the Commissioner. It came home to him with a vengeance
on the evening of 17 July.

Gerard Curry was angry as he drove through Auckland towards
his office in the centre of the city. There were about ten people
and five cars pursuing him. The Turenges, in the back, were
startled and ill at ease. When the car stopped at lights at the
intersection of Princes Street and Waterloo Quadrant, a television van pulled up alongside. The side door rolled back and
television lights glared into the car. This was too much for
Curry. He regarded it as a gross invasion of privacy, an indication that the Turenges were not going to be dealt with fairly
in a manner that the international community would believe
was consistent with notions of justice. He was close to getting
out of the car and making an immediate speech to that effect
to the assembled media; then he decided against it. Instead,
he sat through a green sequence of traffic lights, then shot off
when they turned amber, hoping that the convoy would be cut
off by the red light.

Some of the cars came through the intersection regardless
and continued the pursuit to Russell McVeagh's premises.
When Curry got there, he drove in through a parking building
at the rear of the office and had a caretaker bring down a barrier to prevent other traffic following. That other traffic
included Terry Batchelor and another detective, and a prison
van not far behind. Batchelor ran to the metal grille and asked
the caretaker to let him in. The caretaker declined with considerable conviction.

'Look,' said Batchelor, presenting his identification. 'Police
Department. Will you let me through, please.' This was said
more sternly and the caretaker gave way. Batchelor and his
colleague, convinced that the Turenges could escape, raced
through the carpark and into the building's back lift. Once
they were inside, they realised they did not know what floor
the Russell McVeagh office was on. They would have to stop
at each one. On the first floor there was somebody waiting
at the lift and Batchelor asked for directions. But the man was

Japanese and said something incomprehensible. Finally they arrived at the 15th floor and found the office.

The first person they saw was one of the firm's junior associates. He asked them to wait one floor down in the conference room. Batchelor was not going to be fobbed off and said no, he would remain where the Turenges were. Then one of the partners came out and, smiling, also invited him to repair to the conference room.

'I'm afraid I've got to insist,' said Batchelor. 'I must see them.'

'Why?'

'Because I've been directed to re-arrest them.'

The lawyer asked what for and Batchelor told him the new charges: bringing property into the country which had been dishonestly obtained. The lawyer was appalled.

'But that's simply a duplication of the immigration charges.'

'I'm not in a position to comment,' Batchelor told him, feeling he was being further stalled. 'I'm only carrying out orders.'

The partner then agreed to take him to the Turenges, but asked that they be allowed to confer with their lawyer for 20 minutes. Batchelor agreed. He went down the corridor to an adjacent office and confirmed that the couple were there. The Turenges' faces visibly dropped when they saw him. 'Whenever you come, it is bad news,' Sophie was to tell him later. Then he posted the other detective outside the door and rang Superintendent Galbraith.

Half an hour later the Turenges emerged from the office and Batchelor formally arrested them on the new charges. He escorted them down to the carpark and out through a basement exit into Durham Lane, avoiding the journalists who had the building encircled. The Turenges climbed into the police van and were taken back to Mt Eden. They were not released from custody again.

The initial problem the police faced with the Turenges was an unusual one: they had caught their suspects before establishing a chain of evidence that linked them to the crime. Hence the need for passport, immigration and property charges. These were holding actions only.

Two weeks later, the situation had changed. More evidence had come to the police from the public that placed the Turenges in significant locations in suspicious cirumstances. Eight policemen sent to Norfolk Island had interviewed the *Ouvéa* crew and returned with forensic evidence that explosives had been stored in the yacht's hold. Documents from the *Ouvéa* indicated meetings between the crew and the Turenges. The police were now able to establish evidence of conspiracy involving the Turenges, of arson, and – by implication – of homicide. Detectives had also gone to Sydney to interview Xavier Maniguet; and to Papeete to speak to François Verlet. Further supporting evidence was expected from police despatched to New Caledonia, Switzerland and France.

At Mt Eden Prison on 23 July, therefore, in the presence of their lawyer, Detective Sergeant Batchelor was able to formally charge Alain and Sophie Turenge with conspiracy to commit arson, with wilfully damaging the vessel *Rainbow Warrior* by means of explosives, and with the murder of Fernando Pereira. The charges were heard in court the following day and this time there was no possibility of bail. The couple were remanded until 14 August. Further remands would see them remain in custody until a depositions hearing more than three months later. The New Zealand police would need that time to conduct their largest-ever investigation, to gather evidence from around the globe. Sophie and Alain Turenge, who, their lawyer said, 'proclaimed their innocence to the world', accepted the outcome stoically.

Louis-Pierre Dillais, alias Jean Louis Dormand, leader of the French sabotage team, flew out of New Zealand from Christchurch the day before the Turenges were charged with murder. The bombers themselves, Jacques Camurier and Alain Tonel, left Mt Cook the same day and travelled via Wellington and Rotorua to reach Auckland on 26 July. Why did they return

to Auckland from the South Island? Was consideration given
to a plan to spring their colleagues from custody? Alain
Turenge was to tell a police officer subsequently that in any
country other than a 'friendly' one, he would have been rescued
by fellow agents. They would arrive, take hostages, and simply
shoot them until their colleague was released.

Tonel and Camurier, however, flew out of Auckland for
Papeete. No word was heard of them again. French authorities
subsequently refused to answer questions about them from the
New Zealand police, and this after information had been passed
on, albeit reluctantly, about Cabon, Maniguet, Verge, Barcelo,
Andries, Alain Mafart and Dominique Prieur. The 'third team'
was to prove strictly off-limits as far as official co-operation
was concerned. Even Bernard Tricot was unable to find out
anything about it, other than to make passing reference to
Dillais. And it was Admiral Lacoste's and Charles Hernu's
inability or unwillingness to relay information about members
of that team to French Prime Minister Laurent Fabius that
caused those men to resign and sabotaged President François
Mitterrand's declared intention to obtain information and
'justice at the highest level'. Some secrets were never to be
revealed – at least not by the officials responsible for devising
them.

FOUR

France on Trial

July–September 1985

It took less than 24 hours for a representative of the government most strongly suspected of complicity in the *Rainbow Warrior* bombing to dissociate his country from the sabotage – and in the most emphatic terms. 'In no way was France involved,' the political counsellor at the New Zealand French Embassy declared to the press on 11 July. 'The French government does not deal with its opponents in such ways. France is not worried by the anti-Mururoa campaign planned by Greenpeace, which said it would respect international law.' He added the embassy's sympathies to the crew of the *Rainbow Warrior* for their double bereavement, the loss of a boat and of a shipmate.

In spite of other theories (that the CIA might have been involved because of the Rongelap evacuation, for example) logic did suggest a French connection: who had something to gain by stopping the *Rainbow Warrior* reaching Mururoa? But when evidence of that connection began to accumulate, it seemed so transparent that the New Zealand police initially considered the possibility that clues had been planted to frame the French government: the Zodiac abandoned on Tamaki Drive, the oxygen bottles with French markings, the highly visible antics of the *Ouvéa* crew (of which more was heard each day), and the easy apprehension of the Turenges, who would have left New Zealand but for shoddy documentation and a total ignorance of the New Zealand legal system. Could all this be the result of activities planned by one of the Western world's major intelligence agencies? Or the work of amateurs, mercenaries perhaps? Or a calculated attempt to fraudulently implicate the French Socialist Government in an effort to embarrass it and bring it down?

The most fruitful opportunities to resolve these questions would come from interrogation of the Turenges and an investigation of their activities; and apprehension – if possible – of the *Ouvéa* crew. The Turenges were in custody; the yachtsmen had to be intercepted at Norfolk Island or New Caledonia.

Eight New Zealand detectives and one forensic scientist from the Department of Scientific and Industrial Research flew to Norfolk Island on 15 July. They found the *Ouvéa* crew (minus Maniguet, who had flown to Sydney) in rooms at the South Pacific Hotel, at 10 p.m. As had happened in the case of the Turenges, the police were in contact with their suspects before they had sufficient evidence with which to confront and charge them.

The detectives, whose party included two French speakers (one of whom was Constable Nick Hall), interviewed the Frenchmen throughout the night, together and individually. On only two occasions did they feel they were making progress. One was when Velche and Berthelo claimed never to have been in Auckland; presented with evidence that they had been sighted there, they changed their stories and said they had forgotten. The other near-breakthrough seemed to come when Berthelo was questioned on his own. He showed considerable anxiety. Indeed, he appeared close to violence at one point. He exhibited what could only be described as the demeanour of a guilty man.

The next day the *Ouvéa* was searched. Documents were removed, others photocopied. Some would establish meetings with other French agents, especially the Turenges; a map with the address of a Ponsonby art studio that proved to be a link with Christine Cabon; and a photograph was found of Berthelo in a red woollen hat, which appeared to match one of the Tamaki Drive descriptions of the lone frogman in the

Zodiac on the night of the bombing. Fingerprints were taken, footwear checked; forensic swabbings from the bilges picked up what were eventually identified as traces of high explosive, probably from detonator cords.

Analysis of all this material provided ample evidence to arrest the *Ouvéa* crew on grounds of involvement in the conspiracy to bomb the *Rainbow Warrior*. But such analysis was to take some time. Even passport checks, which would have revealed that the documents were false, would take at least five days. Norfolk's Australian administrators warned the New Zealand police that they would have to issue warrants by 2 p.m. on 16 July or allow the yacht to depart as planned that day for New Caledonia, from where the crew intended to fly to France on 26 July. After consultation with Superintendent Galbraith in Auckland, Senior Sergeant Lex Denby reluctantly told the *Ouvéa* crew they were free to leave. The New Zealand police decided to assemble the evidence carefully and then intercept the Frenchmen at Noumea to lay watertight charges.

That evening Velche, Audrenc and Berthelo boarded the yacht at Cascade Pier on the northern side of the island and disappeared into the darkness. The *Ouvéa* was never seen again. Within three weeks the crew was hiding in France, transported there by means that have never been established. The New Zealand police had their evidence, but had lost their suspects.

Xavier Maniguet too escaped arrest. He was intercepted by Australian and New Zealand detectives at a Sydney picture theatre, where he had been sitting (quite by chance, he claimed) next to an Australian Frenchman, a former trade commissioner in the city, who belonged to an organisation that advised the French Senate on expatriate affairs.

A whole night's inteviewing produced numerous inconsistencies in Maniguet's story. But he stuck glibly and politely to the fiction that he had simply hired the *Ouvéa* with its crew and knew nothing about them, nor about the *Rainbow Warrior* bombing. Again, at this stage, there was insufficient solid evidence on which to base a warrant for arrest. He had to be released, and he made his way back to France via Singapore, home of François Verlet.

Next agent to evade the New Zealand police was Christine Cabon, alias Frédérique Bonlieu, working on an American-supervised excavation at Pardes Hanna near Tel Aviv. According to the Israeli police, the telegram from the New Zealand police asking them to hold Bonlieu for questioning by a New Zealand detective arrived the same day, 25 July, as another telegram from France. The French message, which Cabon received first, told her to return home at once because her father was critically ill. An American student working on the excavation with Bonlieu said that the Frenchwoman came into her dormitory looking pale and anxious, and announced that she had to leave for France immediately. She flew out of Israel the following day.

In fact, of course, her father was already dead. The telegram was a coded message from the DGSE warning her to leave Israel before the New Zealand police got to her. That she received it before the Israeli police acted on the request from New Zealand raises a strong possibility that they co-operated in her escape. Given that she had worked previously for the Israeli Secret Service, this would not be surprising.

Back in New Zealand, the *Auckland Star* was on to a story about Bonlieu's infiltration of Greenpeace and the fact that she was being sought by the police.* The *Star* was asked by the police not to run the item because of the danger that it might alert Bonlieu to the fact that she was under suspicion. The paper went ahead and published it, however, on the grounds that too many people now knew about the infiltration, and that if the *Star* withheld it, others would publish (the *New Zealand Herald* ran it the following day). When Bonlieu *was* found to have disappeared, the police's first reaction was to

---

*It was strange that the *Star* broke this story. One of the *New Zealand Herald* reporters covering the investigation, Karen Mangnall, had lived with Bonlieu/Cabon.

blame the *Star* story. It appeared several hours before the time
Bonlieu left Israel; someone could have been supplying her with
information from New Zealand by telephone.

On 26 July, the New Zealand police obtained warrants for the
arrest of the *Ouvéa* crew on arson and murder charges – the
same as those on which the Turenges had been arrested three
days earlier. By this time the yacht had disappeared, however.
Its last message had been radioed to New Caledonia on 21 July,
and was clearly false (a crew member claimed they were 50
kilometres north-west of the Ile des Pins). A search by a Royal
New Zealand Air Force Orion and a private plane failed to
locate the vessel.

It is believed that American authorities declined to act on
a New Zealand request to locate the yacht through use of one
of its KH11 military satellites. This apparent refusal to assist
the New Zealand investigation – in spite of the United States'
repeated and strong condemnation of international terrorism
– is thought to have been linked to the American administration's strong disagreement with New Zealand over port
access for nuclear ships. It was matched over the following
weeks by an extreme slowness on behalf of the State Department and Interpol in Washington to act on a request from New
Zealand for information about associates of Christine Cabon
in the United States, particularly one contact in Los Angeles.
New Zealand authorities attributed this too to fallout from
the Anzus row.*

There were strong suspicions among members of the New
Zealand government, intelligence agencies and police, that co-
operation with American and British authorities was being
limited because of New Zealand's non-nuclear policy. This
suspicion was enhanced by the unwillingness of both allied
governments to condemn the bombing, even when it was

---

*The FBI eventually staked out a Los Angeles apartment belonging to a Greek
woman, Antigone Zournatzis, who had taken part in the Pardes Hannah excavation with Cabon in July. Subsequent to the bombing of the *Rainbow Warrior*,
she too disappeared.

acknowledged to have been the work of the French government. Subsequently, both the former US Ambassador to the United Nations, Jeane Kirkpatrick, and the British Prime Minister, Margaret Thatcher, were to deny that the bombing had represented state-sponsored terrorism. 'The two are totally different,' Margaret Thatcher asserted, but would not specify in what way. This was a position with which the New Zealand government strongly disagreed.

By the third week of the *Rainbow Warrior* investigation, New Zealand police were in Europe (England, Switzerland, and France briefly) and a three-man team would soon be dispatched to France for a lengthy stay. The French enquiries were to prove most difficult. After initial co-operation from Interpol France, the New Zealand police were told they would have to proceed by way of laborious Rogatory Commissions.* Information and queries from the New Zealand police were required to go from the New Zealand Secretary of Foreign Affairs to his counterpart in Paris. If the validity of the questions was accepted on the basis of supporting evidence, the French judicial police were engaged to carry out the actual enquiry. The queries and evidence were then divided up according to French judicial districts, and judges were appointed to hear evidence gathered by the judicial police in those districts. The judges themselves then made reports on the evidence *they* had heard, and these constituted the Rogatory Commission's reports.

New Zealand police in France were allowed (at least in theory) to co-operate with French investigators, to suggest lines of enquiry and who should be interviewed, and to draw attention to significant evidence already gathered. They were not permitted to conduct independent enquiries, to interview anyone, to take statements, or to keep copies of French statements. In effect, they could not gather any kind of evidence that would

---

*Previous New Zealand police enquiries in France had not been channelled through the Rogatory Commission system. Being required to do so in this instance slowed the investigation considerably.

be admissible in a New Zealand court. It was a frustrating situation in which to work (or – as was frequently the case – to be unable to work).

In the first week in August, events unrelated to the *Rainbow Warrior* enquiry may have had the effect of further impeding investigations in France, and possibly in the United States. On 7 August, eight countries signed the South Pacific Nuclear-Free Zone Treaty at the South Pacific Forum in Rarotonga. This document, initiated by Australia and New Zealand, sought to prevent the storage, dumping, manufacture and testing of nuclear weapons in the South Pacific. Its protocols, which the nuclear powers themselves would be asked to sign, called for an end to nuclear testing in the Pacific and for the renunciation of the use or threat of use of nuclear weapons against any nation in the region.

The French government made no immediate response to the treaty (and was expected to ignore it). Within the American State Department, however, there was some relief that it was a milder document than had been anticipated, and officials joked that they expected to be informed about its text via messages in floating bottles. Clearly, the American administration was not going to regard it as anything more serious than an irritant. It *was* a serious matter for the states of the South Pacific, however, who were trying to ensure that whatever the superpowers did elsewhere, their region would not become an arena for nuclear warfare nor a dumping ground for radioactive waste. It was also a further attempt to prick the conscience of France, testing its weapons so far from its own borders and so close to the backyards of other nations.

By the second week in August 1985, allegations in the French media that representatives of the French government had planned and ordered the *Rainbow Warrior* bombing were becoming more frequent and more insistent. French journalists were uncovering confirmation of what the New Zealand police and Security Intelligence Service had been able to deduce three days after the Turenges had been taken into custody: it *was* a French government operation. As the French accusations became more specific, naming the DGSE and authorities 'high in the military intelligence command', President François Mitterrand decided the time had come to stop leaks that were fertilising the growth of rumours: rumours that would soon implicate the Elysée Palace. He ordered his Prime Minister, Laurent Fabius, to conduct a 'rigorous enquiry' into the affair. On 8 August, Fabius announced that the enquiry would be carried out by 65-year-old Bernard Tricot, a former secretary-general of the Elysée Palace in the time of President de Gaulle. This appointment was expected to be acceptable to all political factions in France. Initially, it was.

Mitterrand, meanwhile, wrote to New Zealand Prime Minister David Lange in terms which suggested he himself had had no part in the operation:

> I wish to tell you . . . how much I and the Government of the republic abhor the criminal attack committed on your territory which no excuse can justify . . . The Prime Minister . . . has given orders for all possible extra help to be given your investigations, while we are also naturally pursuing our own. I intend that this matter should be handled with the greatest possible severity and that your country should be able to count on the full collaboration of France.

While Bernard Tricot got down to work, calling for relevant files and interviewing senior military and intelligence personnel, a process of disinformation began. It was initiated by the French intelligence agencies and carried into the French media largely by journalists with links with the DGSE (Pascal Krop, co-author of a history of the French intelligence services, alleged that at least 50 French journalists were DGSE collaborators in 1984).

The first story was that the *Rainbow Warrior* was destroyed because Greenpeace was being manipulated by 'communist states' and that Fernando Pereira himself was a KGB agent. It was also claimed that the British, Australian and New

Zealand secret services knew of the operation and allowed the bombing to take place to discredit France. Other versions claimed that the Russians had blown up the vessel, the British MI6, the CIA, the South African Secret Service, even the Japanese (to protect the whaling industry): anyone, in fact, except France. These other agencies had allegedly set out to frame the French government.

The stories about Fernando Pereira were especially vicious and untrue. Because he had worked for a short time for a communist paper in Amsterdam, he was identified as a communist and by extension as a terrorist, who not only had links with the KGB but also with the Baader-Meinhoff gang. From this information, it could be deduced that the act of killing him was deliberate, that he was the main target of the bombs that destroyed the boat.

The New Zealand press too was coming up with some misleading stories. Karen Mangnall had alleged in the *New Zealand Herald* that the *Rainbow Warrior* bombers 'may be French mercenaries – former soldiers from an agency like the Foreign Legion who are available, for big money, for sabotage assignments'. In a subsequent story, she claimed that a mercenary known as Chabnes, who had links with right-wing settlers in New Caledonia, had come to New Zealand early in July to help plan the bombing. Later still, she reported that Frédérique Bonlieu, now unmasked as Christine Cabon, was undergoing plastic surgery because 'once her photograph was published in connection with the *Rainbow Warrior* bombing she was targeted to be killed' (in fact, Cabon had undergone surgery *before* she came to New Zealand).

The wildest conspiracy theories retained some credence after Bernard Tricot released his report on 20 August (after only a fortnight's deliberation). Predictably, it reflected an attempt at an orchestrated cover-up. It concluded that the French government had not ordered the sinking of the *Rainbow Warrior*, that there was no reason to believe that the DGSE instructed its agents to bomb the vessel, and that the crew of the *Ouvéa* (who presented themselves to the French police the day the report was released) could not be extradited to New Zealand to stand trial because they were French citizens. The report did concede that up to six DGSE agents had been sent to New Zealand; but Tricot alleged that their sole function had been to gather intelligence on Greenpeace.

In addition to giving the *Ouvéa* crew most of their correct names and listing details of their service records, the report also identified the Turenges, naming them as Alain Mafart and Dominique Prieur and thus confirming earlier stories in the French press. It emphasised that they too were in New Zealand in an intelligence gathering role only.

There were many errors and omissions (or deliberate false-hoods) in the Tricot report. It claimed that Dillais (identified as 'Dubast') had not gone to New Zealand, that none of the *Ouvéa* crew had visited Auckland, and that the agents had not met one another in New Zealand. There was no mention of the third team: Verlet, Tonel and Camurier.

Bernard Tricot himself seems to have had doubts about his totally misleading conclusions. He covered himself by noting: 'I am . . . obliged not to exclude the hypothesis that these officers might have conspired to keep part of the truth from me. I must also not ignore the possibility that the texts of the instructions for the missions . . . were not complete or could have been accompanied by oral comments which could have altered their meaning.'

After release of the report, Tricot told journalists that he had been given exactly the same story by everybody he had interviewed. Was this too an indication that he suspected a conspiracy to deceive?

The Tricot report generated widespread disbelief and cynicism in France and New Zealand.* 'Tricot Washes Whiter' one

---

*One victim of the report's reception was Tricot's daughter Marie-Claude, who committed suicide on 6 September because she had been 'badly affected' by the disbelief and then scandal that surrounded her father's whitewash.

French newspaper proclaimed. It had admitted that at least five DGSE agents had been in New Zealand on or about the time the *Rainbow Warrior* had been blown up. To imply that this was mere coincidence – that they had had no part in the bombing – was more than most people could accept. The consensus in the French press was that it raised more questions than it answered. Further, because it was based on the testimony of the most senior defence and intelligence personnel, particularly Defence Minister Charles Hernu and DGSE Director Pierre Lacoste, it followed that should information in it prove to be incorrect, those men would be shown to have lied.

David Lange was angered by the transparent duplicity of the report, much of which he knew to be wrong in detail, and by the admission of an 'outrageous violation of our territory' by French agents, for which there had been no apology. As if aware of the need to mollify the New Zealand Prime Minister, Laurent Fabius wrote to him:

> We understand the emotion which a criminal outrage has raised [in New Zealand]. This emotion exists also in France . . . But the identification of those who committed that outrage has not yet been able to be made. We hope that the New Zealand authorities will arrive as quickly as possible at discovering the truth . . . The guilty, whoever they be, will have to pay for this crime . . . If it were to appear that criminal acts have been committed by French nationals, judicial action will be immediately exercised. The French Government is determined that no element should remain in the dark.

Fabius followed this statement with an announcement on 5 September that he had instructed Defence Minister Hernu to hold a new enquiry into allegations that the DGSE had mined the *Rainbow Warrior*. He emphasised that he wanted the truth; and that it would be unacceptable if it transpired that French agents had sunk the boat and caused loss of life.

While rumours about l'Affaire Greenpeace continued to simmer in the world's press, the French Cabinet appeared to decide on a propaganda offensive. Charles Hernu announced on 6 September that his country would continue its nuclear testing programme in the Pacific, and he confirmed that France was now capable of building neutron bombs – enhanced radiation weapons that killed people while minimising damage to buildings.

That same week President Mitterrand announced that he and Hernu would travel 14,000 kilometres to visit Moruroa on 14 September, to meet French ambassadors and high commissioners in the region and to emphasise his country's determination to maintain a strong strategic presence in the Pacific. The South Pacific prime ministers regarded this gesture as arrogant and provocative. Their view seemed confirmed when a spokesman for the president said on the atoll that opponents of nuclear tests there would be ignored, and that anyone who opposed French interests would be seen as an adversary. This was too much for David Lange, who responded the following day:

> We are an enemy of the nuclear threat and we are an enemy of testing nuclear weapons in the South Pacific. New Zealand did not buy into this fight. France put agents into New Zealand. France put spies into New Zealand. France lets off bombs in the Pacific. France puts its President in the Pacific to crow about it. It is not the New Zealand or Pacific way of doing things, but apparently it is the French way to win a French election.*

This statement, and the announcement the next day that France had postponed the visit to Paris by the New Zealand Deputy Prime Minister, Geoffrey Palmer, marked the lowest ebb of French-New Zealand relations since the *Rainbow Warrior* was sunk. Both countries seemed locked in a wrestler's embrace that neither could break. Then, four days later, came further developments which appeared to return the moral and political advantage to New Zealand.

---

*National Assembly elections were due the following March.

On 19 September *Le Monde*, which until this time had been exceedingly cautious in its coverage of l'Affaire Greenpeace, ran a lead story that shook the French government. It claimed that Hernu and two senior officers – one an aide to President Mitterrand – had authorised or had advance knowledge of the *Rainbow Warrior* sabotage. It quoted further DGSE sources to reveal that three French agents, by then back in France, had taken explosives to New Zealand and delivered them to two further agents. Those two had then passed the explosives to two French military frogmen who sank the Greenpeace boat. The frogmen later escaped from New Zealand by air.

Hernu denied the charges, apparently angrily. But reverberations continued. President Mitterrand, fed up with the scandal that would not disappear, ordered Fabius to shake up the 'competent services'. And Fabius in turn asked Hernu to question Admiral Lacoste and senior military personnel about the fresh revelations. The current and former chiefs of staff of the armed forces, General Jean Saulnier and Jeannon Lacaze, indicated to Hernu that they had not given any instructions that could have led to the events described by *Le Monde*.

Lacoste, however, refused to answer the questions put to him: '. . . I would endanger the lives of certain officers and warrant officers who have carried out particularly dangerous missions recently or in the more distant past. The precedent set by such a disclosure would be likely to dry up later recruitment for secret operations and endanger the entire security system . . .' Which officers would be endangered? Clearly not those already named in the Tricot report. The only conclusion to be drawn from Lacoste's stance was that he was unable to deny the allegations in *Le Monde*, because in substance they were true; and that he was protecting the as yet unnamed members of the 'third team', responsible for the actual bombing.

Subsequent events moved with the force of inevitability. The following day Prime Minister Fabius proposed to President Mitterrand that Admiral Lacoste be dismissed from his directorship of the DGSE; and that the president accept the tendered resignation of Charles Hernu as Minister of Defence.* These recommendations were accepted. Two days later Fabius appeared on television with his new Defence Minister, Paul Quilès, to announce that DGSE agents *had* sunk the *Rainbow Warrior*, that they had been acting under orders, and that there had been a cover-up of the whole operation. In a separate message conveyed to the Prime Minister of New Zealand by the French Ambassador in that country, Fabius added that he was 'deeply sorry' that the affair had affected relations between New Zealand and France. He proposed a meeting in New York between the French External Relations Minister, Roland Dumas, and the New Zealand Deputy Prime Minister, Geoffrey Palmer, to begin discussions on the question of compensation.

L'Affaire Greenpeace had reached its climax. The dominoes had toppled backwards from the Turenges to the minister responsible for their service and to its director. They would go no further. It was never subsequently established that Fabius and Mitterrand knew of the bombing in advance; the weight of evidence appeared to confirm that they did not. In New Zealand, David Lange had seen a chain of involvement from the agents to the French government, of which he had been aware for two months, finally acknowledged by that government: not as a result of the release of evidence by the New Zealand police (this was being reserved for the agents' trial), but as a consequence of the persistence of the French press. Lange felt vindicated and toned down his rhetoric accordingly. While he now described the bombing as 'a sordid act of international state-backed terrorism', he commended the French government for finally getting to the bottom of the affair and openly acknowledging responsibility. The issue now became one of compensation, he said. Under international law the

---

*Subsequently, Fabius confirmed that it was Hernu who had given the verbal order to 'neutralise' the *Rainbow Warrior*. The former Defence Minister was down but not out: six months later he was awarded the Legion of Honour and was being spoken of as a likely Socialist candidate to succeed Mitterrand. He showed no sign of being repentent or dishonoured by his involvement in the *Rainbow Warrior* sinking.

consequences of the declaration of responsibility which the French had made were compensation for the aggrieved nation and an offer of reparation for an affront to its sovereignty. The next moves in l'Affaire Greenpeace, it was assumed, would be judicial ones. And they would include the trial of the 'Turenges' on charges of arson and murder.

In the months leading up to the trial of Alain Mafart and Dominique Prieur, the New Zealand Justice Department's major worry was that French commandos or hired mercenaries would attempt to remove them from custody or kill them to ensure their silence. Intelligence warnings about such possibilities came from two sources. Auckland police knew of locally based mercenaries who claimed to have been offered $25,000 to spring the French couple from Mt Eden prison, enlisting the help of other inmates. If the mercenaries' claims were true, it was assumed the initiative had come from right-wing sources in New Caledonia. The mercenaries themselves were quoted as saying that the payment proposed for the job was 'ludicrously small'.

Far more serious was a threat communicated by the SIS from external intelligence sources. These reports indicated that elements within the French military and security services were prepared to go to any lengths to prevent a trial taking place – with all the revelations and attention that entailed – and to remove the possibility that the 'Turenges' might reveal who they were, the nature of the operation on which they had been engaged, and the fact that it had been an official one. This danger was regarded as especially strong at the time when the French government had *not* admitted responsibility for Operation Rainbow Warrior; and while the couple were still in Mt Eden, because of that prison's relative lack of security. Even after Fabius admitted his government's role in the affair, the danger remained, intelligence reports suggested, because some of Mafart's and Prieur's colleagues resented the manner in which they had been neglected by their service and left to take responsibility for the *Rainbow Warrior* bombing, and planned to rescue them.

The external threat had to be taken seriously. Mafart himself had already admitted that he would have expected to be rescued quickly by his colleagues from an 'unfriendly' country. And Mt Eden could be penetrated without undue difficulty. A police officer described one possible scenario:

> The best time to arrive would be during visiting hours, because people walk literally up to the main gates. The first thing you are confronted with is a barrier and a man in an office who controls it. If he approaches you, you simply say, 'I've come to see so-and-so' (not mentioning the French prisoners), and he wouldn't question it. Then you proceed to the male quarters, arrive at the gate and press the buzzer. A small door within the door opens and a prison guard asks what you want. Again, you say you have come to see so-and-so. Then he'd just open the door and let you in.
>
> At this point you would turn hard left, towards the security block. You'd pull a gun on the prison officer and he would be obliged to do your bidding. He would take you to Mafart and you'd then get him out of there, continuing to use the prison officer as a hostage. Someone might lose his head and want to tackle you on the way out, but you'd probably get away with it.

The New Zealand government's committee on terrorism weighed the evidence from external intelligence and considered steps to circumvent the threat. Until early September, however, their options were limited by the fact that Mafart and Prieur had to appear weekly in court for remands. This meant they could not be moved from Auckland, and that it was convenient for them to be in the same institution, close to Auckland city, so that journeys to and from court would be as short and secure as possible.

Meanwhile the police on Operation Rainbow had evidence that the Turenges were communicating in cypher, and wondered whether this too might represent a threat to security. The prisoners played chess, informing one another of moves by letter. When police referred the moves to people experienced in the game, they were found to be illogical – they certainly did not represent the kind of tactics that would win games. In addition, in other letters the couple exchanged, there were whole phrases that did not make sense, or which seemed densely proverbial. Again, police concluded it was some kind of cypher. But their experts were unable to make sense of it without an overall frame of reference.

The police had similar difficulties with a pocket computer that had been taken from the couple when they were arrested. This had the capacity to store as many as 1,400 characters. The police could extract nothing from it, and the manufacturers in Auckland were unable to do any better, other than to determine that 250 characters were stored in the computer's secret mode, which could not be opened without the programming code. Finally, experts in Japan did break the code but could release only 254 decimal points arranged in lines of varying length. Code specialists were unable to say what – if anything – they might signify.

A related matter that gave the police cause for further concern was the apparent interception of a micro-dot of the drug LSD sent to Dominique Prieur on a page of the paper *Le Monde*. The material was heart shaped and coated in cellophane. When it was referred to the Department of Scientific and Industrial Research for tests, scientists reported that they were 99 per cent certain that the substance was LSD. After a second test, they said the results were inconclusive. One more test was necessary for complete certainty, but they had already used up the entire sample, which had amounted to about 400 milligrams.

When Prieur was questioned in Mt Eden about this material, she was shocked at the implied accusation and got up and walked from the interview room. Police were baffled by the incident. The idea that she would ingest the drug herself, or make use of it as prison 'currency', just did not not fit with what they had observed of her character and demeanour. They took the matter no further, deciding that either the DSIR analysis had been wrong, or that someone had sent the drug to her without her knowledge or approval.

The incident did have public relations consequences. The French lawyer sent by the DGSE to observe the couple's earliest court appearances, Phillipe Derouin, claimed that the drug accusation and the taking of newspapers for examination was a technique used by the New Zealand police to break the prisoners psychologically. He further claimed that they were being treated like 'common law criminals' and being held by the New Zealand government simply to put pressure on French authorities. In reply, New Zealand police rejected the notion that people charged with major criminal acts should receive special treatment simply because they were army officers; they said a New Zealand officer would be in exactly the same position.

The prisoners themselves had no complaints about their treatment, although they were not coping equally well with the experience of incarceration. Alain Mafart seemed relaxed and philosophical about his fate. He accepted circumstances that could not be altered. He occupied a single cell in the maximum security block at Mt Eden, with a bed, table and stool. During the day he wore loose prison-made jeans and a baggy brown jacket. He was allowed into the exercise yard mornings and afternoons with three or four other prisoners and used it to walk and jog. Otherwise he spent his time in the cell reading or playing chess.

People who spoke to him were impressed by his imperturbability. He told Terry Batchelor that he held no grudge against the New Zealand police. Mafart was a professional, so was the detective; both had simply been doing their jobs. 'As long as you have your health', he kept repeating, 'that is all that really matters.' On another occasion, smiling, he said to Batchelor, 'You have no idea the number of things that went wrong here.' In fact, he said, things had gone wrong in France too. And he had had to go to the funerals of many, many friends. 'It has been a bad year, a very bad year.' And yet he said it resignedly as one who came to terms with such things.

He remained equable when he was subjected to banter or even insults. He told Batchelor that every bad thing people did put a black spot on their hearts. Batchelor replied that involvement in the *Rainbow Warrior* bombing must have bespeckled Mafart's organ, and the agent just smiled. He also smiled when another detective, English-born and handcuffed to him in the holding cells at the District Court, said: 'You're nothing but a dirty little French spy. Do you know the French have never won a battle in the past 500 years?'

When a journalist managed to insinuate his way into Mt Eden as a visitor, Mafart remained relentlessly polite. He sat down in a visitor's booth, divided by a pane of glass, and said hello through his telephone. Told he was speaking to a journalist, he kept smiling and said, 'I'm sorry. You will have to talk with my lawyer. You understand I cannot say anything.' Asked by the journalist if he knew he was accused of being a spy, he shrugged and smiled again: 'I'm sorry you will have to talk to my lawyer. That is all I can say. I'm sorry.' And he hung up his phone, shrugged, smiled again, and sauntered away with his hands in his jacket pockets.

Dominique Prieur, confronted by the same journalist, was far more abrupt. She was brought to him in a large interview room with about a dozen chairs. 'I don't know him,' she told prison officers. Them recognising him from a court appearance, she cried out '*Journaliste!*' and left the room at once.

Unlike Mafart, Prieur was permitted to wear her own clothes. She slept in a cell detached from those of other inmates and was allowed out for ten hours each day (to his two and a half). She helped with domestic chores in the women's section, read prolifically (French fiction) and jogged and played netball with other prisoners. On weekends she was allowed to listen to radio or watch television in the afternoons.

According to those who spoke with her, however, she was not as well adjusted to her circumstances as Mafart. She burst into tears when Batchelor told her that Auckland Airport was not under specific police observation the day she was taken into custody, and that they would probably have been able to leave New Zealand if they had not returned the camper van. She agreed with Batchelor that it had been a bad mistake to carry passports that could so easily be proved to be false, and she said she would take this up with the appropriate authorities when she returned to France.

But although she could and would chat, she gave an impression of being profoundly sad, close to depression. And unlike Mafart she had a spouse, Paris fireman Joel Prieur, and she missed him terribly. He for his part had only come to know of her arrest when he saw her photograph (taken by an *Auckland Star* photographer) on French television news. It had been a sharp shock.

Weekly court appearances in Auckland were no longer necessary once Mafart and Prieur had, through their lawyer, agreed to a 4 November date for the preliminary hearing of charges against them. At that point, still worried about the relative insecurity of Mt Eden for prisoners of their status, the police and Justice Department decided to place them in separate institutions. On 5 September, Alain Mafart was moved to New Zealand's only maximum security prison, at Paremoremo, 30 kilometres north of Auckland; Prieur was flown to the Women's Prison in Christchurch, over 600 kilometres away.

As the sole remand prisoner in Paremoremo, Mafart was kept apart from other inmates who had been convicted on a range of New Zealand's most serious crimes (murder, rape, robbery with violence). But he was not in 'solitary confinement', as some French newspapers alleged, nor was he languishing in spartan conditions. The cell included a chair, a foam rubber mattress on a latticed bed, and a radio. He had access to a communal television and had morning and evening papers delivered to him. He was allowed to make and receive telephone calls to and from his lawyer and the French Embassy. He could eat chocolate and smoke cigarettes provided he paid for them himself. Meals included a choice of roast beef or chicken, with roast potatoes, pumpkin and green peas or silver beet, followed by custard and plum duff and jelly. As before, Mafart adjusted rapidly to his new circumstances. In addition to his reading, which now included New Zealand poetry, he resumed playing the classical guitar and began investigating learning Spanish and playing the bagpipes. Staff found him relaxed and co-operative. He was a popular prisoner.

Again, Dominique Prieur was less happy. She was still missing contact with her husband and her mother (Mafart's parents were dead), and her fellow prisoners at Christchurch, with whom she was allowed to mix, seemed a poor lot: women convicted of violent offences, some of them appearing to her to be mentally defective. In addition, she was separated from her lawyer, who was now more than an hour's plane journey away in Auckland.

Accepting the validity of some of her reservations and realising that she would have to be back in Auckland for her preliminary hearing and trial, the Justice Department decided to fortify the armed services corrective establishment at Ardmore, South Auckland, especially for her. More than 70 soldiers were put to work ringing the barracks with barbed wire, and jumbo bins were placed along the driveway to force approaching vehicles to slow and follow a zigzag route. The result, in the words of a nearby resident, was to create a 'mini-Colditz'. Police and prison service officers were to guard Prieur inside the wire, but outside the New Zealand Army's crack SAS unit was based at Papakura, only ten kilometres away.

When Prieur arrived back from Christchurch on 18 September the SAS was very much in evidence, armed and surrounding the paddock where she was landed by helicopter. For a few moments her spirits soared. She had not been told where she was going. As she stepped down into the green grass she thought she was released and that the journey was the first step on her trip home to France. Then she was escorted to a barracks behind the barbed wire 400 metres away where the situation was explained to her.

Ardmore was not a great advance on Christchurch. She could see her counsel more often, and she was removed from contact with people she had found offensive. But she was isolated for most of each day, being the sole prisoner. The announcement on 23 September that she would be visited by her husband before the preliminary hearing lifted her spirits a little. No plans were made for a visit by her father, a down-and-out pensioner who lived in New Caledonia and was long estranged from Dominique and her mother.

By October 1985 it was clear that Mafart and Prieur were the only French agents who would stand trial in New Zealand for the *Rainbow Warrior* bombing. French law did not allow for the extradition of French nationals. Despite Prime Minister Fabius's declaration that 'the guilty, whoever they may be, have to pay for this crime', and President Mitterrand's insistence in August on 'justice at the highest level', the French government showed no interest in handing the *Ouvéa* crew over to the New Zealand judicial system, nor in putting them on trial in France. And there was at that point insufficient evidence for warrants to be issued for the arrest of Louis-Pierre Dillais, Jacques Camurier and Alain Tonel (the New Zealand police had only just become aware of the existence of Camurier and Tonel). At the annual Interpol conference in Washington, the New Zealand Commissioner of Police, Ken Thompson, tried to discuss the *Rainbow Warrior* investigation with the French delegation but made no headway; the Frenchmen would not even speak to him. Meanwhile no information had yet reached New Zealand from the Rogatory Commission hearings in France itself. The three New Zealand police who had remained in France for two months had made little progress and were recalled in the middle of October.

The preliminary hearing of charges against the 'Turenges' was to begin in early November and expected to run for about six weeks. If a Lower Court judge ruled that the evidence was sufficient to warrant the charges, then the couple would be committed for trial to the New Zealand High Court in March 1986, and this would last a further two months.

Almost everybody involved nursed their own anxieties about this procedure. For Mafart and Prieur (and their lawyer), there was a possibility of a conviction and life sentence for murder (which could mean spending up to 15 years in a New Zealand prison). For the French government there was the prospect of months of international publicity arising from the hearing and the trial, which would expose the workings of the French secret service, its objectives and its bunglings. The trial itself would coincide with the National Assembly elections in France in 1986, ensuring maximum political discomfort for the government.

For the New Zealand police the major hurdle was organising a huge volume of complex evidence (more than 1,800 exhibits and just under 100 witnesses, some from abroad) in time for the preliminary hearing; their second problem was guaranteeing the safety of the defendants. External intelligence reports continued to warn that attempts could be made to release or eliminate the agents; locally, there remained the possibility that mercenaries or extremists might attempt to kill them. As if these threats were not enough to worry about, the Justice Department was faced with the prospect of having to cater in court for more than 100 journalists from France, England, Canada and Australia; and almost half that number from local media. The Auckland District Court had room for three journalists and about 20 members of the public.

In mid-October the department announced that the preliminary hearing and trial would be held in the number one courtroom in the old Supreme Court building in Auckland, which had been out of use for three years. This was the largest courtroom of its kind in the city. It offered good security (there were no windows and the prisoners entered the dock from cells underneath the court) and ample room for seating court officials and up to 50 journalists (if an upstairs gallery was used), and 30 members of the public. If there were more journalists than available seats, closed-circuit television could relay proceedings to another floor. There would be a separate press room equipped with 20 telephones, two telex machines and a Bureaufax machine. Airport detector equipment would screen people entering the building, and consideration was given to surrounding the prisoner's dock with wire mesh or a bullet-proof plastic cage.

The trial was not only likely to be one of the largest and most complex in the country's legal history; it would also be a considerable dramatic performance, with an unprecedented international audience.

It was that international audience, particularly the vast French segment of it, that worried the French government. Represent-atives of eleven French national newspapers and magazines were accredited for the trial, including *Le Monde*, *Le Figaro*, *L'Express* and *Paris Match*; plus other journalists from Agence France Press and French radio and television. Coverage of the hearing and trial in France would be of saturation proportions. Somewhere in Paris, at some level of the French government, the word was given that, if at all possible, proceedings ought not to go ahead; the instruction may even have come from the Elysée Palace. The man entrusted to convey this directive to the agents' Auckland counsel was Daniel Soulez Larivière, the latest lawyer to represent the French government. Larivière had been responsible for previous 'damage limitation' exercises involving agencies and departments of that government and was known to some in Europe as 'Red Adair', a reference to the American trouble-shooter who capped burning oil wells. Quite independent of Larivière's instructions, however, counsel Gerard Curry himself was aware of weaknesses in the Crown's case against his clients. The admissible evidence was highly circumstantial and came nowhere near establishing that the 'Turenges' had been responsible for planning the sabotage mission or planting the bombs. After he had taken the briefs of evidence to his remote Northland holiday home for a week-end of intensive study, Curry became convinced that there were grounds for negotiating a reduction of charges.

   If the Crown proceeded with the original charges, the prosecution ran the risk of not convincing the jury and seeing the
French couple acquitted of murder; in the same circumstances,
the defence's risk was that an emotionally involved jury might
sustain the charges, even though evidence might not justify
such a verdict. All sides had something to gain from a plea
of guilty to manslaughter: the French government would not
be embarrassed by a lengthy trial; the New Zealand police
would be assured of a conviction; and the French agents would
avoid the risk of a murder sentence.
   In a fortnight of negotiations, Curry was able to persuade
the country's Solicitor-General,* the Crown Solicitor in
Auckland, the Commissioner of Police and Detective Superintendent Galbraith of the merit of such a course. Meanwhile
the agents were given their instructions by Larivière. Curry went
further and tried to have the wilful damage charge dropped,
but did not succeed. The police and Crown felt that evidence
for the latter was sufficiently strong, even if some of it was
contested by the defence.
   The agents had little option but to accept the recommendations put to them. They were totally dependent on Curry for
local legal advice; and on Larivière for an indication of what
their employers expected of them. If they were to be looked
after by the French authorities after their eventual release and
compensated for their time in prison, they would have to do
what their superiors required of them, a decision that should
not have been too difficult for experienced army officers;
although there is evidence that Alain Mafart resigned himself
to it with greater ease than did Dominique Prieur.

Completely unaware of these negotiations and the bearing they
would have on legal proceedings, journalists began to assemble
in locust-like numbers in the days leading up to the preliminary
hearing. In all, 147 were eventually accredited, 80 from outside New Zealand; in addition to the French, the latter included

---

*A non-political office in New Zealand.

representatives of the *New York Times, Time, Newsweek*, Associated Press and Reuters. Most of the out-of-towners booked into the Hyatt Kingsgate Hotel (where they had been preceded by Louis-Pierre Dillais, Alain Mafart and Dominique Prieur), because it was within a few minutes' walking distance of the Supreme Court building.

A briefing for the press was held on 3 November in the Hyatt Kingsgate. There to offer advice and answer questions on the New Zealand legal system were officers of the New Zealand and Auckland Law Societies, Justice Department officials and a senior policeman. It began with a touch of lunacy when a representative of the Auckland District Law Society asked if there was anybody present who could not speak English. After a long, puzzled pause, several voices said, 'Oui'.

The lawyers explained the procedures of the preliminary hearing and the trial proper, identified who would be in court, and gave information on the manner in which court officials should be referred to and addressed. A Justice Department representative spoke on protocol ('ties are not out of place in a New Zealand court'), detailed the arrangements for seating the press and sending out copy, and outlined parking facilities ('all over Auckland and wherever you can find one'). The police officer spoke of identity procedures: all journalists would have to wear accreditation cards on their lapels and pass through metal detectors entering the courthouse. It was forbidden to take cameras or electronic equipment inside.

The press gave every appearance of developing into a mutinous rabble as the briefing wore on. Overseas television crews expressed shock and disgust that they would not be allowed to film inside the court (a practice prohibited in New Zealand), the first some of them had heard of this. They tried to argue a case there and then for changing the rules and were advised to make application in writing to the presiding judge, Ron Gilbert. More widespread consternation was caused by the revelation that some journalists would not get a seat in the body of the court (the *New Zealand Listener* was bracketed with NHK Japan and Radio Rhema in this category) and most others would have to share a place by rotation. Permanent positions went to the New Zealand national media (except the *Listener*), Auckland media, the agencies, Radio France, Radio Europe I, the *Melbourne Age*, the *Australian* and the *Sydney Morning Herald*. There was considerable aggression displayed as aggrieved representatives fought their way into queues to complain about these allocations, jostling less assertive colleagues to one side. All journalists not accommodated could watch proceedings on three video screens in an upstairs courtroom.

There was no hint at this stage, 18 hours before the hearing began, that it would not run its full course. None of the officials briefing the journalists knew of the reduction in charges agreed between the prosecution and the defence. But one New Zealand journalist had discovered that witnesses had not been put on standby to attend the hearing; that meant that something unusual was in prospect. He kept the news to himself. A large part of the fourth estate repaired to the hotel's bars; others converged on David McTaggart, who had just entered the lobby. In spite of the anger of some pressmen that they were not as well catered for as they had expected, there was a smell of excitement. Evidence released at the hearing would constitute one of the major international stories of the decade.

Like religion, the law has tended to be effective in direct proportion to its capacity to inspire awe; if it inspires awe, it inspires respect. The architecture of courthouses used to be as important in this role as that of cathedrals.

The old Auckland Supreme Court building, constructed of brick in 1868, is like a cathedral. It has concrete Gothic arches and windows and a high tower of Norman derivation. Its façade is lined with gargoyles, many of historic personages: Queen Victoria and Prince Albert glare at plaintiffs and defendants alike as they walk through the main entrance. 'There was always a sense of occasion and ceremony associated with appearing there,' one veteran Auckland lawyer remembered as the *Rainbow Warrior* hearing was about to begin.

Inside, the atmosphere was even more churchlike: light

streaming through the Gothic windows, deep arcades off high corridors, and a number one court designed as if for worship. The judge sat under a carved wooden canopy with finials and the New Zealand coat of arms blazed across its centre. The seats in the body of the court were long and resembled pews. As journalists and court officials found their places shortly before 10 a.m. on 4 November, after negotiating rigorous security checks at the entrance, the ecclesiastical atmosphere was not enhanced by the sound of a Zip heater boiling water for morning tea in a kitchen somewhere behind the judge's chair.

Outside, a festive air prevailed in spite of a chilly temperature and intermittent drizzle. Greenpeace protestors were taking advantage of the presence of foreign media teams, particularly French television, to stage a demonstration. Some members raised banners and placards (' "Justice at the Highest Level", François Mitterrand, August 1985'), some held balloons, and one, dressed as a gendarme, offered bogus Swiss passports for sale. Uniformed police, suited lawyers, court officials and journalists weaved their way through the ranks of casually dressed protestors.

The first moment of drama came with the arrival of the defendants. It was like a scene from an American television police thriller ('Thank God,' muttered one Australian camera-man, waiting; he had feared he would have nothing on film to show for a morning's work). Three sets of blue lights and sirens flashed and blared their way along Waterloo Quadrant. As they turned at speed into the narrow court driveway, they resolved themselves into two police escort cars sandwiching a box-like van with no windows. The latter had been especially built to move the prisoners each day to and from Mt Eden.

The convoy passed the team of journalists and cameramen, and the van backed into a newly constructed steel enclosure around the defendants' entrance to the building. One para-military guard with a pistol on his left hip stood at the front passenger door, keeping watch. The defendants emerged quickly from the back of the van, blankets over their heads. Then the doors closed and they were gone.

Inside the basement level, which some court officials referred to as 'the dungeons', the scene was different again. The floor was packed with members of the Police Armed Offenders Squad responsible for protecting the defendants and ensuring that the hearing was not interrupted violently. They were armed with hand- and machine-guns. At the first hint of trouble, they would race to the courtroom, guns drawn. The New Zealand Justice and Police Departments did not want to risk losing their star defendants in full view of the world's media; or at least not without a fight. Judge Gilbert had been told to hit the floor if shooting broke out: there was no telling where it might be directed.

With the availability of the video and with the upstairs gallery in the courtroom sealed off, it had been decided that there was no need to enclose the defendants in the specially built bullet-proof cage. Further, their lawyer had argued strongly against its use, stressing that his clients were army officers, not terrorists; while such steps might be taken for their own protection, it would imply a degree of established guilt.

Waiting in the tiny white-washed holding cells below the courtroom, handcuffed to their escorts, Alain Mafart and Dominique Prieur had time to think before they were thrust into the spotlight of international attention. Both had been transferred back to Mt Eden for the course of the hearing. Dominique had spent two long sessions there in the company of her husband the previous day, and this had cheered her. They had talked mostly about the new apartment he had organised for them in Paris, a move made possible with assistance from the French government. Looking at a sketch plan, she made suggestions to Joel about where to put their table, the chest of drawers, all the books.

Later in the day, both defendants had taken a call from the Minister of Defence, Paul Quilès. He had told them to be of good heart, that the French government and people were proud of them, and that they had done – and were doing – no more than their duty. '. . . the government and myself will do our best to make sure that things move as quickly as possible. I must tell you, though, you are quite right not to count your chickens before they are hatched. I think one must remain very cautious.'

Other famous criminals had sat in these same cells: murderers, who had walked up the polished wooden steps into the court to be sentenced to death by hanging (New Zealand abolished capital punishment in 1961); Rua Kenana, the Maori prophet who had tried to establish a community in the Urewera independent of Pakeha influence and control; Arthur Allen Thomas, tried twice for a murder he did not commit and finally released with a Queen's pardon and one million dollars compensation. The trial judge's ringing condemnation of Rua Kenana in 1916 was intended as a warning to anyone contemplating criminality in the then-British Dominion of New Zealand. It echoes still in the corners of that old building:

> Now you learn that the law has a long arm, and it can reach you however far back into the recesses of the forest you travel, and that in every corner of the great Empire to which we belong, the King's law can reach anyone who offends against it.

The defendants were held in the cells more than half an hour longer than planned because the paperwork was not in order upstairs. As they fidgeted and wondered about the delay, the journalists too became more restless, wandering between the number one courtroom, the press communications centre and the room upstairs with three video screens. Judge Gilbert, the Solicitor-General Paul Neazor, the Crown Prosecutor David Morris and Gerard Curry, were preparing and reorganising the documents needed to accommodate the altered charges. Part of the delay was caused by the fact that the court building was designated a District Court for the hearing, but did not have a District Court registry; procedure required that a charge of manslaughter had to be laid formally in a District Court registry, some distance away. Another part of the problem was that, as things had been arranged, Judge Gilbert could have found himself dealing with the immigration charges first, convicting the agents and remanding them – as he was legally obliged to do – pending deportation under the Immigration Act. Such an outcome would have made the New Zealand judicial system appear ludicrous in the eyes of the watching press. And so papers were redrafted and procedures clarified; eventually the proceedings that one New Zealand newspaper had already called 'the trial of the century' were able to begin.

Shortly after 10.30 officials and lawyers took their allotted places in the court like figures in a minuet. The muffled conversation from the 36 journalists inside and an almost equal number of people in the public seats ceased. (The latter included David McTaggart and a small contingent of Greenpeace officials.) Everybody rose as Judge Gilbert entered the court, a squat, stern-looking figure in thick-rimmed glasses; they sat when he sat. The court was in session. Alain Mafart and Dominique Prieur then tramped up the circular stairs in the well in the centre of the room to emerge in the dock. He was in the tweed jacket he had worn the day he was taken into custody; she wore light brown slacks and a beige jacket. She immediately placed headphones over her ears to hear a simultaneous translation of proceedings in French. Both seemed relaxed.

For the onlookers, the shock was immediate. Gerard Curry, red haired, solid, built like a rugby forward, got to his feet and announced that the murder charge had been replaced with manslaughter and arson by the alternative charge of wilful damage, and that his clients were ready to plead on both. Judge Gilbert accepted this. The defendants were then identified by their correct names and occupations and asked to plead. Both said guilty in English, but in voices so low that the journalists upstairs monitoring the videos did not hear and became totally confused as to what was happening. Downstairs, a number of their colleagues left their seats and rushed to the phones to convey this unexpected turn of events to the world outside.

They were not the first to announce it. Peter Kingston, a Radio New Zealand reporter, had seen an official post a charge sheet at the court's public counter shortly after ten o'clock. Curious, he wandered over to read it. It detailed the new charges, not the expected ones. Kingston rushed into court, where proceedings had yet to begin, briefed another radio reporter, then hurried out to ring his newsroom. The result was that his network ran the story simultaneously with Curry's announcement in the court.

Back inside, the Solicitor-General, a short monkish-looking man who speaks deliberately and outside court hardly ever has his pipe out of his mouth, took the floor. He told the court that on evidence available, the Crown could not establish that the defendants had intended to kill anybody on the night of the bombing. He said that they had indicated through their lawyer their willingness to plead guilty to the charges of manslaughter and wilful damage, and that this course of action was acceptable to the Crown. 'While larger questions do arise from the sinking of the *Rainbow Warrior*, this hearing is concerned only with the criminal responsibility of the two defendants under New Zealand law.'

Paul Neazor went on to say that Mafart and Prieur had had meetings with the *Ouvéa* crew. The Crown contended that, in the course of these meetings, a Zodiac inflatable and Yamaha engine were handed over to the defendants and relevant information exchanged about the *Rainbow Warrior*. On the night of the bombing itself, the Crown had been unable to determine the defendants' role other than in support of those who actually placed the explosives, and the identity of those persons had not been established. There was the further complication that Fernando Pereira had died, not as a direct result of either explosion on the *Rainbow Warrior*, but from drowning. For these reasons, the Crown decided to accept the defendants' plea on the lesser charge of manslaughter.

After the Solicitor-General's presentation of the summary of evidence, Mafart and Prieur made no plea to the additional charges of entering New Zealand on forged passports and they were remanded to appear in the Auckland District Court on 25 November. They would appear again in the High Court for sentencing on manslaughter and wilful damage three days before that date.

The result of the hearing generated considerable confusion. Greenpeace spokespersons were angry and felt that Mafart and Prieur were being 'let off the hook'. Privately they speculated whether some sort of deal had been made between the New Zealand and French governments. Overseas journalists were irate, having come thousands of kilometres for a one-hour hearing. French reporters in particular were convinced that they had been deprived of their trial (and of their long expense-account stay in New Zealand hotels) by some kind of judicial conspiracy. They began asking questions about the precise nature of the relationship between defence lawyer Curry and Solicitor-General Neazor.*

Accusations that there had been a government-to-government agreement to reduce the charges against the agents and thus help secure their early release were published in the French press. They were given weight by the claim of Defence Minister Paul Quilès and Foreign Minister Roland Dumas that the latter had suggested such a deal when he spoke to the New Zealand Deputy Prime Minister in New York.

The New Zealand Prime Minister and his deputy denied emphatically that any such agreement had been struck. The New York discussions had been solely on the question of New Zealand's compensation claims. They rejected even more force-fully the allegation that a 'lamb-chop spy swap' deal had been made, as some European papers alleged. The French minister's

---

*Strangely enough the two men did have a connection, although the press never uncovered it. Both had sisters who were nuns in the same convent in the Roman Catholic order of the Sisters of Compassion.

allegations, they said, were either based on a misunderstanding of how the New Zealand judicial system worked, possibly on a belief that the Solicitor-General was a government position like that of Attorney-General; or were designed for domestic political impact. To reduce the likelihood of further confusion, David Lange postponed the New York reparation discussions 'until the judicial process has run its course'. Meanwhile, Gerard Curry appeared on television to affirm that the 'plea bargaining' resulting in the reduction of charges had taken place outside the political arena: it had been solely a matter for the defence, the Solicitor-General, the Auckland Crown Counsel and the police.

A degree of frustration was apparent in public reaction to the outcome of the hearing, however. People felt cheated that there had been no trial, no unfolding of evidence, no process by which to make sense of the whole confused affair; no conviction for murder and hence an unequivocal scapegoat at the end of the process. New Zealanders, having shared the national trauma of the first act of terrorism committed within their borders, needed the catharsis of a full trial to release pent-up emotions and see justice done. The truncated hearing, with its release of minimum evidence and its reduced charges, was far from providing such relief. Worse, it raised possibilities that something other than justice was being seen to be done. And the prospect that the French agents could receive a light sentence and be deported to serve it in France (a legal possibility mooted by the press) became a source of anger; it was certainly something different, something nobody had counted on.

The old Supreme Court building filled again with the same participants and observers on 22 November for the passing of sentence on the French agents. The only difference was that this time it was designated a High Court sitting, and the presiding judge was Sir Ronald Davidson, the country's Chief Justice. Raised high above the floor on his red-backed chair, long-faced, bewigged, dark-robed, Sir Ronald looked – as one French journalist remarked – like a sombre, hanging judge.

Was that an omen?

Gerard Curry opened proceedings with a plea in mitigation on behalf of his clients. Speaking in a deliberate, nasal voice, he outlined the reasons why the agents should be treated leniently: 'Their role was supportive, they acted on orders, they believed no one would be injured, they believed they acted in the interests of France, they expressed remorse at the drowning of Fernando Pereira, they have acknowledged their role and thereby avoided for all concerned a very lengthy and costly trial, and they have already spent four months in a foreign gaol far from family and friends.'

There were, Curry noted, marked differences between New Zealand and French perceptions of what steps could be taken for the defence of one's country. '[France] has experienced the crush of the oppressor's jackboot and even today forces behind the Iron Curtain are assembled only 300 kilometres . . . from her borders. In contrast, New Zealand's borders have never been breached by the oppressor, and geographically we occupy the safest position in the world.'

The defendants had been conditioned by their proximity to war zones and war experience. 'One of [Prieur's] cousins fought for the French Resistance, was captured and imprisoned in Buchenwald concentration camp where he was subjected to medical experimentation. Three of her grandparents and one great-aunt were shot as hostages by the forces of oppression that invaded France. They were shot in front of their children and they were shot just ten days before France was liberated in the Second World War.' But while Captain Prieur had an outstanding academic and army record, Curry said, at home she was a person who performed tasks familiar to New Zealand housewives: 'She cooked, shopped, knitted and made jam.'*

Sketching a portrait of Mafart, Curry said the major came

---

*Further details of Prieur's domestic life emerged from the magazine L'Express, quoting her husband: 'Dominique is a superwife who at home wears blue jeans and a sloppy pullover, is a supercook whose star turn is crab and cheese soufflé, is a superdancer – from rock to pasodoble and Vienna waltz, and a classical music buff.'

from a family with a medical and military tradition. 'His grandfather was a decorated French hero of the First World War and his father was a decorated medical practitioner in the French Army . . . He has a concern for the quality of the environment and an interest in marine ecology. During his leisure time he made a particular study of whales, including six weeks on the coast of British Columbia photographing and following orca whales and some three weeks observing, photographing and swimming with grey whales in Scamon Lagoon in Mexico during their breeding season.' This depiction of Mafart as a whale-loving ecologist produced the only major interruption of the day: snorts of amusement and disbelief from Greenpeace members in the public seats.

Finally, Curry drew the Chief Justice's attention to the New Zealand Criminal Justice Act 1985, which had come into force only six and a half weeks before. This permitted greater flexibility in sentencing, to avoid the destructive effects of imprisonment; and it allowed deportation of foreign offenders to their home countries. In the case of his clients, he concluded, 'a short term of imprisonment and a recommendation for deportation would be appropriate'.

The Crown Solicitor, David Morris, followed with arguments in favour of a long custodial sentence for the agents. Speaking more rapidly than Curry, in a voice clipped by a Scottish accent, Morris emphasised that the defendants had been an integral part of an operation whose purpose involved high risk of injury and loss of life. 'No warning was given about the bomb and this failure is inexcusable.' Experience outside New Zealand had indicated that such warnings saved lives, he said.

Morris then noted that Alain Mafart held the rank of major, a senior position, and that no evidence had been presented to the court that a higher ranked officer had taken part in the operation. This, he implied, would place a larger degree of responsibility for the planning and execution of the operation on Mafart than the defence had admitted.* He closed by submitting that the deterrent aspect of sentencing was of great importance in the case. 'There is a clear need to express public condemnation of such offending, and to give a clear warning to persons of like mind, and their political masters and over-lords, that terrorist activities of any kind will be met with stern reaction and vigorous punishment.'

Mafart and Prieur had stood impassively throughout the sub-missions until Morris got into his stride. As he argued for a strong deterrent sentence and cited British precedents, Prieur began to wilt. Several times she turned her head to catch the eye of her husband, sitting at the side of the court in front of her. He smiled encouragingly, but wanly. Just when she appeared most discouraged, Sir Ronald Davidson called a midday adjournment.

The court resumed for the Chief Justice's sentencing at 12.20 p.m. Sir Ronald began a lengthy judgment by comment-ing on public speculation over the reduction of the murder charge to manslaughter. He traced the process by which this had occurred and concluded: 'The evidence before me coupled with the assurances given by Mr Curry indicate that the negoti-ations which took place between Mr Curry and Mr Neazor were conducted in accordance with accepted New Zealand practice and that nowhere did matters of a political nature intrude . . .'

Moving to the charges against the defendants, Sir Ronald said manslaughter was culpable homicide, but without the intention to cause death. In the case of the *Rainbow Warrior*, explosives had been employed, however, and when such devices were used, the element of danger to life was inevitably present.

Referring to Curry's statement that Mafart and Prieur had been involved in the bombing in a supportive role only, Sir Ronald said one group had brought equipment to New Zealand. The defendants had transported at least some of it to Auckland for use by those who had fixed the explosives. The defendants

---

*Gerard Curry, upset at this suggestion, got to his feet and said the defence had been 'taken by surprise'. Clearly there had been no mention of this factor in earlier discussions between prosecution and defence over evidence.

had also picked up and 'spirited away' at least one of the explosives men afterwards. No one group could have carried out its task without assistance from the others. All were therefore essential to the operation.

'I do not consider one should downgrade too much the part played by the defendants. They were persons holding the ranks of major and captain. Although I am not told of positions they held so far as seniority is concerned, they were certainly in my view not playing a minor role. The planting of the explosives on the vessel was only a part of a joint operation. Without the defendants, it is unlikely that the explosives person could have played his part.'

As the judgment unfolded, it became apparent that the Chief Justice would direct his comments at terrorism in its totality rather than focusing narrowly on the role of the individuals before him. He was also taking care to enshrine in New Zealand law a precedent to deter future terrorism. As this realisation occurred to the defendants, Prieur sagged in her chair and seemed to become terribly fatigued. Mafart, as always, kept his back straight and stared straight to the front.

'This was a deliberate, planned operation of a terrorist nature, carried out for political and ideological motives, using explosives in circumstances where there was a high risk of injury and possibly loss of life, and where heavy damage was caused to the vessel involved,' Sir Ronald continued. 'It is the first offence of its type that has occurred in New Zealand, although elsewhere terrorist activities are a common fact of everyday life. The sentence imposed must give a clear warning to such as the defendants and their masters that terrorist-type activities will be met with a stern reaction and severe punishment . . . . People who come to this country and commit terrorist activities cannot expect to have a short holiday at the expense of our government and return home as heroes.

'Taking all factors into account and giving such weight as I am able to the matters of mitigation . . . and to the remorse which the defendants expressed by their counsel, the sentence of the Court is that on the charge of manslaughter you are each sentenced to ten years' imprisonment; on the charges of wilful damage you are each sentenced to seven years' imprisonment; the terms to be served concurrently.'

In the heightened silence of the court the Chief Justice added only one more comment. He noted Gerard Curry had submitted that he ought in passing sentence make a recommendation that Mafart and Prieur be deported. He declined to do so, he said, and regarded it as appropriate that the question of deportation should be dealt with by the Minister of Justice.

For a few seconds nobody in court moved or spoke. Then Joel Prieur's head slumped into his hands; Dominique Prieur and Mafart turned abruptly to leave the dock but were restrained until the Chief Justice had risen and left the court, at which point they hurried on to the staircase, Mafart stumbling slightly but expressionless, Prieur close to tears as she disappeared from view. Greenpeace observers looked grim – there was no sign of jubilation – but nor were they dissatisfied. Other participants scattered quickly and had few remarks for the waiting press. One who did comment was Daniel Soulez Larivière. Asked if his clients were resigned to ten years in gaol, he said sharply: 'They are soldiers.'

Two days later the agents pleaded guilty to five passport-related charges and were convicted on those too. There were no additional penalties: they were simply remanded to the prisons where they would serve their initial sentences, Paremoremo and Mt Eden. Just over a month later, Dominique Prieur would return to Christchurch Women's Prison where she had previously been so unhappy. There was no recommendation for early release or deportation from either the court or the Minister of Justice.

In spite of Gerard Curry's assurance at the sentencing that the French government was close to a compensation settlement with Greenpeace for the loss of the *Rainbow Warrior*, and that discussions on reparations had commenced with the New Zealand government, both questions remained unresolved six months later. With the severity of sentencing, political and public opinion in France swung against such settlements.* Opinions hardened with the approach of the National Assembly elections in March 1986. After right-wing parties had increased their representation and forced President Mitterrand to call on Jacques Chirac to help form a government, the chances of France paying reparations to New Zealand diminished. The new government was not only more remote ideologically from New Zealand's Labour administration, it felt in no way bound by the admission of responsibility and guilt for the *Rainbow Warrior* operation made by its predecessor. New ministers spoke increasingly of l'Affaire Greenpeace as if it had been a crisis of New Zealand's making, and they authorised what were at first unofficial trade sanctions against that country. Some, like those against New Zealand lambs' brains, eventually achieved official approval; in May 1986 France hinted that it would seek to prevent sales of New Zealand butter to EEC countries until Major Mafart and Captain Prieur were released. The New Zealand government's position remained consistent. The agents had pleaded guilty to a crime, for which they had been convicted; David Lange affirmed neither they nor the New Zealand judicial system were up for sale.

---

*Although the French had paid an undisclosed sum of money in November to the widow and children of Fernando Pereira.

Place of Great Secrecy

September 1966

There is no such place as 'Muruora Atoll'. The horseshoe reef of islands in the Tuamotu group 1,200 kilometres south-east of Tahiti is actually called 'Moruroa' – in Mangarevan dialect, 'the place of great secrecy'. The word was transcribed incorrectly by a nineteenth-century French cartographer and transferred to early maps as 'Mururoa'. The indigenous people of French Polynesia still know it as Moruroa. And – since 1966 – it has been a place of even greater secrecy than before. That year the French government began to explode nuclear weapons over the atoll, in defiance of the Nuclear Test Ban Treaty which had banned atmospheric tests since 1963, and in defiance of majority opinion among Polynesians of French Polynesia.

Ironically, the President of the Fifth Republic, General Charles de Gaulle, decided to visit the French territory that year, to mark the beginning of the Pacific testing programme. It was ironic because when he had received a hero's welcome in Tahiti ten years before, he had told a predominantly Polynesian audience in Papeete that there was 'a universal desire among peoples and ethnic groups to preserve their own culture and determine their own destiny'. Many of the listeners interpreted this as meaning that he was in favour of political independence for the territory. He continued the era of nuclear energy held no dangers for his audience because 'being protected by vast, invulnerable expanses of surrounding ocean, tomorrow Tahiti may well become a refuge and a centre of rebirth for our whole civilisation'. The applause was tumultuous.

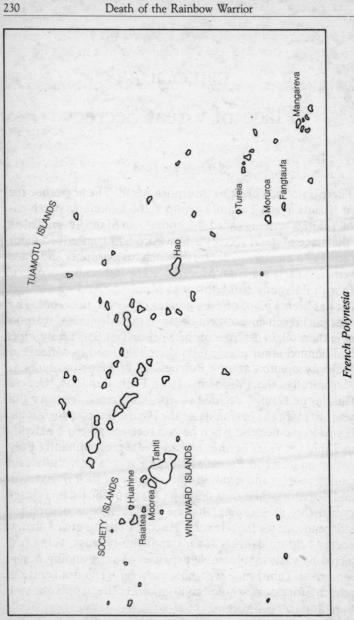

TUAMOTU ISLANDS

Mangareva

Tureia

Moruroa

Fangtaufa

Hao

SOCIETY ISLANDS

Huahine

Raiatea

Moorea

Tahiti

WINDWARD ISLANDS

French Polynesia

The applause was not tumultuous in 1966. None of the
expectations raised by the earlier speech, when de Gaulle had
come as a private citizen, had been realised. French Polynesia
was still under the strong arm of metropolitan France. Its most
charismatic indigenous leader, former First World War hero
Pouvanaa a Opua, was in enforced exile. The local elective
Territorial Assembly was not empowered to discuss or vote
on 'political' issues. And French nuclear testing had been
imposed on the territory against strong local opposition: the
Governor had threatened to dissolve the assembly if it continued to protest against the programme.

This was the climate in which the president was received in
Papeete on 6 September 1966. About 1,000 Tahitians turned
out to welcome him, but journalists noted that 'many young
Tahitian boys shouted "Vive de Gaulle!" then turned to friends
to mutter dirty names in Tahitian'. Tuamotuan and Marquesan
chiefs brought specially to Papeete at government expense
shook hands silently with the general then abruptly turned their
backs on him.

Worse was to come. The following day, de Gaulle was
received by the recognised leader of the indigenous Tahitians
and representative in the National Assembly, John Teariki,
at the new government council room in Papeete. At this private
audience, Teariki pulled out the text of a prepared speech and
read it to his head of state:

Mr President!

Ten years ago you honoured us with a visit. You were then a simple
citizen, but at the same time, in the eyes of many of your fellow
countrymen the greatest living Frenchman. For us Polynesians,
who were once among the first to heed your appeal to continue
the fight for freedom, you were not only the heroic leader of Free
France but also, and above all, the liberator who proclaimed for
the first time at Brazzaville the right of the inhabitants of the
French colonies to equality, freedom, and self-government . . .

[Now] a widespread uneasiness exists in Polynesia and is
worsening from day to day. It is due to the Fifth Republic's policy
since you took over the helm, a policy consisting right from the

beginning of a long series of attacks against our liberties, threats and acts of force aimed at reinforcing the colonial system and the military occupation of our islands . . . as has become evident, your policy has had only one aim, that of being able to freely dispose of our country as a testing ground for your nuclear weapons. Since then our destiny, our health, our social, economic and political institutions have been geared to your military needs . . .

You made this decision without consulting us Polynesians, although our health and that of our children will suffer from the tests. This is a serious breach against the French constitution and the charter of the United Nations. Your propaganda department disregards the most elementary truths by alleging that these atomic and thermonuclear blasts are completely harmless to our health. I do not have enough time, here and now, to refute all of these propaganda lies. Suffice it to say that the reports of the UN Scientific Committee on the Effects of Atomic Radiation for 1958, 1962, and 1964 have firmly established that each radioactive dose, however small, is harmful to those exposed to it, as well as for their descendants – that it is consequently recommended to avoid increasing natural radioactivity – that there exists no efficient method of protection against the harmful effects from widespread radioactive fallout from the explosion of atomic and nuclear bombs. Which is why all these reports reaffirm the necessity of stopping all nuclear tests . . .

Mr President, please apply here in French Polynesia the same noble principles that you enumerated in Pnom Penh for the benefit of the Americans and re-embark your troops, your bombs, and your aeroplanes at once. If you do so, you will never be accused of having caused cancer and leukaemia here in our islands. If you do so, our descendants will not blame you for the birth of monstrously deformed children. If you do so, the friendship of neighbouring peoples will not be tarnished by any atomic clouds. If you do so, France will become a model for the whole world. For this would mean that, for the first time in history, a great nation will have renounced freely, without having been motivated by fear of blackmail, or gain, the use of nuclear power for mass murder, thereby proclaiming its faith in reason and inciting other nations to follow suit. If you do so, we Polynesians shall be proud and happy to be French citizens and we shall again become your best and most faithful friends.

Moved by his own eloquence, swayed by his own logic, Deputy John Teariki walked forward and handed a copy of his speech to the president, who had listened without betraying any sign of emotion. Then the deputy stepped back and waited for the general's response. De Gaulle, however, put the speech in his pocket, shook Teariki's hand silently, swivelled on his heel and strode out of the room followed by his entourage.

The official government bulletin announcing the meeting to the press noted simply: 'The head of state also received the deputy of French Polynesia, John F. Teariki, in the new council building, amounting to a sort of inauguration. The latter touched upon . . . topics with which he is much pre-occupied . . .'

Two days later President de Gaulle flew to Morurua to observe the nuclear explosion devised to coincide with his visit. The decision to test in the Tuamotus had been precipitated by the independence of Algeria in 1962 (in the preceding two years France had detonated four atmospheric bombs and 13 under-ground explosions in the Algerian Sahara). Work to develop the uninhabited Morurua site had begun in 1964. The following year, the director of the Centre d'Expérimentation du Pacifique assured the people of French Polynesia that 'not a single par-ticle of active fallout will ever reach an inhabited island'. The authority of this claim was severely undercut in May 1966 when the CEP's first map of the danger zone for the first nuclear test – to be held in July – included seven inhabited atolls. The map was altered.

On 9 September, President de Gaulle landed on an atoll that had been transformed beyond recognition. Kilometres of it were sealed in concrete – some of it to provide landing strips for military aircraft, other sections to stabilise the ground for building blockhouses (also in concrete), offices, accommo-dation for service personnel, aircraft hangars and wharfs. Two huge towers had been built for electronic observation of explo-sions. Pylon-like aerials also reared into the sky. It was a landscape out of science fiction. Here and there, between the concrete welts, clusters of palms and marine grass survived, reminders that the atoll was not after all manmade. Further along the chain, small islets were still untouched and unspoiled, sprouting luxuriant vegetation and surrounded by clear water. After six years of atmospheric nuclear tests, the whole atoll would be described as a lifeless planet.

The general was to watch a 120-kilotonne explosion from the huge cruiser *De Grasse*, at a distance of about 30 kilometres from the blast centre. He boarded the vessel as soon as he reached the atoll in the late afternoon and *De Grasse* put to sea almost at once, to be in position before nightfall. Early the following morning, however, the sky was overcast and a strong wind was blowing to the west – the wrong direction; it would carry radioactivity to neighbouring Pacific islands. The admiral explained to an impatient de Gaulle that the test would have to be postponed. The general's mood became even blacker when *De Grasse* returned to Moruroa and he saw that the device to be exploded, hanging from a helium-filled balloon, did not look anything like a bomb. One commentator described it as 'an iron box the size of a family refrigerator'.

At sunrise the next day the general was back on *De Grasse*'s bridge, wearing his antiflash goggles and grey protective overalls. The test would have to take place that day, he declared emphatically. He had pressing business in Paris and could delay his return no longer. The admiral was in a quandary. The winds were still westerly, at every altitude. He had to weigh up the risk of radioactive contamination of inhabited islands against the general's wrath. Eventually, he began the countdown. Before the day was out, the plutonium device code-named Betelgeuse had been detonated from the cruiser's bridge, specially equipped for the purpose. The mushroom cloud billowed into the heavens and the general was pleased.

The inhabitants of other Pacific territories were less delighted. As Tahitian anthropologists Bengt and Marie-Thérèse Danielsson noted:

The radioactive fallout reached all the islands west of Moruroa in a matter of hours or days. For instance in Apia . . . 2,000 nautical miles downwind, the radioactive content of the rainwater catchment tanks four days later was estimated by the National Radiation Laboratory of New Zealand . . . to be 135,000 picocuries per litre. Almost equally alarming measurements were made in the Cook Islands and Fiji. The exact amount of radioactive fallout received by the inhabitants of French Polynesia, living in the shade of the atomic mushroom, has never been announced . . .

The Centre d'Expérimentation du Pacifique refused to divulge *any* information about contamination in the French territory itself. Prior to 1966, records of public health statistics in French Polynesia had been published monthly; after the tests began they were not, and anyone requesting them in Tahiti was reported to the police.

That same year the French authorities began secretly to build atomic shelters on the islands east of Moruroa, outside the keyhole-shaped area defined as the danger zone. No fallout shelters were built on islands closer to Moruroa, such as Tureia. But in 1968, the entire population (50 people) was evacuated without warning to Tahiti for a three-month 'holiday'. Residents were allowed to return after superficial decontamination of the island.

These accidents and subsequent ones, the steady buildup of radiation in the central Pacific and the illegal declaration of the 260,000 square kilometre exclusion zone around Moruroa, led to the earliest Greenpeace protests off the atoll in 1972 and 1973.

The 1985 Greenpeace protest, the Pacific Peace Flotilla, did reach Moruroa without its mother ship, the *Rainbow Warrior*. But its composition changed and the individual vessels were later leaving Auckland and arriving off the atoll because of the bombing.

Of the original fleet, *Django* and *Kliss II*, the smallest yachts, pulled out in the absence of the support that the *Rainbow Warrior* would have provided. The scow *Alliance* left Auckland for Moruroa on 3 August, *Vega* on 24 August and *Varangian* on 28 September. An additional vessel, the 30-metre brigantine *Breeze*, sailed on 7 September. The whole venture became viable again once Greenpeace International announced on 17 August that its converted tug *Greenpeace* would sail to Moruroa en route for its 1985/86 Antarctic expedition. Among those who made it to the territorial limit around the atoll were four *Rainbow Warrior* crew members: skipper Peter Willcox was with Grace O'Sullivan on *Vega*, Bunny McDiarmid flew to Curaçao to join the *Greenpeace* crew, and radio operator Lloyd Anderson was on *Varangian*.

Vega arrived first (22 September) followed by *Greenpeace*, *Breeze* and *Alliance*. The crews had rapturous reunions as each vessel appeared over the horizon. Then they got on with the serious business of cruising just outside the 12-mile limit, pursued by French naval ships and helicopters. A large contingent of journalists on board *Greenpeace* recorded every step in the nautical ballet and wired their stories around the globe, keeping world attention fixed on the issue of French testing.

The fleet was together only briefly, however. One of *Greenpeace*'s two generators broke down and it was forced to make for Tahiti for repairs. The French High Commissioner forbade it to enter territorial waters. She was followed by *Breeze*, also seeking entry to Papeete after springing a leak. This request too was turned down, then granted temporarily – for one hour. Both vessels, after makeshift repairs, had to run for New Zealand; but only after they had been welcomed and congratulated at sea by Oscar Temaru, mayor of Faa, accompanied by a group of Tahitian well-wishers in a fishing boat.

Meanwhile *Varangian* joined *Vega* off Moruroa and both vessels learned that Prime Minister Laurent Fabius and other members of his cabinet would arrive at the atoll to observe a bomb test on 24 October. After much agonising over the likely consequences, *Vega* decided to enter the territorial zone and make a run for the lagoon, in an effort to delay the test.

The Greenpeace yacht, veteran now of five Moruroa protests and two previous arrests, breached the zone at 1 a.m.,
taking advantage of darkness. She was closely followed by the
warship *Taape*. The yacht tacked around the atoll for several
hours, agitating the French sailors in pursuit. Finally, just
before dawn, *Vega* made a run for the lagoon itself. As David
McTaggart had been in 1973, the crew was intercepted by armed
commandos in an inflatable. But this time the French wanted
no martyrs; there were no beatings. With their wrists tied, the
four Greenpeace members were transferred to the *Taape* and
the *Vega* towed into Moruroa lagoon behind them.

Later that same morning the underground test went ahead,
observed by Prime Minister Fabius on the ground and by the
new Defence Minister, Paul Quilès, in a helicopter. In the afternoon, the ministers swam in the lagoon with other French par-
liamentarians to demonstrate confidence in their claim that the
tests did not result in dangerous radioactivity.

Vega was now in the hands of the French Navy for the third
time. The crew were taken to the military base on Hao Atoll,
and eventually deported – a confusing process, because each
of the four was of a different nationality, and they had hidden
their passports on the yacht. Greenpeace was ordered to pay
a $NZ8,000 fine for the return of *Vega*, a provision the French
authorities later dropped. The yacht was finally returned to
Auckland in the hold of a French freighter in March 1986, the
last of the 1985 Peace Flotilla vessels to reach home.

The argument about whether or not the French underground
tests were having a detrimental effect on Moruroa and the wider
Pacific environment raged with the intensity of a tropical storm.
The French Secretary of State for the Prevention of Disasters,
Haroun Tazieff, claimed on the atoll the day the *Vega* was
arrested in October 1985 that there was no evidence of radioactive pollution there. 'I am scandalised by the moral attitude
of Greenpeace and the New Zealand Prime Minister,' he
snarled. 'I hate lies.' He cited the conclusions of the so-called

'Atkinson report' in support of his views (the 'Report of a New Zealand, Australia and Papua New Guinea Scientific Mission to Mururoa Atoll', published in 1984).

While the Atkinson report does indeed conclude that there is no immediate risk of radiation being released into the lagoon or the sea from the French underground tests, it has some disturbing features. First, the scientists who compiled it were allowed on the atoll for only four days in October 1983, were not allowed to visit or record data on certain key parts of it, and had to rely in some instances on French data rather than their own.

Second, in spite of these handicaps, the report still found that the lower levels of the atoll leach more radioactivity into the sea and at a faster rate than French reports have alleged. It indicated that during some underground tests radioactive gases are released into the air. And it confirmed that the lagoon was indeed polluted with radioactive plutonium.

A less guarded report than the Atkinson one was released by three Commissariat à l'Energie Atomique engineers in November 1984. This indicated that radioactivity levels on the atoll had doubled in the previous four years; that the north beach was a vast radioactive rubbish heap measuring 30,000 square metres; that blasts from each test sent shock waves through the atoll's core so that it sank about two centimetres after each explosion; and that storms in March and August 1981 had exposed inadequately covered irradiated waste.

This last revelation pinpointed the factor that most Pacific nations feared about French testing at Mururoa: that whatever precautions French scientists took for their own immediate safety, an accident could all too easily release large quantities of radioactivity into the air or the sea. And there *have* been such accidents. The cyclones in 1981 devastated the atoll, dislodging concrete and asphalt covering radioactive waste and sweeping those wastes into the lagoon and the open sea. Others include a bomb detonating after it had become wedged in its shaft in 1979, which caused part of the reef to break off and create a localised tidal wave; and a fire and explosion in an underground bunker which killed two technicians, seriously injured four others, and scattered plutonium around the atoll.

Added to this is concern about the effect of increased radiation on Moruroa workers and neighbouring islanders. This effect is extremely difficult to calculate, because of the unwillingness of French authorities to release relevant data. ('If it is so safe, what have they got to hide?' non-French scientists have asked again and again.)

The incidence of cancer in Tahiti and surrounding islands appears to have increased dramatically over the past decade. Without verifiable statistics, Tahitian leaders such as Jean Doom (Secretary-General of the Polynesian Protestant Church, embraced by 60 per cent of the Tahitian Polynesian population) says: 'We can only trust our own observation that more and more people are sick now – cancers, leukaemias, all sorts.' Oscar Temaru adds: 'And they're getting younger – we've just had cases of a four-year-old and a 36-year-old with cancer. But we cannot prove anything.'

The difficulty of assessing the problem, and of making causal judgments, springs from the fact that the civilian hospital in Tahiti is staffed by military doctors, who are not permitted to release relevant data. Further, most cancer patients are sent to France for treatment; again, no statistics are published. Autopsies are almost never carried out.

At Mangareva, a mere 900 kilometres east of Moruroa, health problems attributable to the tests seem more acute. According to the mayor, Lucas Paeamara, cancer is on the increase, the rate of birth deformities is growing, and people eating fish from Mangareva's lagoons (in 1985) were suffering from vomiting, trembling and paralysis. Again, no scientific investigation has been carried out; nor can such an investigation be undertaken without the consent of the French government. But nobody forgets that it was on Mangareva in 1966 that bomb shelters had to be built, that they were used on several occasions, and that afterwards the authorities merely hosed down the local population with water.

All these phenomena, plus the obvious danger of long-term

pollution of the Pacific as Moruroa erodes or eventually breaks up, have made Pacific Island leaders cynical about claims that the testing programme is harmless. 'If it is so safe, then the French must conduct their experiments in metropolitan France, where its own citizens can bear the risk,' the Prime Minister of Western Samoa, Tofilau Eti Alesana, commented late in 1985. As he said this, France detonated its seventh test for the year, its 74th since underground tests began, and its 115th since the first atmospheric tests in 1966.

The survivors of the *Rainbow Warrior* bombing found themselves reluctant heroes. They were treated with reverence and respect by other Greenpeace members, and by the peace movement generally. It was considered a coup to secure one of them for a protest boat or for a fund-raising exercise. While this was distasteful to the crew members themselves, they accepted a responsibility to use their experience to spread an awareness of Greenpeace's work and to raise money for Greenpeace campaigns. Those who remained in New Zealand accepted speaking engagements all over the North Island. Within three months of the bombing, local Greenpeace coffers had swollen by more than $200,000. They also made themselves available to an army of journalists and investigators who decided to write books and features or make documentaries on the bombing – there were eight books in progress by the end of 1985.

Hank Haazen and Bunny McDiarmid were the first to follow up the contact that the crew had made with the Rongelap islanders in May 1985. In less than a year they were back there, working with the evacuees to help them settle into new homes on Mejato. They reported serious difficulties: the refugees had been cut off from other islands in the atoll because the engines of their boats were not functioning and they were unable to repair them; this meant fishing was impossible in the deeper parts of the lagoon; the fish around the reef were not as pro-lific as they had at first seemed; the lack of sanitary facilities meant a constant fly problem and a high risk of illness; and there had been a severe shortage of food.

Without expecting to change conditions overnight, Haazen and McDiarmid hoped to accomplish some narrow goals. Haazen arrived at Mejato with spare parts for the boat motors and instruction manuals on how to repair them. He and McDiarmid also tried to devise a simple system of sanitation. And they were aware that outside aid would only be directed to the islanders if the interest that the *Rainbow Warrior* evacuation created was fed by a constant flow of information.

Back in New Zealand, crew members and Greenpeace officials were exercised by the problem of what to do with the *Warrior*. Raised from the sea bed at Marsden Wharf on 21 August, hull patched by the New Zealand Navy, she was running up berthage fees of between $400 and $500 per month at the Viaduct Wharf on Auckland's waterfront. While all members of the crew had felt a relationship with the vessel when she was 'alive', they now agreed that she was a hulk, a corpse: the spirit had gone. What ought to be done with her? Discussion within Greenpeace New Zealand had defined four options: repair the boat, preserve her as a museum, cut her up for scrap, or sink her at sea. On investigation, the first two proved prohibitively expensive unless someone else came up with the money ($700,000 for hull repairs alone, for example) – but nobody did. The third option left the crew feeling uneasy: she was a hulk, yes; but she was *their* hulk. Fernando Pereira had died on her. Cutting her up and selling her in pieces would feel like cannibalising a dead relative. And so Greenpeace investigated the last suggestion, sinking the boat at sea. This would meet crew sensitivities, and it would be a solution befitting the record and the dignity of an old maritime campaigner. It would also cost nothing beyond towing the boat to its final resting place, a service that could be donated.

In September 1985 the Greenpeace International annual council meeting considered and accepted a proposal from the New Zealand Underwater Association. This organisation had offered to turn the ship into an underwater memorial, accessible to divers off an attractive section of New Zealand coastline. The association had already chosen a potential site – Slipper Island off the Coromandel Peninsula – and it would bear the cost of transporting the *Warrior* there.

The issue seemed to be settled and stories about the sinking began to appear in the New Zealand press. But nobody had discussed it with Maori people on Coromandel Peninsula. And they had strong cultural objections to the proposal.

The tangata whenua (indigenous people) of the area were a small tribe called Ngati Hei. Their traditional territory ran from Whitianga in the north to Wharekawa Harbour in the south, about 60 kilometres of coastline. Although their numbers in the 1980s were small (they had been decimated by tribal wars in the late nineteenth century and again in the 1820s), they were none the less regarded by other Maori as the kai tiaki or spiritual guardians of an area that included Slipper Island. And Slipper Island – known to them as Whakahau – had been one of their major tribal burial grounds. As soon as Greenpeace was aware of Maori resistance to their proposal, they arranged for representatives to attend a meeting of the Hauraki District Maori Council at Paeroa in late November.

The visitors were called onto the marae by the cries of local women and stood for a moment in silence, heads bowed, in memory of Fernando Pereira and of the Maori people of the district who had died in the previous months. Then they sat in the sun on wooden forms in front of the meeting house to be formally welcomed in Maori by local elders. Hauraki Member of Parliament Graeme Lee replied on behalf of the visitors and laid on the marae the party's customary koha or monetary donation. After this had been collected by the hosts, the visitors were paraded along the front of the meeting house, past the local people with whom they pressed noses in the traditional Maori greeting. The welcoming (and, in Maori terms, 'decontamination' process) was completed with a lunch of meat, vegetables, salad and apple shortcake in the adjacent dining room. With the ritual out of the way, the meeting proper could begin.

The arrangement of people inside the small meeting house was unintentionally awkward for Greenpeace. The chairman and officers of the Maori council were seated behind a table at the far end of the house, from where they had a clear view of those present and could take notes. The Maori delegates and supporters were prone on mattresses around the walls. Members of Greenpeace and the New Zealand Underwater Association were seated on forms in the centre, uncomfortably: they could lean neither forwards nor backwards and had to remain upright. Perched as they were above and in front of the Maori delegates, they felt 'on display'.

Council chairman Jim Nicholls, a handsome 45-year-old insurance broker who came originally from Thames but now lived in Auckland, rose to open the meeting proper.

'Historically, there is no precedent for what we are asked to decide today,' he began. 'This issue and everything associated with it is new for the Hauraki tribes and new for Maori people throughout New Zealand. Traditionally, our canoes have always been burnt, not sunk. Therefore the country as a whole will be watching the outcome of these deliberations.'

The first speakers in favour of sinking the vessel off the island were Graeme Lee and members of the Underwater Association. Lee said the Coromandel coastline was extensive and beautiful and could accommodate something like the proposal before them. Most important to his mind, it would attract more tourists to the region. The Underwater Association spokesmen assured the meeting that the wreck would act as an artificial reef and bring more fish to that part of the coast, that the owner of Slipper Island was in favour of the proposal, and that there was no sign of burials there.

Finally, Steve Sawyer spoke for Greenpeace. He stressed how important the vessel was to his organisation and how attached members had become to it. The question now was, 'What to do with old bones?' Burial at sea was a time-honoured tradition in the northern hemisphere, and Greenpeace hoped it would be acceptable in this instance. *Rainbow Warrior* crew

members felt that the spirit of the ship could be preserved, but
that it would be more difficult for that to happen if it was cut
up for scrap. Finally, he apologised on behalf of Greenpeace
for not having contacted the local people previously, but said
that the previous four and a half months had been an extremely
stressful time for the organisation.

Maori speakers were slow to respond. Several things had
upset them about the previous speakers' presentations. One
was that all the Pakeha so far had referred to the island as
Slipper rather than Whakahau. Another was the Underwater
Association's suggestion that there were no burials on the
island. The third exacerbating factor was that no one had
addressed a major but unstated Maori reservation, that
Fernando Pereira had died on the ship and therefore it could
(according to Maori belief) bring further misfortune if it was
brought to their district.

While the Maori hosts were simmering, a Pakeha woman
named Dorah Sommerville got to her feet. She turned out to
be the wife of the owner of Slipper Island. Embarrassingly,
she informed the meeting that the island was in fact 'riddled
with skeletons'. She also claimed that the sinking of a vessel
there would drive fish away rather than attract them, and that
a further influx of underwater fishermen would exhaust fish
stocks around the island. Finally, she doubted if the wreck
would remain stable in the position it was proposed to sink
it, because of the combined action of wind and currents.

This contribution seemed to breach a dam containing opposition to the proposal, which a series of Maori speakers now
expressed. One woman asked whether Greenpeace had the permission of the North American Indians, from whom they had
taken the ship's name, to sink it. An elder contradicted the
Underwater Association's claim about graves and said he had
found human remains there, some of them recently. A younger
woman criticised Greenpeace for stripping the ship and auction-
ing its detachable parts to raise funds: you did not do that to
a corpse you respected. 'The money kills the spirit,' somebody
else interjected.

While no formal motion had been framed, the feeling of the meeting was becoming apparent. Nobody from the area had spoken in favour of sinking the vessel in Hauraki waters. Half a dozen people had voiced reservations which neither Greenpeace spokespersons nor members of the Underwater Association had been able to allay. Two members of the audience had shown themselves overtly hostile to the proposal and to Greenpeace itself. Tension was high; emotions on both sides were only just held in check. The only thing that could have swung the meeting Greenpeace's way was an impassioned piece of oratory expressing what the Greenpeace people were all feeling: 'We too care about the land and the sea. We abandoned jobs and family and friends to crusade for the preservation of this planet. We are trying to help your cousins in the Pacific contaminated by radioactivity. We care about the spirit of our ship as much as you have cared about your canoes. We too care about our dead: that is why we are here to plead, that is why we want a decent and dignified burial for our ship and for the spirit of Fernando.'

None of these things were said. Carol Stewart, Judy Seaboyer, Susan Jane Owen and Geoff Bates felt them, but contained them. Steve Sawyer, flushed and tense, replied to the query about seeking North American Indian permission to sink the boat saying that the Rainbow Warrior legend belonged to no single group. But he said little else. The three *Rainbow Warrior* crew members present, Henk Haazen, Bunny McDiarmid and Nathalie Mestre, looked close to tears.

'If there's nothing further to be said I'd ask the visitors to retire,' said Jim Nicholls. 'We have to discuss this among the family.'

Outside on the marae, Haazen threw an arm around Mestre and held her close as they moved away from the meeting house. Bunny McDiarmid answered a query from another visitor absently and walked towards the gate. The tension was still high, unspoken and unspeakable. The Greenpeace case had not been understood. On the part of some people, it had been so sharply misapprehended that the motives attributable to Greenpeace were scarcely credible.

Inside the house it was time for delegates to state their position. First up was Peter Johnston, a 44-year-old engineer from Coromandel. He represented Ngati Hei, the tribe in whose territory Slipper Island lay, on the council. His was the signal most delegates were looking for. 'I speak not for myself, but for Ngati Hei,' he said. 'I rang around before I came here today and the verdict I give you is theirs and it's clear. Ngati Hei is opposed to this proposal. Personally, I don't want to say any more than that. But I would ask our kuia to speak for us.'

Heads swivelled to the other end of the meeting house, near the door, where Tuki Davis, senior female elder of Ngati Hei, was struggling to leave the mattress on which she had been sitting. Two men lunged forward to help set the old lady on her feet. She stood for a moment, struggling mentally and emotionally. In contrast to earlier proceedings, which had been marked by an exchange of asides and whispered private conversations, the silence was now palpable.

When Tuki Davis did begin to speak it was in Maori, and grief and anxiety caused her voice to falter. She was not there for herself, she told the delegates, but to take care of her young people, who could not talk Maori and who had no other elders to speak on their behalf. She, Tuki, was the last one present who remembered the old people of Ngati Hei, now all gone. She remembered especially her mother-in-law, with whom she used to speak for hours at a time in years long past. And she had no doubt that those old people would have opposed the sinking of the *Rainbow Warrior* in their territory.

'There are taniwha in the sea around Whakahau. They're guardians of that place. And they'll wreak havoc if we put that foreign object there, with all its associations. Our old people believed in those spirits and how they should be placated. Are we going to throw all that away now, just because those old people are dead?' Tears ran down her cheeks and she struggled to control her voice.

'It hurts me to say these things, because I fear that they're going to divide us. And because the whole issue has divided us, and we should be a whanau, a family. But this is what is in my heart and I have to speak it.' At this point she broke down entirely and pressed a handkerchief to her face. She backed away towards the door and one of the men went to her and led her gently back to a seat in the centre of the house. There was a long pause. Other women in the house had also pulled out handkerchiefs and were dabbing their eyes.

The contributions that followed were anti-climactic. Most speakers opposed the sinking of the vessel, elaborating on the factors raised by Tuki Davis. Some expressed intense resentment at points made by the Underwater Association: a suggestion that members of the association had been the first conservationists in the country; the apparent disparaging of the existence of urupa there. One elder said that the spirit of a man who died in a ship remained there even after the body had gone; and if that spirit *was* there, it would bring misfortune on all those who used the waters around it, and on those who had allowed the ship to be placed there.

Two speakers stood to urge acceptance of the Greenpeace proposal, including chairman Jim Nicholls. Nicholls dwelt on one of the tribe's traditional concepts, Te Pai O Hauraki (the generosity of Hauraki) and said that much of their mana arose from the fact that – in spite of old traditions and precedents – the people there had always been prepared to do things in the past that nobody else would. They were innovators. They helped people in difficulty. And now was their chance to do such things again. In his view, the issue was not solely a Maori one. 'It's a mixture of things that are taha Maori and other things that represent taha Pakeha, like so much of our life nowadays.'

No sooner had he sat down than a wind of cyclonic proportions hit the meeting house, shaking the walls and rushing air from the door through to the back windows. This was followed by torrential rain, whose sound entirely drowned out the next speaker, also in favour of the Greenpeace case. Maori people, or those who could be considered 'practising Maori', still look to the elements, identified with the old Maori gods, for signs. The significance of this demonstration and its timing was not lost. As one woman delegate whispered to another, it matched the name of Slipper Island, Whakahau – 'to make wind' or 'draw breath'. Almost all the subsequent speakers finished on the same note: 'But I support Ngati Hei. They are tangata whenua in this case. They are the guardians. The decision is theirs.'

This was the basis for the vote that followed. The decision itself was not unanimous, and chairman Nicholls announced he was prepared to resign (an offer dismissed loudly by the delegates). But once taken, the front was united. The Hauraki tribes formally turned down the request from Greenpeace and the New Zealand Underwater Association to sink the *Rainbow Warrior* in their waters. Jim Nicholls abandoned the meeting house for the dining room, where some Greenpeace members remained, awaiting a result. It was 5 p.m. and the decision had taken two hours to reach.

In effect, it was a decision that had been made before the meeting, when members of Ngati Hei decided that their mana had been trampled on because they had not been approached at the outset, that the presence of the boat in their waters would risk misfortune, and that large numbers of additional people coming to the area would increase the risk of desecration of their burial grounds.

Greenpeace now had to find an alternative site for the boat. Jim Nicholls, disappointed by the response of his own people, decided to help the environmentalists. That same night he rang Dover Samuels, an ebullient Maori fisherman, entrepreneur and tribal leader who lived at Matauri Bay in Northland. He knew from newspaper reports that Samuels was considering dumping car bodies off the coast to create an artificial reef to attract fish and to discourage trawlers. He also knew that Samuels wanted to develop tourism at the bay, which he already

advertised as having a 'million-dollar view'. The conversation
was short and pertinent.

'Dover. We have an aitua here that needs putting to rest.
Greenpeace wants to sink the *Rainbow Warrior* and the
Hauraki people won't take it. Can you help us?'

'No problem. Bring it up here. Give the Underwater Association people and Steve Sawyer my number and tell them to
ring me. Then we'll call a meeting to talk about how it can
be done.'

Sawyer was cautious when he spoke with Samuels that night,
wary of having to repeat the Paeroa experience. Allan Fowler
of the Underwater Association was even less happy, feeling
that the distance from Auckland to Matauri Bay was too great,
but he agreed that the most important consideration was finding a resting place for the boat. A meeting was arranged
between Greenpeace, the Underwater Association and Matauri
Bay residents at the bay on 27 November.

Sawyer's anxieties turned out to be misplaced. The discussions at Matauri Bay could not have been more of a contrast
with those held at Paeroa the previous week. This time the
Greenpeace representatives were welcomed with warmth and
enthusiasm and found an already strong predisposition in
favour of their proposal. At 6.30 in the evening, Dover Samuels
took Sawyer and Carol Stewart up to the marae on the hill
overlooking the bay and the Cavalli Islands, so named by the
navigator James Cook. There the Maori tangata whenua were
waiting with a group of Pakeha farmers, fishermen, divers and
old-age pensioners.

Samuels led his guests into the meeting house where, again,
the welcomes were conducted in Maori. Then Sawyer was asked
to speak. He told the meeting about the origin of the *Rainbow
Warrior*, the reasons for the Pacific Peace Voyage and the
Rongelap evacuation. He then stressed how important it was
to Greenpeace and to the *Rainbow Warrior* crew that the
Warrior be laid somewhere where it could be respected and
admired. He stressed too how impressed he was with the beauty
of the bay and of the islands and said he could not think of

a more appropriate location for the boat's final resting place.

This time there was no argument about Greenpeace or its motives. There was not even any discussion with the environmentalists. After Carol Stewart had said a few words, she and Sawyer were asked to withdraw for half an hour while the Matauri Bay community debated the proposal. They went and sat out on the hillside, looking down through the grass and the dusk to the bay that had taken hold on them so quickly and so intensely. It was a classical land and seascape: a long white-sand beach embraced at either end by green headlands; the islands scattered beyond, floating on the water like a vision from the Aegean. It was a view mindful of other times and other places, of past and present; it was redolent of peace.

Twenty minutes later, Dover Samuels fetched them back to the meeting house. A decision had been made and it was unanimous: Matauri Bay *would* take the *Rainbow Warrior*. The people had identified strongly with Greenpeace's affiliation with their ship, the sea, the land, Samuels said. These were qualities that Maoris recognised and understood. The only reservation locals had was that if the area around the sunken vessel was declared a marine reserve, they did not want the government to use that as a means of acquiring the smaller Maori-owned islands to include within the reserve. If that ever happened, Samuels said, they would want Greenpeace help to resist it. Sawyer and Stewart, ecstatic about the course and outcome of the meeting and still entranced by the beauty of the place, agreed.

Dover Samuels' press statement announcing the decision was masterly, pouring oil on waters already troubled and taking steps to ensure new ones were not disturbed.

The Matauri Bay community was anxious to see the *Rainbow Warrior* laid to rest in proper fashion, he said. The plan was to mark the chosen location with a buoy carrying an inscribed tribute to Greenpeace and the ship. A memorial service for Fernando Pereira would be held on board the boat before it was scuttled. He predicted that the probable site would be on

the landward side of the southern Cavallis, about four kilometres offshore.

He went on to say that he and his people fully understood
why the Hauraki tribes had refused to take the boat. 'Here
we do not have a similar situation, though. We have no burial
grounds on our nearby islands.'

Greenpeace and Dover Samuels had hoped to have the *Rainbow
Warrior* at Matauri Bay by New Year 1986, and a festival was
planned to coincide with the ceremonial sinking. The festival
went ahead, on 5 January, but the scuttling did not. Concerned
about a complete absence of progress in negotiations with the
French government over *Rainbow Warrior* reparations, the
New Zealand government announced that it would withhold
permission to sink the ship until it had decided whether or not
to hold a marine inquiry into the bombing. It is doubtful that
this procedure was ever seriously envisaged, however; the
government's legal advisers said at the outset that the circumstances of the *Warrior*'s initial sinking put it outside the
scope of legislation that controlled such inquiries. But, so long
as the *Rainbow Warrior* remained above water, the government argued, there was always a possibility of further revelations that could embarrass the French.

In May 1986, however, that possibility was finally renounced.
The Minister of Transport confirmed that there would be no
inquiry and that Greenpeace was free to dispose of its derelict, rusting vessel. The plan now was to tow it to Matauri Bay
in time to sink it on 10 July, first anniversary of the bombing.

While Greenpeace New Zealand waited for a final environmental report on the effects of sinking the boat at the bay,
Dover Samuels prepared to receive the vessel and its contingent
of mourners. He had the *Rainbow Warrior*'s propeller moved
to the top of a steep hill overlooking the bay, a site that would
also be used for viewing the vessel's final location. Then he
motored out several times to the point of Motutapere Island,
one of the Cavallis, where the *Warrior* would be scuttled.

It was an ideal position, he felt, sheltered and in about 20 metres of clear water. This would make the *Warrior* visible from the surface and easily accessible to scuba and snorkel divers. In addition, it was halfway between Doubtless Bay, where the French navigator de Surville burnt a Maori village in 1769, and the Bay of Islands, where his compatriot Marion du Fresne was killed by other Maoris three years later.

The site was also within six kilometres and full view of Flat Island, scene of the *Ouvéa* crew's only scuba diving expedition in New Zealand waters in 1985. After that expedition, the French yacht had cruised along the Cavallis, within metres of what would be the *Rainbow Warrior*'s last resting place.

ACKNOWLEDGEMENTS

I have many acknowledgements to make for help with the preparation of this book. Some people asked not to be identified because the information they supplied was sensitive, or because professional considerations precluded their being named.

I should note too that while members of the New Zealand Police Department's Operation Rainbow team were of incalculable help confirming or correcting information from other sources, they did not supply me with the interview transcripts quoted, nor with the material on the activities of the New Zealand Security Intelligence Service. I was given this information on the understanding that I did not divulge my sources.

Among those I can name, and thank most heartily for their help, are:

The crew of the *Rainbow Warrior*, especially Martini Gotje, Davey Edward, Hanne Sorensen, Henk Haazen, Bunny McDiarmid and Lloyd Anderson; and members of the Greenpeace organisation, in particular Steve Sawyer, David McTaggart, Elaine Shaw, Carol Stewart, Rien Achterberg, Judy Seaboyer, Athol von Koettlitz, Pip Burch and Monique Davis.

Commissioner Ken Thompson, Detective Superintendent Allan Galbraith, Detective Inspector Maurice Witham, Detective Inspector Bert White, Detective Sergeant Terry Batchelor, Detective Sergeant Neil Morris, Detective Constable Phil Jones, Chief Inspector Joe Dumble, Constable Digby Nash, Constable Archie Clark, Gerry Wright, Gerard Curry, Paul Neazor, Judge R. J. Gilbert, Mervyn Norrish, Sarah Dennis, Pamela Wilkinson, Rhys Richards, Wendy Gregg, John Belgrave, Brian Cooper, Frank MacLean, Des Hall.

David Robie, Darrell Giles, Claire Logan, Peter Kingston, Kim Griggs, Bill Saunders, Terry Carter, Sue Williams, Christine Cole Catley, Nicola Scott, Sharon Crosbie, Jenny Little, Bill Deverell, Michael Field, John Miller, Raewyn Mackenzie, Ray Richards, Antony Alpers, Penny Minchin, Russell Baillie, Rosemary Roberts, Joe Askew, David Young, Trish Gribben.

Jean-Louis Peninou, Frederic Filloux, Franc Depierre, Joel Marc, Roger Chatelain, Germaine Bacon.

Billiet Edmond, Giff Johnson, Ben Abrams, Carol Nash, Jewel Sucich, Joan and Barry George, Hec Crene, Trevor and Erna Rogers, Pat Colenso, Simon Langer, Reva Meredith, Graham MacDonald, Tank Barker, Bill Hopkins, Judy Harrison, Barbara Titchener, Dover Samuels, Jim Nicholls, Carol Fleet, John Hammond.

Dale Wrightson, Tony Knight, Helen Mason, Phyllis Gant, June Allen, Valerie Hogan, John Ormond, Lorraine Cameron, Peter Wills, Doug and Peta Hyslop, Jim Chapple, Rear-Admiral L. G. Carr, David Elworthy, Gerri Judkins, Rachael King.

Kate Pillow and Pamela Prior typed the manuscript; and I owe a special debt of gratitude to Geoff Walker and Graham Beattie of Penguin Books for their suggestions and support.

I would like too to acknowledge the disproportionate assistance of David Robie, in interview, and more especially through his writing in the *New Zealand Times* and elsewhere on Greenpeace, the *Rainbow Warrior*, and Pacific affairs in general. Robie is one of a very small number of journalists in New Zealand to specialise in Pacific matters. More than anybody else, he has been responsible for whatever modest knowledge I have of current affairs in the region. I have drawn too, sometimes in quotation, from his excellent book *Eyes of Fire, the Last Voyage of the Rainbow Warrior*, Lindon Publishing, Auckland, 1986.

Other publications I have consulted and in some instances quoted from are:

Warriors of the Rainbow, Strange and Prophetic Dreams of the Indians, William Willoya and Vinson Brown, Naturegraph Co., 1962.

The Greenpeace Chronicle, Robert Hunter, Picador, 1982.

Greenpeace III, Journey into the Bomb, David McTaggart with Robert Hunter, Collins, 1978.

Collision Course at Kwajalein, Marshall Islanders in the Shadow of the Bomb, Giff Johnson, Pacific Concerns Resource Centre, 1984.

Nuclear Free and Independent Pacific Conference – 1983, Pacific Concerns Resource Centre, 1983.

Moruroa Mon Amour, the French Nuclear Tests in the Pacific, Bengt and Marie-Thérèse Danielsson, Penguin 1977.

Extracts from the Journals of the Ships Mascarin and Marquis de Castries 1772. (Early Eyewitness Accounts of Maori Life 2), transcription and translation by Isobel Ollivier, Alexander Turnbull Library Endowment Trust, 1985.

A CHOICE OF
PELICANS AND PEREGRINES

☐ **The Knight, the Lady and the Priest**
   Georges Duby   £6.95

The acclaimed study of the making of modern marriage in medieval
France. 'He has traced this story – sometimes amusing, often horrify-
ing, always startling – in a series of brilliant vignettes' – *Observer*

☐ **The Limits of Soviet Power** **Jonathan Steele**   £3.95

The Kremlin's foreign policy – Brezhnev to Chernenko, is discussed
in this informed, informative 'wholly invaluable and extraordinarily
timely study' – *Guardian*

☐ **Understanding Organizations** **Charles B. Handy**   £4.95

Third Edition. Designed as a practical source-book for managers,
this Pelican looks at the concepts, key issues and current fashions in
tackling organizational problems.

☐ **The Pelican Freud Library: Volume 12**   £5.95

Containing the major essays: *Civilization, Society and Religion,
Group Psychology* and *Civilization and Its Discontents*, plus other
works.

☐ **Windows on the Mind** **Erich Harth**   £4.95

Is there a physical explanation for the various phenomena that we
call 'mind'? Professor Harth takes in age-old philosophers as well as
the latest neuroscientific theories in his masterly study of memory,
perception, free will, selfhood, sensation and other richly controversial fields.

☐ **The Pelican History of the World**
   J. M. Roberts   £5.95

'A stupendous achievement . . . This is the unrivalled World History
for our day' – A. J. P. Taylor

A CHOICE OF
PELICANS AND PEREGRINES

☐ *A Question of Economics* **Peter Donaldson**   £4.95

Twenty key issues – from the City and big business to trades unions –
clarified and discussed by Peter Donaldson, author of *10 × Economics* and one of our greatest popularizers of economics.

☐ *Inside the Inner City* **Paul Harrison**   £4.95

A report on urban poverty and conflict by the author of *Inside the Third World*. 'A major piece of evidence' – *Sunday Times*. 'A classic: it tells us what it is really like to be poor, and why' – *Time Out*

☐ *What Philosophy Is* **Anthony O'Hear**   £4.95

What are human beings? How should people act? How do our thoughts and words relate to reality? Contemporary attitudes to these age-old questions are discussed in this new study, an eloquent and brilliant introduction to philosophy today.

☐ *The Arabs* **Peter Mansfield**   £4.95

New Edition. 'Should be studied by anyone who wants to know about the Arab world and how the Arabs have become what they are today' – *Sunday Times*

☐ *Religion and the Rise of Capitalism*
   R. H. Tawney   £3.95

The classic study of religious thought of social and economic issues from the later middle ages to the early eighteenth century.

☐ *The Mathematical Experience*
   Philip J. Davis and Reuben Hersh   £7.95

Not since *Gödel, Escher, Bach* has such an entertaining book been written on the relationship of mathematics to the arts and sciences. 'It deserves to be read by everyone ... an instant classic' – *New Scientist*

A CHOICE OF PENGUINS

☐ *The Complete Penguin Stereo Record and Cassette Guide*
Greenfield, Layton and March   £7.95

A new edition, now including information on compact discs. 'One of the few indispensables on the record collector's bookshelf' – *Gramophone*

☐ *Selected Letters of Malcolm Lowry*
Edited by Harvey Breit and Margerie Bonner Lowry £5.95

'Lowry emerges from these letters not only as an extremely interesting man, but also a lovable one' – Philip Toynbee

☐ *The First Day on the Somme*
Martin Middlebrook   £3.95

1 July 1916 was the blackest day of slaughter in the history of the British Army. 'The soldiers receive the best service a historian can provide: their story told in their own words' – *Guardian*

☐ *A Better Class of Person* **John Osborne**   £2.50

The playwright's autobiography, 1929–56. 'Splendidly enjoyable' – John Mortimer. 'One of the best, richest and most bitterly truthful autobiographies that I have ever read' – Melvyn Bragg

☐ *The Winning Streak* **Goldsmith and Clutterbuck**   £2.95

Marks & Spencer, Saatchi & Saatchi, United Biscuits, GEC... The UK's top companies reveal their formulas for success, in an important and stimulating book that no British manager can afford to ignore.

☐ *The First World War* **A. J. P. Taylor**   £4.95

'He manages in some 200 illustrated pages to say almost everything that is important ... A special text ... a remarkable collection of photographs' – *Observer*

A CHOICE OF PENGUINS

☐ *Man and the Natural World* **Keith Thomas**   £4.95

Changing attitudes in England, 1500–1800. 'An encyclopedic study of man's relationship to animals and plants . . . a book to read again and again' – Paul Theroux, *Sunday Times* Books of the Year

☐ *Jean Rhys: Letters 1931–66*
    Edited by Francis Wyndham and Diana Melly   £4.95

'Eloquent and invaluable . . . her life emerges, and with it a portrait of an unexpectedly indomitable figure' – Marina Warner in the *Sunday Times*

☐ *The French Revolution* **Christopher Hibbert**   £4.95

'One of the best accounts of the Revolution that I know . . . Mr Hibbert is outstanding' – J. H. Plumb in the *Sunday Telegraph*

☐ *Isak Dinesen* **Judith Thurman**   £4.95

The acclaimed life of Karen Blixen, 'beautiful bride, disappointed wife, radiant lover, bereft and widowed woman, writer, sibyl, Scheherazade, child of Lucifer, Baroness; always a unique human being . . . an assiduously researched and finely narrated biography' – *Books & Bookmen*

☐ *The Amateur Naturalist*
    Gerald Durrell with Lee Durrell   £4.95

'Delight . . . on every page . . . packed with authoritative writing, learning without pomposity . . . it represents a real bargain' – *The Times Educational Supplement*. 'What treats are in store for the average British household' – *Daily Express*

☐ *When the Wind Blows* **Raymond Briggs**   £2.95

'A visual parable against nuclear war: all the more chilling for being in the form of a strip cartoon' – *Sunday Times*. 'The most eloquent anti-Bomb statement you are likely to read' – *Daily Mail*

PENGUIN REFERENCE BOOKS

☐ *The Penguin Dictionary of Troublesome Words* £2.50

A witty, straightforward guide to the pitfalls and hotly disputed issues in standard written English, illustrated with examples and including a glossary of grammatical terms and an appendix on punctuation.

☐ *The Penguin Guide to the Law* £8.95

This acclaimed reference book is designed for everyday use, and forms the most comprehensive handbook ever published on the law as it affects the individual.

☐ *The Penguin Dictionary of Religions* £4.95

The rites, beliefs, gods and holy books of all the major religions throughout the world are covered in this book, which is illustrated with charts, maps and line drawings.

☐ *The Penguin Medical Encyclopedia* £4.95

Covers the body and mind in sickness and in health, including drugs, surgery, history, institutions, medical vocabulary and many other aspects. Second Edition. 'Highly commendable' – *Journal of the Institute of Health Education*

☐ *The Penguin Dictionary of Physical Geography* £4.95

This book discusses all the main terms used, in over 5,000 entries illustrated with diagrams and meticulously cross-referenced.

☐ *Roget's Thesaurus* £3.50

Specially adapted for Penguins, Sue Lloyd's acclaimed new version of Roget's original will help you find the right words for your purposes. 'As normal a part of an intelligent household's library as the Bible, Shakespeare or a dictionary' – *Daily Telegraph*